FRENCH
Family Cooking

Françoise Bernard

FRENCH
Family Cooking

Françoise Bernard

PHOTOGRAPHS BY J. J. MAGIS

MACMILLAN PUBLISHING COMPANY   NEW YORK

TRANSLATED BY MARGUERITE THOMAS

French language edition © 1985 Hachette

English language edition copyright © 1986 by Macmillan Publishing Company, a division of Macmillan, Inc.

Macmillan Publishing Company
866 Third Avenue, New York, N.Y. 10022
Collier Macmillan Canada, Inc.

Library of Congress Cataloging-in-Publication Data
Bernard, Françoise, fl. 1965–
French family cooking.
Includes index.
1. Cookery, French.   I. Title.
TX719.B4138   1986   641.5944   86-5205
ISBN 0-02-510180-3

First Printing 1986

Printed and bound by Graficromo s.a., Cordoba, Spain

INTRODUCTION

Twenty years ago I wrote my first cookbook, *Family Recipes (Recettes Familiales).* Its great success in over one million kitchens led me to specialize in good home cooking, always simple but also subtle and refined. In this book I offer you the best traditional French cooking, leaving to the great chefs the burden of communicating the more arcane secrets of gastronomy.

Although the number of family recipes is practically infinite, French cuisine can define and contain them by the kinds of ingredients used (meat, fish, vegetables, etc.) and by the methods used in preparing them. I am tempted to say French cuisines, since regional France possesses ten or twenty, but fortunately they all share a unique combination of audacity and good taste to complement them.

France, country of mountains and plains, of seas and forests, of sunshine and rain, produces on its land and in its waters everything edible to delight the palate. Modern transportation provides Mediterranean bouillabaisse to the land-bound city of Lille and salt-marsh-bred lamb to the sunny shores of Nice. And most important, more than one third of all French families grow herbs and vegetables in their own gardens.

In the majority of homes, women are still doing the cooking. And French home cooking is privileged in its history. Not until the French Revolution did restaurants appear to take the place of mere way stations. These restaurants served a "restoring" cuisine that originated, especially in the provinces, with simple home cooking. The nineteenth century certainly possessed more bourgeois family cooks than chefs, and the grandmothers of Lyons still remind us of the change from cooking "for one's own" to cooking "for others." We must remember that most of the basic themes of French cuisine developed around the family hearth or oven. And in a time where great chefs are treated as demigods it is only fair to underline that their complex recipes take root in ground that has been laboriously prepared by innumerable unknown cooks. Curnonsky, despite (or perhaps because of) his title "Prince of Gastronomes," has often said that nothing pleased him more than a simple (but good) home-cooked dish.

Because in a cookbook a dish must be tasted with the eyes as well as the imagination, we have garnished each recipe with a beautiful and instructive photograph. Grateful acknowledgment must be given to the magical talent of photographer Jean-Jacques Magis, who provided these magnificent images.

Finally, remember that cooking is a living art. These recipes are themes on which you can improvise. So if your results differ from mine from time to time, it is because of your imagination and individuality expressed through the medium of the recipe.

Françoise Bernard

CONTENTS

FIRST COURSES

SEAFOOD

POULTRY AND GAME

MEATS

VEGETABLES · PASTA · RICE

DESSERTS

FIRST COURSES

Bisque de langoustines SHRIMP BISQUE

[For 4 people]

2 pounds *langoustines* or
    1 pound shrimp*
2 tablespoons oil
1 onion, chopped fine
1 carrot, chopped fine
3 tablespoons Cognac
1 tablespoon rice
2 tomatoes, chopped coarse
1 teaspoon tomato paste
⅓ cup white wine
Bouquet garni
Salt to taste
Freshly ground black pepper to taste
2 tablespoons *crème fraîche*

Preparation and cooking time: 1 hour and 15 minutes

Separate the shrimp heads from the tail. Cook both rapidly in a little very hot oil, along with the chopped onion and carrot. Sprinkle with half the Cognac. Flame the mixture over the heat.

Add the rice, fresh tomatoes and tomato paste, 5 cups of water, wine, bouquet garni, salt, and pepper.

After simmering 4 to 5 minutes, remove the shrimp tails from the bisque, but cook the rest 10 more minutes.

Peel the shrimp tails. Dice the flesh.

Process the bisque in a food mill or food processor to crush the heads and extract as much of the essence as possible; push through a strainer if pieces of shell remain. Return the bisque to the heat a few seconds with the diced shrimp, remaining Cognac, and *crème fraîche*. *See *Langoustines* in Miscellaneous Notes.

Bouillabaisse MEDITERRANEAN-STYLE FISH SOUP

[FOR 6 TO 8 PEOPLE]

Preparation and cooking time: 1 hour

4½ pounds assorted fish*
3 onions, chopped coarse
3 tomatoes, chopped coarse
4 tablespoons oil
1 small sprig fennel or 1 teaspoon dried
1 bay leaf
1 sprig or 1 teaspoon summer savory (or thyme)
1 small piece orange peel
2 big pinches saffron
Salt and pepper to taste

ROUILLE SAUCE
About ½ cup fresh bread crumbs (French bread or homemade-type white)
1 cup warm milk
1 to 2 small hot peppers (fresh or dried)
½ cup oil
Salt and pepper to taste

GARNISH FOR THE BROTH
24 small slices French bread

Clean and rinse the fish. Cut the largest in chunks. Chop the onions. Peel and cut up the tomatoes.

In a casserole, slowly heat the oil. Add the chopped onions. Cook 5 minutes without coloring. Add the fish. Shake the casserole so the fish gets well coated with oil. Then add the tomatoes, fennel, bay leaf, savory or thyme, orange peel, saffron, salt, and pepper. Cover with boiling water (which should reach just a little above the fish).

Boil rapidly, over high heat, uncovered, for 15 to 20 minutes.

ROUILLE SAUCE: Soak the bread in a little warm milk. When saturated, squeeze thoroughly. Using a mortar and pestle, mash the garlic and hot peppers. Add the bread, then beat in the oil, drop by drop. Add salt and pepper. The *rouille* will thicken like mayonnaise. This entire procedure may be done in a food processor.

Place the bread slices in a soup tureen. Pour the broth over them. Serve the fish separately, in a deep platter, and the *rouille* separately. Serve immediately.

My advice: This is one of many bouillabaisse recipes. Some add potatoes, others remove the fish heads—except *rascasse*—and prepare separately a broth of fish heads to "moisten" the bouillabaisse. I substitute a shot of *pastis* (anise-flavored liqueur such as Pernod) for the fennel.

*See Fish for *Bouillabaisse* in Miscellaneous Notes.

Remarks: Saffron is a spice so rare and expensive that it is sold by the half-gram.

For the garnish, you might use bread that is slightly stale or toasted and rubbed with garlic.

Gratinée au fromage

ONION SOUP

[FOR 4 PEOPLE]

3 large onions, chopped fine
1½ tablespoons butter
1 tablespoon flour
½ cup dry white wine
6 cups water
1 cube beef broth
Salt to taste
Freshly ground pepper to taste
4 thin slices French bread
¼ cup port
1 to 2 egg yolks
¾ cup grated Gruyère cheese

Remarks: It goes without saying that, whenever possible, you'll use homemade beef stock instead of a bouillon cube.

Preparation and cooking time: 45 minutes

Mince the onions. Cook them very slowly in the butter, in a covered casserole. When the onions are golden, sprinkle them with flour. Stir with a wooden spoon just until the mixture browns lightly, no more.

Add the wine, water, bouillon cube, salt, and pepper. Simmer 20 minutes. Toast the bread.

In an ovenproof soup tureen, whisk together the port and egg yolks. Pour, little by little, over the scalding onion soup, stirring constantly. Float the toasted bread on top. Sprinkle with grated Gruyère. Place in a very hot broiler until the cheese is melted and lightly browned and serve immediately.

My advice: The gratin is even more appetizing and easier to serve in individual bowls. But they must fit in the broiler without breaking!

Petite marmite de queue de bœuf   OXTAIL STEW

[FOR 4 PEOPLE]

Preparation and cooking time: 3 hours and 15 minutes

1 oxtail, cut into small chunks (2 to 3
    pounds)
Salt to taste
3 leeks, 3 carrots, 2 turnips, 1 stalk
    celery, chopped coarse
1 onion
4 whole cloves
1 clove garlic
Bouquet garni
1 cup Madeira
3 tablespoons butter
12 thin slices French bread*

In a large pot place cold water and pieces of oxtail tied together with string. Bring to a boil. Discard this first water. Return to the pot and cover again with about 8 cups of cold water. Add salt and return to the heat.

Peel and wash the vegetables. Cut them in pieces. Drop them into the simmering soup along with the spices: the onion stuck with 4 cloves, garlic, and bouquet garni. Cover and cook 3 hours.

Add the Madeira 5 minutes before the end of cooking.

Butter the bread slices. Toast them under a broiler a few minutes until golden brown.

Serve the strained broth in bowls with, separately, the toasted bread, the meat, and the vegetables.

*The recipe calls for slices of *baguette*, the traditional narrow, round French loaf. If you can't find this size, cut larger slices of French bread in halves or quarters.

Potage glacé au concombre   COLD CUCUMBER SOUP

[FOR 4 PEOPLE]

1 cucumber, about ¾ pound
½ clove garlic
Minced fresh herbs (parsley, tarragon,
    chives, chervil, basil, e.g.)
2 cups unflavored yogurt
Juice of ½ lemon / Pepper, salt to taste
A few ice cubes

Remarks: If you replace the herbs with 5 to 6 leaves of minced fresh mint, some raisins, and ½ teaspoon of cumin you will have a delicate Oriental dish.

Preparation time: 10 minutes

Peel, seed, and dice the cucumber. Salt it and, if possible, let it stand for 1 hour to draw out the juices. Rinse with cold water. Drain and sponge dry.

Place in a food processor the diced cucumber (reserve a few pieces for garnish), garlic, fresh herbs of your choice, yogurt, lemon juice, pepper, and a pinch of salt. Process to a fine puree. About halfway, add some not-too-large ice cubes.

Serve in individual bowls with a few pieces of cucumber and a pinch of minced fresh herbs.

Soupe aux moules à la crème et au safran

MUSSEL SOUP WITH CREAM AND SAFFRON

[FOR 4 PEOPLE]

2 quarts mussels
1 shallot, chopped fine
½ cup dry white wine
2 cups water
Bouquet garni
Salt to taste
Freshly ground black pepper to taste
2 leeks (white part only), chopped fine
1 tablespoon butter
Pinch saffron
2 ounces vermicelli
½ cup *crème fraîche*

Preparation and cooking time: 45 minutes

Scrub and wash the mussels. Steam them open over brisk heat in a pot with the minced shallot, wine, 2 cups of water, bouquet garni, salt, and pepper. Remove them from the cooking liquid. Put this through a metal strainer lined with paper towels to completely remove any sand.

Wash and mince the white part of the leeks. Cook, covered, over very low heat with the butter. Do not let the leeks brown. Pour in the mussel broth (6 cups at least, or make up the difference with water). Cover and cook 15 minutes.

Add the saffron and vermicelli to the boiling soup. Stir. After 5 minutes of simmering, when the vermicelli is cooked *al dente*, add the shelled mussels and the cream. Stir a few seconds over the heat. Check the seasoning and serve.

My advice: If you omit the saffron, your soup will have a different but still excellent flavor. You might also replace the vermicelli with a teaspoon of cornstarch for a velvety texture.

VEGETABLE SOUP WITH BASIL AND GARLIC

Soupe au pistou

[FOR 4 PEOPLE]

Salt to taste / 1 zucchini
¼ pound green beans / ¼ pound leeks
¼ pound carrots / ¼ pound turnips
¼ pound celery root / 2 tomatoes
2 ounces spaghetti or large vermicelli

PISTOU

2 cloves garlic
A few leaves fresh basil
½ cup grated Parmesan or Gruyère
    cheese
½ cup olive oil

Remarks: If fresh basil is unavailable, use ½ teaspoon of dried basil, but it won't be as good.

Preparation and cooking time: 1 hour and 30 minutes

Boil 6 cups of salted water in a pot. Wash, peel, and dice all the vegetables, then add them to the boiling water. Cover and simmer 1 hour.

Add the pasta, broken into pieces. Bring to a boil again and cook according to the directions on the package, until *al dente.*

PISTOU: With a pestle, crush the garlic and basil. Add the grated cheese, then, little by little, the olive oil, mixing it like mayonnaise (this may be done in a food processor).

In a soup tureen, stir together the unstrained soup and the *pistou.*

My advice: I find this mixture goes well with the *pistou:* Dutch cheese (such as Edam or Gouda) and Gruyère grated together. Put some in a small bowl on the table for those who wish to add it to their dish.

Soupe de poisson FISH SOUP

[FOR 4 PEOPLE]

2½ pounds rockfish or other lean fish*
4 tablespoons olive oil
2 onions, cut in quarters
2 tomatoes, chopped coarse
3 cloves garlic, crushed
Bouquet garni
1 small sprig rosemary or ½ teaspoon dried
8 cups water
1 tablespoon *pastis* (anise-flavored liqueur such as Pernod)
Salt to taste
Freshly ground black pepper to taste
2 teaspoons saffron
3 tablespoons vermicelli (optional)
Garlic croutons
Grated Gruyère cheese

Preparation and cooking time: 1 hour and 15 minutes

Clean the fish. Do not remove the heads. In a large pot, heat the oil and lightly brown the quartered onions, chopped tomatoes and garlic, bouquet garni, and rosemary. Add the fish. Continue cooking over medium-high heat. Mash occasionally with a wooden spoon.

After 10 minutes, when the fish has been cooked to a pulp, add 8 cups of water, the *pastis*, salt, pepper, and saffron. Bring to a boil and simmer for 30 minutes, uncovered.

Put the soup through a food mill or food processor to crush the bones as much as possible.** (You may thicken it with large vermicelli, if you wish: bring the soup to a boil, add the pasta, boiling 3 minutes, until *al dente*) Serve with croutons rubbed with garlic and grated Gruyère.

My advice: Mash the fish with a wooden spoon to reduce to a pulp; this will release all the juices that give an incomparable flavor. For smoothness, keep a strong boil going during the entire cooking period.

*See Fish for Fish Soup in Miscellaneous Notes.
**It is not always possible to grind up all the fish bones, so you may want to force the soup through a very fine sieve.

Velouté d'avocat AVOCADO SOUP

[FOR 4 PEOPLE]

1 can or cube chicken broth
1 very ripe avocado / 1 egg yolk
Salt, pepper to taste
1 slice firm white bread, cubed
2 tablespoons butter

Remarks: Don't let this soup cool off because it's always risky putting a soup or sauce back on the heat after thickening it with egg yolk.

Preparation and cooking time: 15 minutes

Prepare the chicken broth according to instructions.

Puree the avocado flesh in a food mill or food processor. Immediately beat in the egg yolk. Add it, little by little, to the scalding soup, off the heat, whisking vigorously. Lightly salt and pepper.

Serve immediately in cups, with little cubes of bread sautéed in butter.

Avocats farcis de langouste

[FOR 4 PEOPLE]

1 lobster tail (frozen)

COURT BOUILLON
2 cups water
1 onion / 1 carrot, chopped coarse
1 whole clove
1 teaspoon vinegar
Bouquet garni
4 whole peppercorns, crushed
Salt to taste

1 cup mayonnaise
A few drops Tabasco sauce or 2 pinches
  cayenne pepper
Fresh herbs (minced parsley, chives)
Juice of 1 lemon plus 1 slice
½ sweet pepper, preserved in oil
1 teaspoon capers
Salt to taste
Freshly ground black pepper to taste
2 avocados / 4 lettuce leaves

AVOCADOS STUFFED WITH LOBSTER

Preparation and cooking time: 45 minutes, plus 1 hour waiting time

To cook the frozen lobster, put it, still frozen, in cold water with all the ingredients of the court bouillon. Bring to a boil very slowly. Keep it gently simmering for 5 to 7 minutes, then chill completely in the court bouillon.

Shell the lobster. Cut 4 thin slices out for decoration, and the rest in more or less regular dice.

Make the mayonnaise, or use store-bought, adding Tabasco sauce or cayenne pepper, fresh herbs, lemon juice, minced sweet pepper, capers, diced lobster, salt, and pepper.

Shortly before serving, cut the avocados in half. Cover them with a lettuce leaf, some lobster salad, and a thin slice of lobster. Cut a thin slice of lemon. Split it up to the center with a knife. Twist it slightly to arrange it on horseback on the stuffed avocado.

My advice: Frozen lobster will have more flavor if it cooks gently in a very aromatic court bouillon, and cools off in it. It can even stay in it until the next day, in the refrigerator.

Cocktail de crevettes aux kiwis

[FOR 4 PEOPLE]

½ pound peeled shrimp
1 teaspoon rum
2 tablespoons mayonnaise
1 tablespoon *crème fraîche* or sour cream
Minced chives
2 pinches cayenne pepper or a few drops
   Tabasco sauce
5 to 6 lettuce leaves
2 kiwis
Juice of ½ lemon

4 small serving bowls or goblets

SHRIMP COCKTAIL WITH KIWIS

Preparation time: 20 minutes

Macerate the shrimp in the rum about 20 minutes.

Mix the mayonnaise (home-made or store-bought) with the *crème fraîche*, minced chives, and cayenne pepper or Tabasco sauce. Gently stir in the shrimp.

Wash and dry 5 to 6 lettuce leaves. Roll them up and, on a cutting board, slice them in thin strips with a large knife.

In 4 serving glasses or bowls, arrange in layers the lettuce, shrimp with mayonnaise, and lettuce.

Peel the kiwis. Slice them in rounds. Arrange them in a crown, on top of the cocktails. Sprinkle with lemon and refrigerate them until just before serving.

Variation: You can enrich this cocktail with an avocado cut into small cubes or balls. Sprinkle with lemon juice immediately so it won't darken, and add pepper before mixing in the salad.

Cocktail de langouste à la mayonnaise rose

LOBSTER COCKTAIL WITH PINK MAYONNAISE

[FOR 4 TO 6 PEOPLE]

2 raw lobster tails, about ½ pound (frozen)

COURT BOUILLON

½ bottle dry white wine
2 cups water
½ carrot, 1 onion, sliced in rounds
Bouquet garni
10 whole peppercorns, crushed
Salt to taste
1 small stalk celery

PINK MAYONNAISE

1 cup oil
1 egg yolk
2 teaspoons Dijon-type mustard
Salt to taste
Freshly ground black pepper to taste
1 teaspoon sherry vinegar
1 tablespoon Cognac
1 tablespoon ketchup
A few drops Tabasco sauce or 2 pinches cayenne pepper

GARNISH

A few lettuce leaves
2 small firm tomatoes, sliced thin
4 to 6 shrimp, unpeeled (optional)

4 to 6 stem glasses

Remarks: The lobsters may be cooked still frozen (see Avocados Stuffed with Lobster, p. 20) or defrosted completely and cooked right away. But once cooked, they can be safely kept in their cooking court bouillon for a few hours and even until the next day in the refrigerator.

Preparation and cooking time the day before: 1 hour, plus 5 hours for defrosting

The day before, defrost the lobsters 5 to 6 hours at room temperature. Meanwhile simmer all the ingredients for the court bouillon 30 minutes. Let cool.

Plunge the lobster tails into the court bouillon. Boil rapidly about 8 minutes. Let cool in the court bouillon.

PINK MAYONNAISE: Prepare a spicy mayonnaise according to the above proportions (see the recipe for mayonnaise, p. 26).

With scissors, cut out the mushy underside of the lobster tails. Then remove the lobster meat. Cut off 8 to 12 slices, then dice the rest. Mix the diced meat with the mayonnaise. Reserve the slices.

To serve, roll the lettuce leaves up and shred them on a cutting board. Arrange a few in the bottom of each stem glass. Cover with mayonnaise and lobster. Cover with the rest of the lettuce and a thin slice of tomato. Finish with 2 slices of lobster topped with a layer of mayonnaise. You might decorate each glass with a large shrimp hooked over the edge.

Coques d'avocat   AVOCADO SHELLS

[For 4 people]

Preparation and cooking time: 20 minutes

2 avocados
2 ripe tomatoes
1 onion, chopped fine
1 teaspoon capers
1 tablespoon mild white cheese (such as ricotta or small-curd cottage cheese)
Juice of 1 lemon
1 tablespoon olive oil
Salt to taste
Freshly ground black pepper to taste

Cut the avocados in half. Carefully take the flesh out of the skins without damaging the skins. Sprinkle the empty shells with lemon to avoid darkening. Put them in an airtight plastic container in the refrigerator. Peel and seed the tomatoes. Cut the tomato and avocado flesh into small dice.

Mix thoroughly with the minced onion, capers, cheese, lemon juice, oil, salt, and pepper. Chill.

Just before serving, arrange this salad in the avocado shells.

Couronne de légumes et crevettes en aspic   CROWN OF VEGETABLES AND SHRIMP IN ASPIC

[For 4 to 6 people]

Preparation time: 30 minutes, plus 1 hour defrosting and refrigeration

About ½ pound frozen shrimp, peeled
Juice of ½ lemon (reserve 1 tablespoon)
A few drops Tabasco sauce
1 small (8-ounce) can or 1 package frozen mixed vegetables (about 1 cup)
½ cucumber / 2 to 3 small firm tomatoes
¼ sweet pepper / Salt to taste
1 tablespoon (1 package) unflavored gelatin
Freshly ground black pepper to taste
2 hard-boiled eggs, sliced
Lettuce leaves or watercress

1 crown-shaped mold

Remarks: To easily unmold a jellied dish, you need only dip the bottom of the mold in very hot water 3 to 4 seconds—no more—and invert it immediately on the serving platter.

Sprinkle the shrimp with lemon juice and a few drops of Tabasco sauce. Let the shrimp defrost at room temperature, about 30 minutes.

Thoroughly drain the mixed vegetables. Blot them lightly with paper towels. Cut the seeded cucumber in slices, the tomato in quarters, and the pepper in strips. Add salt and refrigerate.

Prepare the gelatin according to package instructions. Add to it 1 tablespoon of lemon juice, salt, and pepper. Pour about ¼ inch of it in the bottom of the mold. Tip the mold to coat the sides with gelatin. Refrigerate for 5 minutes.

When the layer of gelatin has stiffened in the mold, fill it with vegetables mixed with the well-drained shrimp, pressing a few shrimp and slices of egg and cucumber against the sides so they'll be visible after unmolding. Slowly pour on the rest of the cold, but still liquid, gelatin. Let set in the refrigerator.

Serve the crown of aspic unmolded on lettuce leaves that have been left whole or sliced in thin strips, or else on a bed of lightly seasoned watercress. You can unmold it in advance, but put it back in the refrigerator until just before serving.

Écrevisses gourmandes en salade CRAYFISH SALAD

[FOR 4 PEOPLE]

Preparation and cooking time: 45 minutes

20 to 24 crayfish
Salt to taste

VINAIGRETTE
4 tablespoons oil
1 tablespoon sherry or wine vinegar
½ tablespoon lemon juice
1 small shallot, chopped fine
Chervil or tarragon, chopped fine
Salt to taste
Freshly ground black pepper to taste

½ pound young green beans
A few leaves of assorted salad greens
    (Boston or Bibb lettuce, watercress,
    corn salad, e.g.)
1 small can *girolle* mushrooms*
2 slices foie gras

4 large plates

Wash the crayfish. Plunge them into boiling salted water 5 minutes. Drain and shell them, reserving a few unshelled ones for garnish.

Whisk together all the ingredients of the vinaigrette.

Cook the green beans in a large amount of very salted boiling water, 8 to 10 minutes only. Drain them immediately and flush them generously with cold water so they stay firm and green. Pat them dry and dress with half the vinaigrette.

Wash and spin-dry the salad greens. Distribute a few on each plate along with the drained mushrooms. Sprinkle with the remaining vinaigrette. Top with small groups of green beans, diced foie gras, and the crayfish tails. Garnish with the reserved crayfish.

My advice: *Girolles* may be replaced by fresh cultivated mushrooms, sliced and sprinkled with lemon juice. At the last moment, a little diced beet wouldn't harm this salad. The green beans are still *al dente* in this recipe. Cook them longer if you prefer but, still, not too much.

*Canned *girolle* or *chanterelle* mushrooms may be found in many specialty food stores. Or see "My advice."

Hors-d'œuvre de langoustines à la rouille PRAWNS WITH *ROUILLE* SAUCE

[FOR 4 PEOPLE]

Preparation and cooking time: 30 minutes

20 *langoustines* or prawns   *t*
Bouquet garni / Liberal seasoning salt
Freshly ground black pepper to taste
½ pound small pasta (shells or spirals)
1 tablespoon oil

ROUILLE SAUCE
2 to 3 cloves garlic
1 egg yolk / Salt to taste
1 fresh hot pepper or cayenne pepper
1 teaspoon tomato paste
1 cup oil (preferably olive oil)
1 teaspoon water

1 head lettuce (such as Boston or Bibb)
4 small tomatoes
12 black olives / 1 celery heart
Toasted slices of French bread

Remarks: Be careful! With some food processors you can make mayonnaise or similar sauces by using a whole egg, not the yolk only as this recipe indicates.

To cook the *langoustines,* or prawns, put them in cold water with the bouquet garni, a lot of salt, and some pepper. Simmer 3 to 5 minutes, depending on size. Drain them.

Boil the pasta in a large amount of salted water. Stir. As soon as it is cooked but still firm to the bite, drain it. Mix immediately with a little olive oil so it won't stick together while cooling.

ROUILLE SAUCE: Crush the garlic. Add the egg yolk, salt, crushed hot pepper or cayenne, and the tomato paste. Using an electric mixer or food processor, beat until the mixture is thoroughly blended. Then add the oil, almost drop by drop in the beginning. When the sauce begins to thicken, pour the oil in more liberally. Toward the end, add 1 teaspoon of cold water to stabilize it.

Mix a little *rouille* with the cold pasta. Arrange the lettuce leaves on a large platter, the pasta in the middle. Garnish the border with quartered tomatoes, prawns, olives, and the quartered celery heart. Serve the rest of the *rouille* in a sauceboat accompanied by toasted rounds of bread for spreading.

Mayonnaise de langouste

[FOR 6 PEOPLE]

2 frozen lobster tails
1 large (16-ounce) can or 2 packages frozen mixed vegetables (about 2 cups)

MAYONNAISE
2 egg yolks / Salt to taste
Freshly ground black pepper to taste
2 teaspoons Dijon-type mustard
2 cups oil / 2 teaspoons vinegar

1 heart Boston or Bibb lettuce
¼ pound shrimp / ½ lemon

Remarks: For successful mayonnaise, all the ingredients should be at the same temperature to encourage emulsification; a little vinegar or boiling water, added at the end, stabilizes it. This liquid softens the mayonnaise slightly; if it is too hard it has a tendency to separate.

LOBSTER MAYONNAISE

Preparation and cooking time: 45 minutes

Cook the lobster tails in court bouillon (see Avocados Stuffed with Lobster, p. 20). Drain the vegetables in a colander, then on a kitchen towel.

MAYONNAISE: * In a bowl, beat with a whisk the egg yolks, salt, pepper, and mustard just until the mixture is thoroughly blended. Add the oil almost drop by drop to start. When the mixture begins to gather a little consistency, pour the oil in more liberally. Whisk steadily without rushing during the entire preparation. Add the vinegar toward the end to stabilize it. Mix half the mayonnaise with the vegetables. Pack into a deep but narrow mold (such as an electric mixer bowl).

To serve, unmold on a platter. Arrange lobster slices around it, with a few lettuce leaves at the top. Stick the hard point of the shrimp into the lemon peel. Place on the lettuce. Serve a sauceboat of mayonnaise separately.

*May be done in a food processor.

Mousse froide de saumon

[FOR 6 TO 8 PEOPLE]

THICK BÉCHAMEL SAUCE
2 tablespoons butter / ¼ cup flour
1 cup milk / Salt and pepper to taste

1½ pounds salmon (fresh or frozen)
Pinch cayenne pepper / 1 egg + 1 yolk
½ cup *crème fraîche* / Juice ½ lemon

GARNISH
Mayonnaise (p. 26)
Vinaigrette (see Crayfish Salad, p. 24)
1 head Boston or Bibb lettuce
8 small tomatoes / 1 cucumber
4 hard-boiled eggs / 16 olives

COLD SALMON MOUSSE

Preparation and cooking time: 1 hour and 15 minutes the day before; 30 minutes that day

THICK BÉCHAMEL SAUCE: In a saucepan, over low heat, mix the butter and flour. Add the milk all at once, salt, and pepper. Whisk just until it boils. Let cool.

Remove the skin and bones from the fresh or defrosted salmon. Mix it with a pinch or two of cayenne pepper, the egg and egg yolk, the *crème fraîche*, lemon juice, and the béchamel. Check for seasoning. Pour into a buttered 9-inch loaf pan. Place in hot (450°) oven with enough boiling water to come about halfway up the sides of the mold and bake about 40 minutes. Chill overnight.

That day, prepare the mayonnaise and vinaigrette. Line a platter with lettuce leaves. Arrange slices of salmon mousse on the lettuce. Garnish the border with slices of tomato, cucumber, hard-boiled eggs, and olives. Sprinkle lightly with vinaigrette. Serve the mayonnaise separately.

Pamplemousse au crabe

[For 4 people]

¼ cup rice

MAYONNAISE

1 egg yolk
1 cup oil
1 teaspoon Dijon-type mustard
1 teaspoon vinegar
Salt to taste
Freshly ground black pepper to taste
Pinch cayenne pepper (optional)

2 large grapefruit
1 small (6-ounce) can lump crabmeat
16 green or black olives
Salt to taste
Freshly ground black pepper to taste

CRAB WITH GRAPEFRUIT

Preparation and cooking time: 45 minutes

Cook the rice 15 to 18 minutes in a large amount of salted water. Immediately rinse with cold water to cool it completely and drain.

Prepare the mayonnaise according to the proportions given above (see Lobster Mayonnaise, p. 26).

Cut the grapefruit in half lengthwise. Separate the fruit from the skin without tearing the rinds (which will be used later). Separate the grapefruit sections, peeling off the thin white membrane.

Combine the crab, grapefruit sections, rice, a few chopped olives, salt, pepper, and mayonnaise. Just before serving, fill the half-rinds with this salad. Place an olive in the center of each one.

My advice: You can prepare all the ingredients in advance as long as you chill them separately in the refrigerator. At the very last minute, combine the ingredients and fill the grapefruit rinds.

SALAD WITH TUNA AND TOMATOES

Salade niçoise

[FOR 4 PEOPLE]

4 boiled potatoes
4 hard-boiled eggs
1 can tuna packed in oil
1 can anchovy fillets
4 firm tomatoes
2 white onions
1 cucumber
1 green pepper
20 green or black olives

VINAIGRETTE

4 tablespoons olive oil
1 tablespoon vinegar
A little Dijon-type mustard
Salt to taste
Freshly ground black pepper to taste

Preparation time: 20 minutes

Peel the potatoes. Shell the eggs. Open the cans of tuna and anchovies.

Cut the tomatoes and eggs in quarters, the onions, cucumber and potatoes in slices, the pepper in thin strips after removing the seeds.

To serve: In a salad bowl, arrange the potatoes into a dome surrounded by the cucumber slices. Scatter over them the quartered tomatoes and eggs, the tuna, pepper strips, olives, and onion slices. Arrange the anchovy fillets into a star. Sprinkle with vinaigrette. Serve immediately (if necessary the salad can stay in the refrigerator a short time, but eventually it will juice up too much).

Variation: I recommend long crusty chunks of French bread drenched with olive oil, rubbed with garlic, and spread with anchovy paste that you add to the dressed salad.

CHICKEN SALAD

Salade de poulet

[FOR 4 PEOPLE]

1 cup mayonnaise (p. 26)
About 2 cups cold leftover chicken
1 stalk celery
10 green or black olives
½ teaspoon paprika
Salt to taste
Freshly ground black pepper to taste
Pinch cayenne pepper

GARNISH

4 to 8 lettuce leaves
2 tomatoes
2 hard-boiled eggs
A few radishes

Preparation time: 30 minutes / *Chilling time:* 1 hour

Pour the mayonnaise into a salad bowl. Add the chicken cut into small dice, the celery in small sticks, the seeded olives, paprika, salt, pepper, and pinch of cayenne pepper. Mix together and chill for 1 hour.

Before serving, arrange 1 to 2 lettuce leaves in goblets or on dessert plates and top with the chicken salad and a few quarters of tomatoes and hard-boiled eggs. Decorate with the radishes.

My advice: Add to your chicken salad anything the season offers and your fantasy inspires: cucumber, pickles, minced fresh herbs, pimientos, chunks of raw fennel, and even slices of potato. The mayonnaise should be fairly liquid. If necessary, dilute it with a little lemon juice, vinegar, or water if you're concerned that it will be too acidic.

Salade verte aux chevrotins grillés

GREEN SALAD WITH GRILLED GOAT CHEESE

[FOR 4 PEOPLE]

1 heart from a head of salad greens
4 small goat cheeses* / A little oil

VINAIGRETTE

3 tablespoons oil
1 tablespoon wine vinegar
1 small shallot, chopped fine
Salt and pepper to taste

Preparation and cooking time: 15 minutes

Wash and dry the salad greens thoroughly. Dress and toss them in a salad bowl. Keep chilled.

Shortly before serving salad, coat the small cheeses with oil. Place them under the broiler, 3 to 4 minutes on each side. Remove before they begin to collapse.

To serve, toss salad lightly with vinaigrette, crush the cheeses slightly, and arrange them on top. *See *Chevrotins* in Miscellaneous Notes.

Tomates aux crevettes

[FOR 4 PEOPLE]

4 large firm, ripe tomatoes
Salt to taste
½ pound peeled shrimp (fresh, frozen,
    or canned)
Juice of ½ lemon
Freshly ground black pepper to taste
½ cup mayonnaise (p. 26)

GARNISH

4 sprigs parsley

TOMATOES STUFFED WITH SHRIMP

Preparation time: 15 minutes

Cut a large slice off the top of each tomato, from the side opposite the stem. Hollow the tomatoes out with a teaspoon, without tearing the skin. Rub them inside with a bit of salt and turn them upside down on a plate to let them drain 10 minutes in the refrigerator. The cold will keep them firm.

Defrost the shrimp, if necessary. Sprinkle them with lemon juice and pepper.

Prepare a stiff mayonnaise or use store-bought mayonnaise.

Mix the shrimp with ¾ of the mayonnaise. Fill the tomatoes with it. Top with a touch of mayonnaise and a sprig of parsley.

Beignets de gambas (langoustines ou grosses crevettes) SHRIMP FRITTERS

[FOR 4 PEOPLE]

Preparation and cooking time: 20 minutes / *Deep-frying temperature:* 325°

24 peeled shrimp or prawns

LIGHT BATTER

2 egg whites
2 pinches salt
A few drops lemon juice
1 heaping tablespoon plus 1 level tablespoon flour or potato starch

Oil

LIGHT BATTER: Just before using, beat the egg whites with 2 pinches of salt and the lemon juice until stiff peaks form. Add the flour in a steady stream, folding it in carefully with a wooden spoon.

Dip the still-frozen shrimp in the batter. Plunge it into moderately hot oil so that it can defrost while cooking. (But if it has already defrosted, toss it into very hot oil.)

Variation: Try marinating the shellfish, lemon juice, herbs (fresh basil, for example), pepper, and a little oil for about 1 hour. Excellent!

Bouchées à la Reine

[FOR 4 PEOPLE]

1 pound veal sweetbreads
1 small carrot, 1 onion, chopped fine
2 tablespoons butter
½ cup dry white wine
1 teaspoon thyme
1 bay leaf
Salt to taste
Freshly ground black pepper to taste
¼ pound mushrooms
1 teaspoon lemon juice

VELOUTÉ SAUCE

1 tablespoon butter
1 tablespoon flour
Mushroom-cooking liquid
About ¼ of the sweetbread-cooking
    liquid

1 small can chicken *quenelles**
Pinch nutmeg

4 prebaked puff pastry shells

SWEETBREADS IN PUFF PASTRY SHELLS

Preparation and cooking time: 1 hour / *Oven temperature:* 350°

Place the sweetbreads in a pot of water. Bring slowly to a boil. Simmer 2 minutes. Rinse in cold water and drain. Trim off the fat, connective tissue, and cartilage. Mince the carrot and onion. Sauté them in about ½ tablespoon of hot butter. Add the sweetbreads, 1½ cups of water, the wine, thyme, bay leaf, salt, and pepper. Cover and simmer over very low heat 20 minutes.

Meanwhile trim the sandy bottoms off the mushrooms. Wash and slice them. Put them in a pan with the remaining butter, the lemon juice, salt, and pepper. Add just enough water to cover. Simmer 5 minutes.

VELOUTÉ SAUCE: Melt, over moderate heat, 1 tablespoon of butter. Add the flour. Stir over the heat a few minutes until the mixture is foamy. Add 1 cup of the cooking liquid from the mushrooms and the cooking liquid from the sweetbreads. Simmer over extremely low heat, stirring frequently, about 8 minutes, or until it thickens.

Combine the sauce, the diced sweetbreads, the mushrooms, the *quenelles*, and a little nutmeg. Keep warm in a double boiler.

Ten minutes before serving, heat the pastry shells in a moderate (350°) oven. Fill them with the sweetbread mixture. Put their caps on. Serve immediately.

*Since it is virtually impossible to find these delicate little chicken dumplings in the U.S., you'll either have to make your own or leave them out.

Escargots bourguignonne

[FOR 4 PEOPLE]

SNAIL BUTTER
1 clove garlic, crushed
1 shallot, chopped fine
¼ cup minced parsley
8 ounces (2 sticks) butter
1 teaspoon salt
Freshly ground black pepper to taste
2 tablespoons dry white wine

4 dozen snails (canned)
4 dozen empty snail shells
1 cup dry white wine

4 *escargot* pans

SNAILS WITH BUTTER AND GARLIC

Preparation and cooking time: 45 minutes / *Oven temperature:* 450°

SNAIL BUTTER: Mince the garlic, shallot, and parsley. Knead the butter with a wooden spoon until it is creamy. Blend in the garlic mixture, salt, pepper, and 2 tablespoons of the wine.

Drain the snails. Add to each empty shell a bit of the stuffing, a drained snail, and some more stuffing, packing it in well. Arrange them as you go along in little dishes with indentations made especially for *escargots*. If you don't have them, you can use egg-poaching pans with indentations.

Fifteen minutes before the meal, preheat the oven to 450°. Pour 2 teaspoons of the wine into each *escargot* pan. Put them in the oven 5 to 10 minutes, until the stuffing is hot and bubbly.

Gratin de langoustines

[FOR 4 PEOPLE]

2 pounds raw prawns or large shrimp
2 tablespoons oil
1 small carrot, 1 shallot, 1 clove garlic, chopped fine
3 tablespoons Cognac
2 cups dry white wine
1 tablespoon tomato paste
3 cups water
Bouquet garni
Salt to taste
Freshly ground black pepper to taste
Pinch cayenne pepper
1 egg yolk
1 cup *crème fraîche*

4 ovenproof porcelain ramekins or baking dishes

PRAWNS WITH *CRÈME FRAÎCHE* AND WINE

Preparation and cooking time: 1 hour and 30 minutes

In a large skillet, sauté the prawns over high heat in oil. Add the minced carrot, shallot, and garlic. Sprinkle with Cognac. Flame the mixture over the heat. Add the wine, tomato paste, water, bouquet garni, salt, pepper, and cayenne. Cover and simmer gently 3 to 4 minutes.

Peel the prawns, reserving the shells. Arrange the prawns in the ramekins and keep them warm.

Pulverize the shells in a food mill or food processor. Add the cooking liquids. Cook over medium-high heat 20 minutes, uncovered. Strain this sauce through a strainer lined with paper towels.

Blend together the egg yolk and cream. Stir into the sauce off the heat. Pour over the shrimp. Place the ramekins under the broiler or in the top of a very hot (450°) oven 2 to 3 minutes and serve.

My advice: If you feel your sauce is too thin before adding the egg yolk and *crème fraîche*, there is still time to mix in a spoonful of butter kneaded into the same amount of flour. Boil for an instant. Then add the egg yolk and cream, off the heat.

Mousselines de foies de volailles CHICKEN LIVER MOUSSELINES

[FOR 4 TO 6 PEOPLE]

Preparation and cooking time: 50 minutes / Oven temperature: 425°

THICK BÉCHAMEL SAUCE
1 tablespoon butter
1 heaping tablespoon flour
1 cup milk
Salt and pepper to taste

1 onion or shallot, chopped fine
1 tablespoon minced parsley
½ pound chicken livers / 1 egg
2 tablespoons *crème fraîche* or whipping cream
Salt and pepper to taste
¼ teaspoon nutmeg
⅛ teaspoon cinnamon
1 teaspoon butter

GARNISH
2 tomatoes / 1 teaspoon butter
A few bunches parsley

6 small ovenproof ramekins or molds

THICK BÉCHAMEL SAUCE: Over medium heat, stir the butter and flour together until the mixture foams. Add the cold milk, salt, and pepper. Stir until thick.

Mince the onion or shallot and parsley. Process them in a food processor with the chicken livers, béchamel, egg, cream, salt, pepper, nutmeg, and cinnamon.

Butter the molds. Fill them with the mixture up to about ½ inch below the rim of the mold (they puff up in cooking). Place the molds in a bain-marie and bake in a hot (425°) oven 30 minutes.

Meanwhile peel and seed the tomatoes. Sauté them in 1 teaspoon of butter, salt, and pepper until they are reduced to a fairly thick puree.

Unmold the liver mousselines. Garnish them with the tomato puree and little bunches of parsley.

Variation: Instead of tomatoes, a mushroom cap or sliced mushrooms, preferably sautéed in butter or simmered in water, makes a nice garnish. Pour a little warmed *crème fraîche* over them.

Pannequets au roquefort

[FOR 8 CRÊPES]

CRÊPE BATTER

1 cup flour
2 to 3 eggs
2 cups water
1 tablespoon oil
½ teaspoon salt

ROQUEFORT BÉCHAMEL SAUCE

2 tablespoons butter
1 heaping tablespoon flour
1 cup milk
Freshly ground black pepper to taste
3 ounces Roquefort cheese
2 tablespoons *crème fraîche*

Grated Gruyère or Parmesan cheese
1 tablespoon butter

8- or 9-inch skillet
Paper towel soaked in oil

ROQUEFORT CRÊPES

Preparation and cooking time: 45 minutes, plus resting time for the batter / *Oven temperature:* 450°

CRÊPES: In a mixing bowl or food processor, beat together all the ingredients for the batter until they are blended into a fairly runny batter. Let it rest in the refrigerator, 1 hour if possible. Cook the crêpes over high heat, in a very hot pan, greasing it between each cooking with the oiled towel.

ROQUEFORT BÉCHAMEL SAUCE: Whisk together, over low heat, the melted butter and flour. As soon as the mixture bubbles, add the cold milk all at once, and pepper (no salt). Whisk until the mixture comes to a boil. Let simmer a couple of minutes. Off the heat, stir in the crumbled or grated Roquefort and the *crème fraîche*.

Place a spoonful of this mixture on each crêpe. Roll up the crêpes and tuck the ends under. In a shallow buttered baking dish, arrange the crêpes as you make them, side by side, seam side down. If any sauce is left over, spread it over the top. Sprinkle with grated Gruyère or Parmesan cheese and dot with butter. Brown in a very hot (450°) oven or broiler about 5 minutes.

My advice: The number of crêpes depends on the thickness of the batter and the size of the pan. If you love crêpes, don't hesitate to buy a good small skillet made especially for cooking them, either in sturdy cast iron or with a nonstick surface.

Pissaladière PROVENÇALE PIZZA

[For 6 to 8 people]

CRUST
2 cups flour / ½ teaspoon salt
8 tablespoons (1 stick) butter or margarine
About ½ cup water

or 1 pound frozen pie dough

TOPPING
2 medium onions
3 tablespoons butter
Salt and pepper to taste
12 anchovy fillets packed in oil
20 black olives

10- to 12-inch pie pan (preferably with
low sides such as a quiche pan)

Preparation and cooking time: 1 hour, plus resting time for the dough / *Oven temperature:* 450°

CRUST: Mix the flour, salt, and pieces of butter by pressing and rubbing your hands together. Add a little water to this coarse-grained mixture. Knead vigorously. Form into a ball, then flatten it with the palm of your hand. Roll it into a loose ball again. Do this rapidly 3 times. Roll or press the dough into a thin crust in the pie pan and refrigerate it, 1 hour if possible.

Peel the onions (under cold water to avoid crying). Cut them in thin slices. Cook them until golden in a deep pot with 3 tablespoons of butter. Then add 1 cup of water, salt, and pepper. Cover and simmer 15 minutes.

Spread the cooked onions in the pastry-lined pie pan. Top with anchovy fillets laid out in a star pattern and black olives. Bake in a hot (450°) oven 30 to 40 minutes. Remove from the pan and serve hot or warm.

Quenelles de poisson

[FOR 4 PEOPLE]

¾ pound fish fillets (pike or silver hake)*
2 egg whites
Salt to taste
Freshly ground black pepper to taste
Pinch cayenne pepper
2 tablespoons *crème fraîche*

MORNAY SAUCE

2 tablespoons butter
¼ cup flour
2 cups cold milk
Salt to taste
Freshly ground black pepper to taste
¼ teaspoon nutmeg
½ cup grated Gruyère or Swiss cheese
¼ cup *crème fraîche*

1 tablespoon butter

FISH QUENELLES

Preparation and cooking time: 35 minutes, plus at least 1 hour waiting time / *Oven temperature:* 450°

Coarsely chop the fish fillets. Process to a fine puree in a food processor. Scrape into a large mixing bowl.

Add, little by little, the unbeaten egg whites, stirring vigorously with a wooden spoon 5 minutes. The mixture should develop the consistency of very thick mayonnaise. Add salt, pepper, cayenne pepper, and *crème fraîche*. Mix and refrigerate for at least 1 hour (or even overnight).

Prepare the Mornay sauce (see the recipe for Poached Eggs with Ham, p. 49).

Poaching: In a pot of salted water (just on the verge of boiling) drop, by tablespoonfuls, the chilled *quenelle* mixture. Don't put in too much so that they can puff up easily. Let simmer without boiling 8 to 10 minutes. Drain thoroughly on paper towels.

Arrange the *quenelles* in a shallow baking dish. Cover with creamy Mornay sauce, dot with butter, and bake in a hot (450°) oven about 10 minutes.

My advice: The *quenelles* may be cooked a few hours in advance. Leave them in their poaching water in the refrigerator. Just before serving, simply cover them with sauce and put them into the oven to heat and brown.

*Easier to use and more readily available in the U.S. are other sturdy and somewhat gelatinous fish such as halibut, ocean cod, or firm-fleshed varieties of ocean flounder.

Quiche aux courgettes et tomates

[FOR 4 PEOPLE]

PASTRY DOUGH WITH EGG:

1 cup flour
¼ teaspoon salt
½ cup soft butter or margarine
1 egg

FILLING

3 small zucchini
About 3 tablespoons oil (preferably olive oil)
Salt to taste
Freshly ground black pepper to taste
4 tomatoes (not too ripe)
10 to 12 fresh basil leaves
2 eggs
1 cup milk

1 quiche pan, 10 to 12 inches in diameter

ZUCCHINI AND TOMATO QUICHE

Preparation and cooking time: 1 hour / Oven temperature: 450°

PASTRY DOUGH WITH EGG: Mix the flour, salt, and pieces of butter, pressing and rubbing the palms of your hand together to produce a coarse-grained mixture. Add the egg. Knead vigorously and form into a ball. Flatten with the palm of your hand. Gather it up into another ball. Do this 3 times. If the dough isn't adhering properly, dampen it with a spoonful of water worked in rapidly. Roll out the dough. Fit it into the buttered quiche pan. Prick the bottom all over with a fork so that it doesn't bubble up in cooking. Bake in a hot (450°) oven about 25 minutes.

Meanwhile cut the zucchini, unpeeled, into slices about ¼ inch thick. Place them in a single layer in a large skillet containing half the oil, warmed. Cook over moderately high heat, 4 to 5 minutes on each side. Add salt and pepper. Transfer the zucchini to a plate.

Pour the remaining oil into the skillet. Cut the tomatoes in half. Squeeze them gently to drain off any excess juice. Place them, cut side down, in the hot skillet. Fry them 4 to 5 minutes.

Scatter the basil leaves over the baked crust. Arrange the zucchini and tomatoes over it. Beat the eggs and milk together. Check the seasoning. Pour over the filled tarte and bake 15 minutes in the oven. Serve hot or warm.

Quiche lorraine à la crème

[FOR 6 TO 8 PEOPLE]

PASTRY DOUGH

2 cups flour
½ teaspoon salt
12 tablespoons (1½ sticks) butter or
    margarine
About ½ cup water

or 1 pound frozen pie dough

FILLING

¼ pound salt pork or ham
5 eggs
⅔ cup *crème fraîche* or whipping cream,
    or ⅓ cup milk and ⅓ cup cream
Salt to taste
Freshly ground black pepper to taste
¼ teaspoon nutmeg (optional)

1 quiche pan, 12 to 14 inches in diam-
    eter

QUICHE LORRAINE WITH CREAM

Preparation and cooking time: 1 hour / *Oven temperature:* 450°

PASTRY DOUGH: Mix the flour, salt, and pieces of butter by rubbing the palms of your hands together. Add the water to this coarse-grained dough. Knead vigorously. Form into a ball, then flatten it with the palm of your hand. Gather up into a ball again. Do this 3 times. If possible, chill for a while before rolling out the dough and fitting it into the quiche pan. Carefully prick the entire surface with a fork to prevent it from bubbling up during baking.

Dice the salt pork. Plunge it into boiling water. As soon as the water returns to a boil, drain the pieces of salt pork. Scatter them over the pie crust (ham may be put in the crust without preliminary blanching).

Beat together the eggs, cream (or milk and cream), a little salt, pepper, and, if desired, nutmeg. Pour over the quiche. Bake in a hot (450°) oven about 40 minutes. As soon as it comes out of the oven, remove the quiche from pan and serve.

My advice: If the top browns before the quiche is cooked through, cover with a piece of foil to prevent it from browning further.

Quiche moelleuse aux moules

[FOR 4 PEOPLE]

PASTRY DOUGH

1 cup flour
½ teaspoon salt
6 tablespoons butter or margarine
About ½ cup water

FILLING

1½ quarts mussels
½ cup dry white wine
1 small onion, chopped coarse / 2 eggs
3 to 4 tablespoons *crème fraîche* or
    whipping cream
1 tablespoon minced parsley
Pepper to taste / Salt (optional)

CREAMY MUSSEL QUICHE

Preparation and cooking time: 1 hour and 15 minutes / Oven temperature: 450°

Prepare the pastry dough (see the recipe for Quiche Lorraine with Cream, p. 40). Fit it into a buttered quiche pan 10 to 12 inches in diameter. Prick the bottom and refrigerate.

Scrub and wash the mussels. Steam them open over high heat, in a pot with the wine and chopped onion. Remove them from their shells. Pour the cooking liquid through a strainer lined with paper towels to remove any sand. Arrange the well-drained mussels in the crust.

Beat the eggs with the cream, a cup of the mussel broth, and minced parsley. Add pepper, but salt only after tasting. Pour over the mussels. Bake in a hot (450°) oven 30 to 35 minutes.

Soufflé au fromage

[FOR 4 PEOPLE]

THICK BÉCHAMEL SAUCE

2 tablespoons butter
3 tablespoons flour
1 cup cold milk
Salt and pepper to taste

3 eggs, separated / Pinch salt
¾ cup grated Gruyère or Swiss cheese

Remarks: You must beat the egg whites until stiff peaks form. Before beating them, add a pinch of salt; they'll rise better. Fold gently into the béchamel sauce with a spoon or rubber spatula, and not with a whisk. So that your soufflé will rise evenly, run a knife blade around between it and the mold.

Finally, wait until your guests arrive before putting the soufflé in the oven. Remember that "a soufflé doesn't wait, it's the guests who wait for it."

CHEESE SOUFFLÉ

Preparation and cooking time: 45 minutes / Oven temperature: 400°

THICK BÉCHAMEL SAUCE: Melt the butter over low heat. Add the flour. Stir over the heat a few seconds until the mixture becomes foamy. Add the cold milk all at once. Season with salt and pepper. Stir until it begins to boil.

Preheat the oven to 400°. Butter a soufflé mold. Separate the egg yolks from the whites. Add a pinch of salt to the whites. Beat them until very stiff peaks form.

Add to the béchamel, off the heat, the grated cheese and egg yolks, then, very carefully, the beaten egg whites. Pour into the mold. Bake in the oven 25 to 30 minutes.

My advice: Be careful not to get excited too soon! Your soufflé isn't necessarily done just because it puffs up. Leave it in the oven a little while longer, for if it's thoroughly cooked it collapses less rapidly. By your second or third try, making a cheese soufflé will seem easy to you.

ROQUEFORT TARTE

Tarte au roquefort

[FOR 4 PEOPLE]

Preparation and cooking time: 1 hour / *Oven temperature:* 450°

PASTRY DOUGH WITH EGG

1 cup flour
¼ teaspoon salt
½ cup soft butter or margarine
1 egg

FILLING

3 ounces Roquefort cheese
3 eggs
3 to 4 tablespoons *crème fraîche* or whipping cream
Freshly ground black pepper to taste

1 pie or quiche pan, 10 to 12 inches in diameter

PASTRY DOUGH WITH EGG: Mix the flour, salt, and pieces of butter by rubbing the palms of your hands together to make a coarse-grained dough. Add the egg. Knead vigorously and form into a ball. Flatten it with the palm of your hand. Form it into a ball again. Do this 3 times. If the dough doesn't adhere properly, moisten it with a spoonful of water, working it in rapidly. Roll out. Fit into a buttered pie or quiche pan.

Crumble the Roquefort finely with a food mill, sieve, or cheese grater.

Beat together the eggs, cream, and crumbled Roquefort. Add pepper but not salt; the Roquefort is salty enough. Pour into the crust. Bake in a hot (450°) oven about 30 minutes. Serve the quiche as soon as it's done as an entrée, or cold as an appetizer with drinks.

Tourte au crabe CRAB TORTE

[FOR 4 TO 6 PEOPLE]

COURT BOUILLON

1 cup vinegar
1 carrot, 1 onion, chopped coarse
3 whole cloves
Bouquet garni
Salt to taste
10 peppercorns

2 large crabs
3 slices firm white bread
½ cup dry white wine
3 scallions or small onions
1 clove garlic
1 small pimiento
½ pound ground pork loin
3 tablespoons butter
Salt to taste
Freshly ground black pepper to taste

PASTRY DOUGH

1⅔ cups flour
1 teaspoon salt
8 tablespoons (1 stick) butter or margarine
¾ cup water

2 eggs
⅓ cup *crème fraîche*

1 pie pan, 10 inches in diameter

Preparation and cooking time: 2 hours and 30 minutes / *Oven temperature:* 450°

Combine the ingredients of the court bouillon. Cook the crabs about 20 minutes in it, then let them cool.

Shell the crabs. Remove the meat from the legs, claws, and cavities in the upper shell. Soak the bread in the wine. Mince the scallions or onions, garlic, and pimiento. Cook until golden, with the ground pork, in 2 tablespoons of the butter. Stir in the crab, the bread (squeezed dry and crumbled), salt, and pepper.

PASTRY DOUGH: Work the flour, salt, and pieces of butter or margarine between the palms of your hands. Add the water to this coarse-grained mixture. Knead vigorously. Form into a ball, then flatten it out again. Form it into another ball. Do this 3 times. Divide it in two halves that you flatten into two circles. Line the pie pan with one.

Spread the crab mixture over it. Cover with the second circle of dough lightly moistened around the edges. Seal by pressing the two layers together. Cut a hole in the center. To keep it open, slip a little foil chimney in it. Brush the surface of the pie with a little beaten egg. Bake in a hot (450°) oven 30 to 40 minutes.

When it's done, mix the beaten eggs with the *crème fraîche*. Pour it inside the pie, through the opening in the chimney. Return to the oven 5 minutes. Serve hot.

My advice: Using canned crab will save you the trouble of shelling. The trade-off is that it won't taste quite as good!

Tourte à la viande   # MEAT TORTE

[FOR 6 PEOPLE]

Marination: The day before / *Preparation and cooking time:* 1 hour and 40 minutes
Oven temperature: 450°

1 pound veal shoulder
½ pound pork loin
Salt and pepper to taste

MARINADE

½ cup red wine
1 carrot, 1 onion, 1 shallot, chopped
  coarse
1 teaspoon thyme / 1 bay leaf
1 tablespoon minced parsley
Salt and pepper to taste

PASTRY DOUGH

1⅔ cups flour / 1 teaspoon salt
6 tablespoons butter or margarine
¾ cup water

2 eggs

The previous day, marinate the meat with all its ingredients.

PASTRY DOUGH: See Crab Torte (preceding recipe). Line the pie pan with one crust.

Drain the meat. Chop it, then salt and pepper. Spread it over the crust. Cover with the second circle of dough lightly dampened around the edges. Seal by pressing the two layers together, then roll them up.

Cut a hole in the center and slide a little foil chimney in it. Brush the surface of the pie with a little beaten egg or water. Bake at 450° about 1 hour.

When the pie is done, beat the egg yolks with ½ cup of the marinade. Pour it inside the pie, through the opening in the chimney. Return it to the oven 5 minutes. Serve hot.

My advice: So that the top crust doesn't open during baking, don't wet the edges too much: too much dampness interferes with proper adhesion.

Vol-au-vent financière

[FOR 6 TO 8 PEOPLE]

1 sweetbread
¼ pound spinal marrow
1 beef brain
Salt to taste
1 teaspoon vinegar
2 tablespoons butter
1 onion, chopped fine
1 carrot, chopped fine
1 tablespoon flour
1 tablespoon tomato paste
2 cups dry white wine
1 cup Madeira
Bouquet garni
Freshly ground black pepper to taste
½ pound mushrooms
1 small truffle
1 can *quenelles**
12 pitted green olives
1 puff pastry shell, about 10 inches in
    diameter

SWEETBREADS AND BRAINS IN PUFF PASTRY

Preparation and cooking time: 1 hour and 30 minutes

Cook the sweetbread according to the recipe for Sweetbreads in Puff Pastry Shells (p. 32).

Trim and rinse the marrow and brain. Place them in a skillet of boiling water with salt and vinegar. Turn the heat down very low. Remove from the heat just before the water begins to simmer. Let them cool in the cooking broth.

Lightly brown the sweetbread in 1 tablespoon of the butter. Remove it from the skillet. Lightly brown the minced onion and carrot, filament from the sweetbread, flour, tomato paste, wine, ½ cup of the Madeira, bouquet garni, salt, and pepper. Add the sweetbread. Cover and simmer 15 minutes.

Wash and quarter the mushrooms. Sauté them rapidly in the remaining butter. Add the finely minced truffle and its juices, diced marrow and brains, thickly sliced *quenelle*, olives, the remaining Madeira, sweetbread cooking liquid, and pepper to taste. Cover and simmer 10 minutes.

Heat the pastry shell in the oven. Fill it just before serving.

My advice: Use truffle juice, not just the truffle, because that's where most of the flavor is.

*Since canned *quenelles* are virtually impossible to find in the U.S. you may just have to leave them out of the recipe.

Bouillabaisse borgne

ONE-EYED BOUILLABAISSE

[FOR 4 PEOPLE]

2 leeks (white part only), sliced in rounds
1 onion, chopped coarse
2 tablespoons oil (preferably olive oil)
2 tomatoes, sliced in rounds
4 firm potatoes, peeled and sliced in
  rounds
4 cloves garlic
1 sprig fennel or 1 teaspoon dried
Bouquet garni
Orange peel
2 big pinches saffron
Salt to taste
Freshly ground black pepper to taste
4 slices stale French bread
4 eggs
Minced parsley

4 soup bowls

Preparation and cooking time: 45 minutes

Wash the leeks and slice them. Chop the onion. In a pot, cook both, slowly, without browning, in the oil.

Slice the tomatoes and peeled potatoes. Add them to the pot along with 2 cloves of the garlic, fennel, bouquet garni, a small piece of orange peel, saffron, salt, pepper, and 4½ cups of water. Boil about 30 minutes.

Rub the bread slices with the remaining garlic. Place one in the bottom of each bowl.

When the vegetable broth is done, strain it without crushing the vegetables and discard the bouquet garni. Pour the broth back into the pot. Arrange the vegetables on a platter and keep them warm.

Bring the broth back to a simmer. Poach the eggs in it 3 minutes. Then remove them gently with a slotted spoon.

Pour the broth into the bowls with the bread. Serve the poached eggs and vegetables lightly sprinkled with parsley separately.

My advice: If fresh tomatoes are unavailable, use 2 teaspoons of tomato paste. But it isn't as good.

Œufs brouillés   SCRAMBLED EGGS

[FOR 1 PERSON]

Preparation and cooking time: 25 minutes

2 to 3 eggs
Salt to taste
Freshly ground black pepper to taste
1 tablespoon butter
1 tablespoon _crème fraîche_ or whipping
    cream (optional)

Beat the eggs lightly in a medium-sized pan with a round bottom. Add salt and pepper.

Cook in a double boiler, or directly over very low heat, stirring constantly with a wooden spoon. The eggs will start to become creamy. Continue stirring, over the heat, blending in little pieces of the butter and, toward the end, the cream, if desired.

Scrambled eggs are done when they look like thick, lumpy cream. Remove them at once from the heat and serve over slices of toast or on warm plates.

My advice: To ensure success with scrambled eggs, cook them over a double boiler (at least until you get the hang of it). Use a thick pan (enamelware, Pyrex, or heatproof porcelain).

Stir with a wooden spoon, not a whisk.

If they start coagulating too rapidly, add a spoonful of cold water to stop the cooking. Meanwhile, don't stop stirring.

Œufs cocotte pastourelle   BAKED EGGS WITH CREAM

[FOR 4 PEOPLE]

Preparation and cooking time: 15 minutes / _Oven temperature:_ 550°

¼ pound fresh mushrooms
1 slice lean ham, minced (optional)
2 tablespoons butter
3 ounces Roquefort cheese
2 to 3 tablespoons _crème fraîche_ or
    whipping cream
Freshly ground black pepper to taste
Pinch salt
8 eggs

8 ramekins

Mince the mushrooms and sauté over medium heat with a little butter, a few drops of lemon juice, salt, and pepper. Heat with the ham in the ramekins along with the butter.

Mash the cheese with a fork, along with the cream to soften it. Add pepper. Salt it very lightly.

Spread this mixture in the ramekins. Break an egg in each one.

Place the ramekins in a baking pan and pour in enough water to come halfway up the side. Bake in a very hot (550°) oven 8 to 10 minutes. You can make the eggs in boiling water on top of the stove, but in that case, cover the ramekins. The cooking time will be a little longer.

Serve the eggs in the ramekins.

Œufs cocotte aux pointes d'asperges

BAKED EGGS WITH ASPARAGUS TIPS

[FOR 4 PEOPLE]

Preparation and cooking time: 20 minutes / *Oven temperature:* 550°

1 small can asparagus tips
2 tablespoons butter / 8 eggs
Salt and pepper to taste

MORNAY SAUCE

2 tablespoons butter
1 heaping tablespoon flour
3 cups milk
Salt and pepper to taste
¼ cup grated Gruyère or Swiss cheese
½ cup *crème fraîche* or whipping cream

8 ramekins

Remarks: You can make these eggs on top of the stove, in a pan of boiling water. Cover each ramekin with foil to create heat on the surface. Count on an extra two minutes of cooking time.

Drain the asparagus tips. Sponge them dry with paper towels. Butter the ramekins generously. Cover the bottoms with asparagus tips. Break an egg over them. Add salt and pepper.

Place the filled ramekins in a baking dish with a little cold water to bake them in a bain-marie, in a very hot (550°) oven, until the whites are firm (8 to 10 minutes).

MORNAY SAUCE: Meanwhile stir the butter and flour over low heat. Add the cold milk all at once, salt, and pepper. Stir with a whisk until it boils. Let simmer 2 minutes. Off the heat, stir in the grated cheese and cream. The sauce will be somewhat more liquid than usual.

Unmold 1 or 2 eggs on each warmed serving plate. Pour a little sauce over it and the rest into a sauceboat. Serve immediately.

Œufs pochés bohémienne

[FOR 4 PEOPLE]

5 eggs (one for garnish)
1 slice boiled ham
3 tablespons butter
4 slices homemade-type white bread

MORNAY SAUCE

2 tablespoons butter
1 heaping tablespoon flour
2 cups milk
Salt to taste
Freshly ground black pepper to taste
¼ cup grated Gruyère or Swiss cheese
1 egg yolk

Remarks: Even out the edges of the poached eggs by cutting them with a large cookie cutter or, simpler yet, with a knife. All the "chefs" do this.

POACHED EGGS WITH HAM

Preparation and cooking time: 45 minutes

Hard-boil 1 egg. Mince, separately, the yolk and the white. Dice the ham.

In a skillet, melt 3 tablespoons of butter. Fry the bread in it until lightly browned on both sides.

MORNAY SAUCE: Over low heat, melt 2 tablespoons of butter. Stir in the flour. Add the cold milk and stir until the mixture comes to a boil. Add salt and pepper. Simmer 2 minutes. Off the heat, add the grated cheese and egg yolk to the hot sauce. Keep warm, but don't place directly over the heat.

Into a pot of unsalted, simmering, acidulated water (1 cup of vinegar to 8 cups of water), carefully break the 4 eggs, one by one, holding them very close to the water. Remove them with a slotted spoon after 3 minutes. Place them on a kitchen towel to drain. Then arrange one on each slice of toasted bread. Cover with Mornay sauce. Decorate with the chopped ham and reserved hard-boiled egg yolk and white.

Omelette fermière au jambon et fines herbes

OPEN-FACED OMELETTE WITH HAM AND FRESH HERBS

[FOR 4 PEOPLE]

1 slice ham
2½ tablespoons butter
6 eggs
Salt to taste
Freshly ground black pepper to taste
2 tablespoons minced fresh herbs (parsley, chives, chervil, tarragon)

Preparation and cooking time: 15 minutes

Dice the ham. Sauté it rapidly over medium heat in a skillet with 1 tablespoon of the butter.

Beat the eggs with salt and pepper. Add the ham and minced herbs. Wipe out the skillet thoroughly, then melt the remaining butter. Stir it into the beaten eggs.

Put the empty skillet back on the heat (without washing it). As soon as it is very hot, pour in the eggs and let them set over medium heat, stirring slowly but constantly with a wooden spoon so that the omelette cooks clear through. As soon as it starts to look dry along the edges, but is still foamy in the center, turn it upside down on a warmed plate.

My advice: Make sure the pan is very hot before pouring the eggs in; otherwise the omelette will stick. But reduce the heat: the omelette should cook slowly, over medium heat, while you stir it through to the bottom so that it cooks evenly.

SORREL OMELETTE

Omelette à l'oseille

[FOR 4 PEOPLE]

1 bunch sorrel
2 tablespoons butter
8 eggs
1 slice ham, chopped thin
1 tablespoon minced chives
Salt to taste
Freshly ground black pepper to taste

Preparation and cooking time: 30 minutes

Remove the stems and tough strings from sorrel. Wash and coarsely chop it.

In a pot, reduce the sorrel over low heat, in 1 tablespoon of the butter. Simmer 5 to 7 minutes, stirring with a wooden spoon. Drain thoroughly.

Beat the eggs. Stir in the minced ham, sorrel, minced chives, salt, and pepper.

Melt the remaining butter in a skillet. Pour it into the beaten eggs. Return the empty skillet to the heat (without washing it). When it is very hot, pour in the eggs. Cook them a few minutes over medium heat, stirring with a wooden spoon to cook the omelette evenly. As soon as the edges begin to set, fold it while turning it upside down on a warmed plate.

OMELETTE WITH CREAM AND HERBS FROM MONT SAINT MICHEL

Omelette du Mont-Saint-Michel

[FOR 4 PEOPLE]

6 to 7 eggs, separated
2 tablespoons *crème fraîche* or whipping cream
Salt to taste
Freshly ground black pepper to taste
1 tablespoon oil
2 tablespoons butter
1 tablespoon minced fresh herbs (parsley, chervil, tarragon)

Remarks: The egg whites should not be stiffly beaten, merely whisked together separately, with a fork.

Preparation and cooking time: 15 minutes

Take two bowls. In one, put the egg yolks, cream, salt, and pepper. In the other, combine the egg whites, salt, and pepper. Beat the contents of both bowls separately.

Heat the oil and 1 tablespoon of the butter in a large skillet. Pour in the yolks, then the whites. Cook rapidly 2 to 3 minutes, stirring gently with a fork.

Fold the omelette. Melt the rest of the butter over it before sliding it on to a long platter. Sprinkle with minced fresh herbs and serve.

My advice: I've chosen the simplest of the omelettes said to be from Mont-Saint-Michel for, of course, many variations are part of the area's gastronomic heritage.

Omelette soufflée au roquefort — FLUFFY OMELETTE WITH ROQUEFORT

[FOR 4 PEOPLE]

3 ounces Roquefort cheese
7 eggs, separated
3 tablespoons *crème fraîche* or whipping
   cream
Freshly ground black pepper to taste
2 tablespoons butter

Preparation and cooking time: 15 minutes

Press the cheese through a strainer—or grate it—to pulverize it. Mix it with the egg yolks, cream, and pepper (no salt).

Beat the egg whites until stiff peaks form. Fold them delicately into the mixture.

Melt the butter in a large skillet. Pour in the omelette. Shake the skillet to prevent sticking on the bottom. When the underside is golden brown, place the skillet under a broiler. As soon as the top of the omelette is lightly browned, serve it.

My advice: The ideal utensil for making a fluffy omelette is an oval skillet with a nonstick surface, generally used for fish. But any nonstick skillet, even a round one, will do. The important thing is to keep the omelette from sticking!

Timbale d'œufs portugaise

[For 4 to 6 people]

3 cups milk
6 eggs
Salt and pepper to taste
Pinch nutmeg

TOMATO SAUCE
3 medium tomatoes
1 bell pepper
2 tablespoons butter
2 cloves garlic, crushed
1 onion, chopped fine
1 tablespoon tomato paste
1 small hot pepper, chopped coarse
Bouquet garni
Salt and pepper to taste

Remarks: The *timbale* must be cooked quickly and timed carefully to avoid letting it boil. The top will bake rapidly in a very hot oven while the bottom stays at a lower temperature because of the bain-marie.

UNMOLDED EGGS WITH TOMATO SAUCE

Preparation and cooking time: 1 hour / *Oven temperature:* 525°

Preheat the oven to 525°. Meanwhile heat the milk. Beat the eggs in a bowl along with the salt, pepper, and nutmeg. Stir in, little by little, the boiling milk. Pour the mixture through a strainer to get rid of any pieces of egg.

Pour into a buttered soufflé mold. Put it in a shallow pan (a bain-marie) filled with cold water. Bake in the oven 20 to 25 minutes.

TOMATO SAUCE: Peel and quarter the tomatoes. Gently squeeze out their juice. Seed the pepper and cut it into thin strips. Heat the butter in a skillet. Toss in the minced garlic and onion, fresh tomatoes, tomato paste, hot pepper, bouquet garni, bell pepper, salt, and pepper. Cook over moderately high heat, uncovered 20 to 30 minutes. Puree in a food mill or food processor when cooked.

Let the egg *timbale* cool slightly before unmolding it on to a platter. Pour a little tomato sauce over it and serve the rest in a sauceboat.

Capilotade de lapin en gelée

[FOR 6 PEOPLE]

1 calf's foot with bone, split in half
1 tablespoon oil
1 tablespoon butter
1 rabbit, about 3 pounds, cut into pieces
¼ pound bacon*
3 shallots, chopped coarse
3 cloves garlic
Salt and pepper to taste
2 whole cloves, chopped coarse
Bouquet garni with extra thyme
2 carrots, cut in halves
2 cups dry white wine

GARNISH

Cornichons
Lettuce wedges

JELLIED RABBIT PÂTÉ

Preparation and cooking time the day before: 2 hours and 30 minutes / Cooling time: 12 hours

Boil the calf's foot 5 minutes and drain it.

In a large casserole, heat the oil and butter. Brown the rabbit in it (3 to 4 pieces at a time) and the diced bacon. Drain off all the grease accumulated in cooking.

Put the meat back in the casserole along with the shallots, garlic, salt, pepper, cloves, bouquet garni, carrots, and the calf's foot. Cover it ¾ of the way up with wine and a little water if necessary. Bring to a boil and simmer, covered, 2 hours.

When the rabbit is done, remove the meat from the bones, shredding it somewhat. Put all of the meat—including the meat from the calf's foot removed from the bone and diced—in 1 or 2 terrines (or loaf pans). Pour the strained cooking broth over it. Let it set in the refrigerator at least 12 hours. Serve, unmolded, with *cornichons* (small French pickles, available in jars) and lettuce.

*The unsalted, unsmoked fresh bacon commonly found in France is not readily available in the U.S. To keep American bacon from overpowering a dish, simmer it in a panful of water about 10 minutes; drain, rinse, and dry it.

Terrine de faisan PHEASANT PÂTÉ

[FOR 1 PHEASANT, ABOUT 3 POUNDS]

Marination time: 24 to 48 hours / *Preparation and cooking time:* 2 hours and 15 minutes
Oven temperature: 350°

½ pound boneless veal
½ pound boneless lean pork

MARINADE
1 cup dry white wine
¼ cup Madeira (optional)
1 carrot, 1 shallot, 1 onion, sliced in
  rounds
1 clove garlic
3 tablespoons oil
Bouquet garni
Freshly ground black pepper to taste

¼ pound bacon*
¼ pound ham
1 can truffle pieces
15 pistachio nuts
¼ pound pork fatback or bacon**

1 terrine, pâté mold, or loaf pan

Marination: Remove the pheasant meat from the bones. Place the meat in a large bowl with the veal and lean pork (cut into pieces) and the marinade ingredients. Refrigerate 24 to 48 hours.

Drain the meats. Reserve a few strips of pheasant. Mince the rest with the bacon and ham. Beat the ingredients together, mixing in a little strained marinade and juice from the truffles until the mixture is thoroughly blended.

Cut a piece the size of the top of your pâté mold out of the fatback. Fold it in half and cut out a few chevrons. Line the bottom and sides of the mold with the fatback scraps. Pack in just enough of the pâté mixture to fill half the mold. Distribute the reserved pheasant strips, small pieces of bacon, pistachio nuts, and truffle pieces over it. Cover with the remaining pâté mixture. Top the very full pâté mold with the piece of foil.

Bake in a bain-marie 1 hour and 45 minutes in a moderate (350°) oven. During the last 15 minutes, remove the cover so the top can brown. Thirty minutes after taking it out of the oven, place a small board or a dish with a weight on it on top of the pâté to pack it down. Let it sit at least 24 hours before eating.

My advice: For a well-seasoned pâté, use 1 teaspoon salt for every pound of meat.

*See the note about bacon on p. 54. **See Miscellaneous Notes on pork fatback.

Terrine de foie de porc

[FOR 10 TO 12 PEOPLE]

2 pounds pork liver
1 pound bacon*
2 shallots
2 cloves garlic
2 teaspoons salt
1 teaspoon pepper
2 cups brandy or Cognac
½ teaspoon allspice
1 large sheet pork fatback**
1 large piece pork caul
Bouquet garni
3 whole cloves

10-cup pâté mold, terrine, or loaf pan

Remarks: If you make it in 2 smaller molds, the second one will keep longer if you don't cut into it.

PORK LIVER PÂTÉ

Preparation and cooking time: 3 hours / *Oven temperature:* 350°

Cut the liver and bacon into small pieces. Mince them in a food processor or meat grinder with the shallots and garlic.

Place the mixture in a large bowl with salt, pepper, brandy or Cognac, and allspice. Stir together vigorously for several minutes.

Blanch the pork fatback and wipe dry. Dip the caul in a bowl of cold water so that it can be unfolded easily without tearing. Spread it out on a kitchen towel to dry, then line the mold with it, letting the edges overlap the sides of the mold.

Pour the forcemeat into the lined mold. Pack it down by tapping it lightly against the counter. Fold the caul all the way over the top of the pâté. Place the bouquet garni and cloves on top of it, then the fatback. Cover with the lid of the pâté mold or a piece of foil. Place in a baking pan filled with water.

Bake in a moderate (350°) oven for about 2 hours and 30 minutes. During the last 15 minutes, remove the cover to brown the top of the pâté. Cool. Lay a piece of foil against the top of the pâté. Cover the mold with its lid or another piece of foil and refrigerate 2 to 3 days if possible.

My advice: If you would like to keep it even longer, cover the pâté with about 1 inch of melted lard and keep it refrigerated.

*See the note about bacon on p. 54.
**See Miscellaneous Notes on pork fatback.

Terrine de foies de volailles   CHICKEN LIVER PÂTÉ

[FOR 4 TO 6 PEOPLE]

¾ pound chicken livers
¼ cup port
¼ cup Cognac
½ teaspoon thyme
⅛ teaspoon nutmeg
Freshly ground black pepper to taste
1 tablespoon oil
¼ pound boneless pork
¼ pound boneless veal
Salt to taste
¼ pound bacon*
1 bay leaf
2 ounces fatback**

6-cup pâté mold, terrine, or loaf pan

Preparation and cooking time the day before: 1 hour and 30 minutes / *Oven temperature:* 350°

The day before macerate the livers with the port, Cognac, thyme, nutmeg, pepper, and oil.

The next day, in a meat grinder or food processor, chop all but 4 of the livers, the pork, and the veal, along with the marinating liquid. Salt and pepper it generously. Cut the remaining livers into small dice.

Line the bottom and sides of the mold with the bacon. Pack in half the forcemeat, then a layer of the diced livers. Finish with the remaining forcemeat. Top with the bay leaf, and the fatback. Cover with a lid or foil. Bake in a baking pan filled with water in a moderate (350°) oven for about 1 hour. Keep the pâté in the refrigerator for a day or two before eating it.

My advice: Any poultry livers may be used: chicken, turkey, duck, or goose.

*See the note about bacon on p. 54.
**See Miscellaneous Notes on pork fatback.

Terrine de lièvre ou de lapin

RABBIT OR HARE PÂTÉ

[FOR ONE 5- TO 6-POUND RABBIT
OR HARE]

Marination time: 24 to 48 hours / *Preparation time:* 1 hour and 30 minutes
Cooking time: 1 hour and 45 minutes / *Oven temperature:* 350°

2½ pounds lean boneless pork
¾ pound bacon or salt pork*

MARINADE
1 bottle white or red wine
½ cup wine vinegar
4 tablespoons oil
1 carrot, 2 onions, 3 shallots, 1 stalk
celery, sliced in rounds
2 cloves garlic, crushed
5 sprigs parsley
1 sprig thyme or 1 teaspoon dried
½ bay leaf
½ teaspoon freshly ground black pepper
2 whole cloves

3 eggs
3 tablespoons cornstarch
Salt to taste
Freshly ground black pepper to taste
2 tablespoons Cognac
½ pound pork fatback**

1 to 2 pâté molds or terrines

Two to 3 days ahead of time, bone the rabbit or hare. Cut the saddle meat into fillets. Cut the remaining rabbit, pork, and bacon into pieces. Combine them in a bowl with the marinating ingredients. Let it marinate in the refrigerator.

One or 2 days ahead of time, drain the meats. Cook the marinade over medium heat, uncovered, 30 to 40 minutes, until it has been reduced to about 1 cup.

Meanwhile sponge the meats dry. Mince them, except for the rabbit fillets. Mix with the eggs, cornstarch, salt, pepper, and Cognac. Beat vigorously. Add a few tablespoons of the reduced and strained marinade (the pâté should not be too runny).

To assemble and cook the pâté, line the mold with fatback or bacon as described in Pheasant Pâté (p. 55) and cook it in a bain-marie in a moderate (350°) oven about 1 hour and 45 minutes.

My advice: To make attractive slices, remove the two rabbit fillets. Wrap each one in a thin strip of fatback and lay them side by side (or end to end) on the pâté when the mold is half filled. Then finish filling it with the remaining forcemeat.

*See the note about bacon on p. 54.
**See Miscellaneous Notes on pork fatback.

Terrine de Saint-Jacques au poivre vert   SCALLOP PÂTÉ WITH GREEN PEPPERCORNS

[FOR 10 PEOPLE]

Preparation and cooking time the day before: 2 hours, plus 6 hours resting time before cooking
Oven temperature: 350° then 400°

THICK BINDING MIXTURE (PANADE)
1 tablespoon flour
1 egg yolk
½ cup boiling milk
1 teaspoon salt
Freshly ground black pepper to taste
¼ teaspoon nutmeg

1 tablespoon green peppercorns (in brine)
½ pound whiting, sole, or flounder fillets
½ pound scallops (including coral, if available)*
3 eggs
½ cup *crème fraîche* or whipping cream
6 tablespoons softened butter

1 pâté mold, terrine, or loaf pan

MAYONNAISE WITH GREEN PEPPERCORNS
1 tablespoon green peppercorns (in brine)
1 egg yolk
Salt to taste
1 cup oil
1 tablespoon lemon juice
1 tablespoon *crème fraîche*

THICK BINDING MIXTURE (PANADE): The day before, in a food processor or deep bowl, beat together the flour and egg yolk. Then slowly add the boiling milk, salt, pepper, and nutmeg. Pour it into the same saucepan the milk was heated in and whisk over heat a few seconds (until it thickens). Let cool. Rinse the green peppercorns. Sponge them dry and mash them.

In the food processor, puree the fish fillets and scallops (reserving the coral if you have any). Beat each egg in thoroughly, then beat in the binding mixture, *crème fraîche*, softened butter piece by piece, and crushed peppercorns, until the mixture is almost smooth. Season if necessary. Generously butter the sides and bottom of the mold. Pack in half the scallop mixture. If you have the coral, lay it over the top. Cover with the remaining mixture. Cover the mold with foil. Let it rest in the refrigerator about 6 hours.

To bake (still the day before serving), place the mold, uncovered, in a shallow baking dish filled with water. Start baking with the oven set at 350°, then raise it to 400°, for 1 hour and 15 minutes. The mixture will rise a little in baking. Cover with foil to prevent it from "crusting." The pâté is done when a knife inserted in the middle comes out very hot, all along the blade. Refrigerate overnight.

Serve entrée in its baking dish thinly sliced with *crème fraîche* or mayonnaise with green peppercorns.

MAYONNAISE WITH GREEN PEPPERCORNS: Rinse and drain the peppercorns. Mash them and put them in a bowl with the egg yolk and salt. Beat a few seconds. Continue beating constantly and pour in oil, very slowly at first, then faster as the sauce thickens. When the mayonnaise is very stiff, add half the lemon juice to soften it somewhat. Beat in the remaining oil and, at the end, the *crème fraîche*. Finally, taste it before adding all or part of the remaining lemon juice.

*Scallops with coral are almost impossible to find in the U.S., so substitute another scallop or two instead.

SEAFOOD

Bar beurre blanc STRIPED BASS WITH BEURRE BLANC

[FOR 4 PEOPLE]

1 striped bass, about 2½ pounds

COURT BOUILLON

8 cups water
½ bottle dry white wine
1 onion, 1 carrot, sliced in rounds
Bouquet garni
Salt to taste
Freshly ground black pepper to taste
A few ice cubes

BEURRE BLANC

12 ounces (3 sticks) butter, diced and
    put in the freezer
2 shallots, chopped fine
1½ tablespoons white vinegar or ⅔ cup
    Muscadet wine
½ cup fish-cooking broth
Salt to taste
Freshly ground black pepper to taste

Preparation and cooking time: 30 minutes

Dice the butter for the *beurre blanc* and put it in the freezer.

COURT BOUILLON: In a fish poacher, simmer 4 cups of water with the wine, sliced onion and carrot, bouquet garni, salt, and pepper 20 minutes. Then add 4 cups cold water and some ice cubes to cool it off quickly.

Place the fish on a fish-poaching rack. Plunge it into the almost cold court bouillon. Bring to a boil and cook very gently, scarcely simmering, about 10 minutes.

BEURRE BLANC: A little ahead of time, or while the fish poaches, slowly cook the minced shallots with vinegar or wine, without letting it color, until the liquid has been reduced to almost nothing. Just before serving, remove the butter from the freezer. Pour ½ cup of the court bouillon into the pan with the shallot-reduction. Add salt and pepper. Turn the heat up high. As soon as it starts to boil, whisk in the butter, 2 to 3 pieces at a time, beating constantly with a wire whisk, over medium-high heat, until all the butter has been used. Remove the pan from the heat from time to time, for 3 to 4 seconds, continuing to whisk as if making mayonnaise. When the *beurre blanc* becomes creamy, serve it right away in a warm sauceboat, or pour it over the fish, on the serving platter.

Brochettes de fruits de mer SHELLFISH BROCHETTES

[FOR 4 PEOPLE]

1 lemon
12 unpeeled prawns or *langoustine* tails
8 sea scallops
8 small cubes lean salt pork / Oil
Salt and pepper to taste

4 skewers

Preparation and cooking time: 20 minutes / *Oven temperature:* 550°

Slice the lemon, then cut each slice in half. On each skewer, alternate 3 prawns, 2 scallops, 2 salt pork cubes, and lemon half-slices.

Brush the brochettes with oil. Salt and pepper them. Broil or bake them in the top of a very hot (550°) oven, 5 to 6 minutes on each side.

Brochettes de Saint-Jacques au bacon

SEA SCALLOP BROCHETTES WITH BACON

[FOR 4 PEOPLE]

16 sea scallops

LEMON MARINADE
2 tablespoons oil
Juice of 1 or 2 lemons plus rinds (minced)
1 teaspoon thyme
1 bay leaf
Freshly ground black pepper to taste

12 slices bacon*
2 large onions, sliced in rounds
A few bay leaves
1 lemon, quartered
2 tablespoons butter

4 skewers

Marination time: 1 hour / *Preparation and cooking time:* 30 minutes

Carefully wash the scallops (the white meat and the coral).* Marinate them 1 hour in the lemon marinade.

Wrap every other scallop with a piece of bacon. Pierce it where the two ends of the bacon meet to keep the scallop wrapped up. Thread, alternately, on the skewer wrapped and unwrapped scallops. Intersperse pieces of onion, bay leaves, and lemon peel between them wherever you wish.

Place the brochettes in a hot broiler—not too close to the heat—about 10 minutes. Turn them over several times, brushing them with the marinade. Serve with a quartered lemon and a sauceboat of melted butter. Rice *timbales* are a good accompaniment.

Note: To make rice *timbales*, butter the interior of the molds—cups, ramekins, or custard cups—and pack cooked rice into them. Invert them on to each plate and place the brochettes and lemon quarters on them.

*See the notes about bacon and scallops on p. 54 and p. 59, respectively.

CALAMARY WITH TOMATO SAUCE

Calmars niçoise

[FOR 4 PEOPLE]

3 pounds calamary (cuttlefish or squid)*
2 tablespoons oil
1 onion, 1 carrot, chopped fine
4 tomatoes, chopped coarse
1 teaspoon tomato paste
Bouquet garni
2 cloves garlic, crushed
2 whole cloves
Salt and pepper to taste
Pinch cayenne
2 cups dry white wine
2 cups water
A few sprigs parsley

Remarks: If you partially freeze the calamary for 2 to 3 hours, you'll have no difficulty removing the insides.

Preparation and cooking time: 1 hour and 30 minutes

Cut the calamary open from top to bottom with a pair of scissors. Remove the ink pockets, entrails, cartilage, and the hard beanlike beak. Wash in generous amounts of water. Remove the thin membrane that covers the fish. Cut the fish in strips. Sponge them dry.

In a pot, heat the oil. Add the strips of calamary, the onion, and the carrot. Stir over high heat.

After a few minutes, add the tomatoes, chopped and lightly crushed, the tomato paste, bouquet garni, minced garlic, whole cloves, salt, pepper, cayenne, wine, and water. Cover and simmer slowly for 45 minutes to 1 hour.

Discard the bouquet garni, and serve the dish sprinkled with parsley.

My advice: Calamary may be prepared the day before and reheated. Boiled potatoes or plain rice go well with the excellent calamary sauce.

*See Calamary in Miscellaneous Notes.

Colin froid à la russe

[FOR 4 PEOPLE]

COURT BOUILLON

8 cups water
¼ cup vinegar
2 onions, cut in quarters
Salt to taste
1 shallot, chopped coarse
1 whole clove, crushed
Bouquet garni

1 whole cod, about 3 to 4 pounds*
2 cups mayonnaise (see p. 26)

2 large (16 ounce) cans mixed vegeta-
    bles or two 16-ounce packages mixed
    frozen vegetables (about 4 cups)
1 can anchovies

COLD COD WITH VEGETABLE SALAD

Preparation and cooking time: 45 minutes, plus 1 hour waiting time

COURT BOUILLON: Boil the water, vinegar, onions, salt, shallot, clove, and bouquet garni 15 minutes. Let cool. Lower the fish into it. Reheat the court bouillon
slowly. Remove from the heat just as it reaches a boil. Let the fish cool in the court
bouillon for 1 hour

Prepare the mayonnaise.

Pour the vegetables into a strainer and let them drain thoroughly. At the last
minute, mix them with about half the mayonnaise.

Drain the fish. Scrape off the skin gently. Arrange the fish on a long platter.
Spoon a little vegetable salad along each side of the fish. Garnish the fish with
mayonnaise and crisscrossed anchovies. Serve the rest of the vegetables in a salad
bowl.

My advice: To make a good-sized fish without a fish poacher, use a large pot.
Wrap the fish in a kitchen towel or piece of muslin and lower it into the court
bouillon. When it is done, grab the ends of the towel to lift it out without mishap.

*Use cod, hake, haddock, or another similar white-fleshed fish.

Coquillages farcis   STUFFED SHELLFISH

[FOR 4 PEOPLE]

Mussels, clams, or bay scallops: 6 dozen
Or sea scallops: 4 dozen

STUFFING I
½ cup butter
1 shallot, chopped fine
2 cups bread crumbs / Minced parsley
Salt and pepper to taste

STUFFING II
6 tablespoons butter
2 cloves garlic, crushed
1 teaspoon curry powder
Juice of ½ lemon
Salt and pepper to taste

Preparation and cooking time: 30 minutes ahead of time, plus 10 minutes before serving
Oven temperature: 550°

Scrub the shells under running water and rinse them again. Open them, raw, with a knife. Detach the empty shells and place the full ones in individual ovenproof pans.

Place a spoonful of stuffing on each one. Refrigerate until just before serving.

At the last minute, brown under a broiler or in the top of a very hot (550°) oven 8 to 10 minutes.

My advice: To make perfect stuffed shellfish, they must be browned very rapidly in a very hot oven. Cooked slowly, they'll end up more like rubber than mollusks! This recipe may be prepared in advance and reheated.

Coquilles Saint-Jacques au champagne

[FOR 4 PEOPLE]

12 to 16 sea scallops

COURT BOUILLON
Bouquet garni
2 shallots, chopped coarse
1 onion
2 whole cloves
Salt to taste
Freshly ground black pepper to taste
½ bottle champagne

SAUCE
4 egg yolks
1 tablespoon *crème fraîche*
1 teaspoon cornstarch
2 cups scallop court bouillon

4 individual serving casseroles

SCALLOPS IN CHAMPAGNE

Preparation and cooking time: 30 minutes

Remove the beard from the scallops, saving only the white nugget of meat and the coral.* Wash them in running water to get rid of any sand. If the scallops are very large, cut them in half across the width. Put them in a large pot with the bouquet garni, chopped shallots, onion stuck with 2 cloves, salt, and pepper. Cover with champagne. Bring slowly to a bare simmer, keeping it just below simmering 2 minutes only. Remove the scallops with a slotted spoon and keep them warm.

Strain the cooking broth. Boil it over high heat, uncovered, until it evaporates by about half (2½ cups maximum).

SAUCE: In a bowl, beat the egg yolks, *crème fraîche*, and cornstarch. Then pour the contents into the pot with the broth, whisking constantly over low heat. As soon as the sauce thickens slightly, remove it from the heat without letting it boil.

Serve the scallops in individual casseroles, covered with sauce. You could accompany them with rice pilaf (see Rice Pilaf with Clams or Mussels, p. 202).

My advice: Don't let the scallops boil in the court bouillon because overly vigorous cooking is likely to make them fall apart and toughen.

*See the note on p. 59.

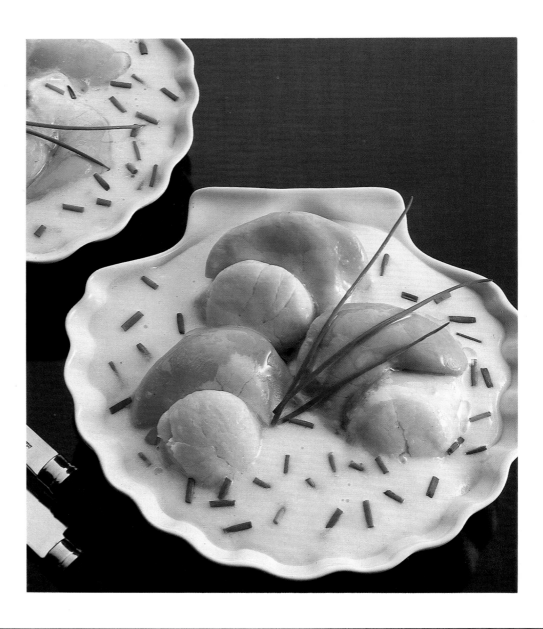

Coquilles Saint-Jacques en pâte

[FOR 4 people]

PASTRY DOUGH WITH EGG

1½ cups flour
4 tablespoons butter
½ teaspoon salt
1 egg

8 clean, dry scallop shells
12 to 16 scallops
A little flour
3 tablespoons butter
1 tablespoon oil
1 shallot, chopped fine
1 tablespoon minced parsley
Salt to taste
Freshly ground black pepper to taste

Remarks: The pastry shells can be prepared the day before and reheated in the oven, just before serving, while the scallops cook.

SCALLOPS IN PASTRY SHELLS

Preparation and cooking time: 45 minutes / *Oven temperature:* 525°

PASTRY DOUGH WITH EGG: Mix all the pastry ingredients in your food processor or mound the flour into a dome. In the middle, knead the softened butter with the salt. Work the egg in until it is creamy. Then rapidly knead in the flour.

Butter 4 scallop shells. Line them with a thin layer of dough, pressing with your fingers to make it stick. Trim the dough around the edges. Press down again. Cover with a second layer of scallop shells. Place in a very hot (525°) oven 10 minutes. Midway through the baking, remove the top shell to let the crust brown.

Meanwhile rinse the scallops and their coral (if available).* Sponge them dry. Cut them across the width in 2 or 3 slices. Flour them lightly. Sauté for 3 to 4 minutes in a skillet, over medium heat, with 1 tablespoon of the butter and the oil. Add the minced shallot, parsley, salt, and pepper, then, at the end, the remaining butter.

Unmold the pastry shells on a platter or on individual serving dishes. Fill them with the scallops and their sauce. Serve immediately.

*See the note on p. 59.

Coquilles Saint-Jacques provençale

SCALLOPS WITH GARLIC AND PARSLEY

[FOR 4 PEOPLE]

Preparation and cooking time: 30 minutes

1 clove garlic, crushed
2 tablespoons minced parsley
12 to 16 scallops
Flour for dredging
2 tablespoons butter
1 tablespoon oil
Salt to taste
Freshly ground black pepper to taste
Juice of ½ lemon

Mince the garlic and parsley together.

Rinse the scallops. Sponge them completely dry.

Dredge them in flour. Shake to remove any excess. Brown the scallops lightly in a skillet with moderately hot butter and oil. Turn to brown lightly on the other side, over moderate heat. Finally, sprinkle with the minced garlic and parsley, salt, and pepper. Cover and cook, over low heat, 5 more minutes. Sprinkle with lemon juice before serving.

My advice: If you've dried the scallops carefully, it isn't absolutely necessary to flour them. However, the flour helps prevent hot grease from splattering. For a milder flavor, substitute a shallot for the garlic.

Dorade farcie aux champignons

SEA BREAM STUFFED WITH MUSHROOMS

[FOR 4 PEOPLE]

1 whole sea bream, 2 to 4 pounds
(cleaned and scaled)*

STUFFING

About 1 cup milk
2 slices stale bread
½ pound mushrooms
1 shallot, chopped fine
3 tablespoons butter
1 egg yolk
1 tablespoon minced parsley
Salt to taste
Freshly ground black pepper to taste

1½ cups dry white wine
2 tablespoons butter
Salt to taste
Freshly ground black pepper to taste
1 lemon

Preparation and cooking time: 1 hour / Oven temperature: 525°

Wash the fish and blot dry with paper towels. If a dark membrane lines the stomach, remove it or the stuffing will pick up a bitter taste.

STUFFING: Pour the warm milk over the bread. Cut off the sandy bottom of the mushroom stems. Wash the mushrooms rapidly and slice them. Mince the shallot. Sauté the mushrooms and shallots over high heat in butter. Lightly squeeze the bread to get rid of any excess milk. Mix it with the egg yolk, parsley, salt, pepper, and mushrooms.

Pack this stuffing into the fish. Sew it up with white kitchen thread or keep the opening closed with a wad of crumpled foil.

Arrange in a buttered baking dish. Add the wine, butter cut into pieces, salt, and pepper. Place into the middle of a very hot (525°) oven 30 to 40 minutes. Baste during cooking. Serve with lemon sections.

My advice: Bake the fish in a serving dish, for there is always the risk of the fish falling apart if it's transferred to another platter.

*Or use hake, porgy, snapper, striped bass, or another lean whole fish.

Écrevisses à la nage

[FOR 4 PEOPLE]

COURT BOUILLON

1 carrot, 1 shallot, 1 onion, sliced in rounds
1 tablespoon butter
½ bottle dry white wine
Bouquet garni
Salt to taste
5 peppercorns, crushed
Pinch cayenne pepper

24 crayfish

CRAYFISH IN BROTH

Preparation and cooking time: 45 minutes

COURT BOUILLON: Slice the carrot, shallot, and onion. Cook them until golden brown in a casserole with the butter. Add the wine, an equal amount of water, bouquet garni, salt, peppercorns, and cayenne. Simmer 30 minutes.

Wash the crayfish in running water. Plunge them into the boiling court bouillon. Cook them 8 to 10 minutes. Remove from the broth and drain.

Cook the court bouillon, uncovered, over high heat until it evaporates by half. Put the crayfish back in this broth, either warm or chilled, to serve them *à la nage*—swimming.

Encornets farcis à la portugaise

[FOR 4 PEOPLE]

8 squid, 4 to 5 inches long
8 toothpicks for holding them closed

STUFFING

1 onion, chopped fine
1½ tablespoons butter
1 slice ham
2 carrots
1 tablespoon minced parsley
2 tomatoes
Salt and pepper to taste
2 egg yolks
10 black olives, crushed

SAUCE

2 tablespoons butter
1 onion, 1 carrot, 1 tomato, cut into strips
Salt and pepper to taste

1 tablespoon vinegar
1 cup dry white wine
1 tablespoon minced parsley

STUFFED SQUID WITH TOMATO SAUCE

Preparation and cooking time: 2 hours and 15 minutes

Clean and wash the squid (see Calamary with Tomato Sauce, p. 65). Sponge them dry.

STUFFING: Mince the onion. Cook it over low heat in a casserole with 1½ tablespoons of butter. Cover. Grind the ham, carrots, squid tentacles, and parsley in a food mill (or food processor, chopping ingredients coarsely first). Peel and seed the tomatoes. Put all of this in the casserole. Add salt and pepper. Cover and simmer 5 minutes. Remove from the heat and stir in the egg yolks. Cook over high heat a few seconds, stirring rapidly to dry the stuffing out without letting it stick. Finally, add the minced olives.

SAUCE: In a pot, combine 2 tablespoons of butter with the onion, carrot, and tomato, all cut into strips. Add salt and pepper. Simmer 10 minutes.

Pack the stuffing into the squid. Keep them closed with toothpicks. Arrange them in the pot with the sauce. Add the vinegar, wine, and parsley. Cover and simmer, over low heat, 1 hour and 30 minutes.*

Serve hot with plain rice or pilaf (p. 202). But this dish is equally good as a cold entrée.

*Americans are likely to find squid tough and rubbery cooked this long. You may prefer to simmer the sauce 1 hour, adding the squid to cook for the last 45 minutes.

Filets de dorade grillés à l'estragon

SEA BREAM FILLETS GRILLED WITH TARRAGON

[FOR 4 PEOPLE]

4 large fillets sea bream, *or see* Variations
6 tablespoons oil
1 clove garlic, crushed
1 sprig tarragon
Juice of ¼ lemon

MAÎTRE D'HÔTEL BUTTER

3 tablespoons butter
1 sprig tarragon, chopped fine
Juice of ¼ lemon
Salt to taste
Freshly ground black pepper to taste

Marination time: 2 hours / *Preparation and cooking time:* 15 minutes

Two hours ahead of time, marinate the fish fillets in the oil, minced garlic, tarragon, and a few drops of lemon juice.

MAÎTRE D'HÔTEL BUTTER: Knead the softened butter with the tarragon, finely minced, a little lemon juice, salt, and pepper.

Arrange the fish in a broiler pan. Place under a very hot broiler and grill 5 to 6 minutes on each side, with the oven door open. Serve each fillet on a warm plate with a chunk of maître d'hôtel butter.

Variations: Fish fillets or steaks (salmon, snapper, halibut, or swordfish) may also be cooked in a cast-iron skillet. Oil them well again before putting them in a very hot pan. Turn them over with a broad spatula because they fall apart easily.

Out of season, fresh tarragon can be replaced by parsley or dried herbs: thyme, rosemary, and marjoram.

Filets de sole Marguery

[FOR 4 PEOPLE]

1 quart mussels
8 fillets of sole
1 cup dry white wine
1 cup water
Salt to taste
Freshly ground black pepper to taste
Bouquet garni
⅛ pound small shrimp, peeled

SAUCE
2 tablespoons butter
1 tablespoon flour
2 cups fish-cooking liquid

GARNISH
⅛ pound small shrimp, unpeeled

Remarks: The white wine used for cooking the fish must be dry. Sweet white wine, because of its high sugar content, is apt to turn grayish in cooking.

Before pouring the sauce over the sole, taste it for seasoning.

FILLET OF SOLE WITH SHELLFISH

Preparation and cooking time: 1 hour

Scrub and wash the mussels. Put them in a pot and steam them open over high heat. Take them out of their shells. Strain the juice and reserve it.

Arrange the fillets of sole in a large skillet. Add the wine, water, cooking liquid from the mussels, salt, pepper, and bouquet garni. Place over low heat. Remove it just as it comes to a boil.

Drain the fillets, reserving the cooking liquid. Arrange them on a warm serving platter. Surround them with the mussels and peeled shrimp. Place the platter over a pot of boiling water to keep warm.

SAUCE: Melt, over low heat, 2 tablespoons of butter. Add the flour. Stir over heat a few seconds, until the mixture is foamy. Add 2 cups of the fish-cooking liquid. Stir until it boils. Simmer, over very low heat, about 10 minutes.

Pour the sauce over the fish. Garnish the dish with unpeeled shrimp.

My advice: To simplify this recipe, which requires a fair number of steps, canned or bottled mussels may be used. Just add them, drained, to the sauce a little before pouring it over the fish.

Filets de sole en paupiettes

[For 4 people]

9 fillets of sole
2 tablespoons *crème fraîche* or whipping cream
1 egg white
Salt to taste
Freshly ground black pepper to taste
½ pound mushrooms, sliced thin
1 teaspoon water
A little vinegar
1 cup dry white wine
1 teaspoon flour
1 teaspoon soft butter

STUFFED FILLET OF SOLE

Preparation and cooking time: 45 minutes / *Oven temperature:* 375°

STUFFING: Puree one raw fillet of sole in a food processor or food mill. Add 1 tablespoon of the *crème fraîche*, the egg white, salt, and pepper.

Spread a little stuffing on each fillet. Roll up the fillets. Tie them in both directions with string. Rinse the mushrooms in water with a little vinegar added to it. Cut them into thin slices. Scatter them over the bottom of a shallow baking dish, the fillets of sole on top. Cover with wine and foil. Bake in a moderate (375°) oven 15 to 20 minutes.

Drain the fillets, reserving the cooking liquid. Remove the strings wrapping the fillets. Arrange the fish on a serving platter and keep warm.

SAUCE: Boil the fish-cooking liquid in a saucepan over high heat. With a fork, thoroughly mash together the flour and the softened butter. Add it to the sauce in tiny pieces. Boil for a moment or two, stirring constantly. Stir in, at the end, the remaining tablespoon of *crème fraîche*. Pour over the fillets of sole and serve with steamed potatoes, plain rice, or a mousse of pureed green vegetables.

Gigot de mer provençale

MONKFISH WITH GARLIC AND PARSLEY

[FOR 4 PEOPLE]

Preparation and cooking time: 1 hour and 15 minutes / *Oven temperature:* 350°

2 pounds monkfish*
3 cloves garlic
Salt to taste
Freshly ground black pepper to taste
Flour for dredging
1 tablespoon butter
1 tablespoon oil
1 carrot
1 onion
½ pound mushrooms
½ cup dry white wine

GARNISH
2 tablespoons butter
Salt to taste
Freshly ground black pepper to taste
1 clove garlic
3 tablespoons minced parsley
3 tomatoes
1 tablespoon oil

Insert pieces of garlic along the length of the monkfish. Add salt and pepper and dust it lightly with flour. Brown it rapidly in a skillet with the butter and oil. Remove from the heat.

Peel and dice the carrot, onion, and stems (only) from the mushrooms. Spread this mixture in a baking dish. Place the monkfish on top of it. Sprinkle with the wine, salt, and pepper. Bake in a moderate (350°) oven for 30 to 40 minutes.

GARNISH: Fifteen minutes before the fish has finished cooking, cut the mushroom caps in thin slices. Sauté them in a skillet with butter. Salt and pepper them. Add the garlic and minced parsley. Keep warm. Cut the tomatoes in half. Cook them in a skillet with very hot oil 5 minutes, cut side down, then 5 minutes on the other side. Salt and pepper them at the end.

Arrange the monkfish on a warm serving platter. Pour ½ cup of water in the baking dish over heat. Stir a few seconds, scraping the bottom of the dish. Pour over the fish. Garnish the platter with sautéed half-tomatoes covered with sautéed mushroom slices.

Serve with steamed potatoes or large shell macaroni.

*Monkfish, also known as anglerfish or lotte, has a lobster-like flavor and texture and is becoming available in U.S. markets.

Homard à l'américaine

[FOR 4 PEOPLE]

1 live lobster, about 3½ pounds
Salt to taste
Freshly ground black pepper to taste
5 tablespoons oil
1 carrot, 1 shallot, chopped fine
1 tablespoon Cognac
3 to 4 tomatoes, chopped coarse
1 tablespoon tomato paste
1½ cups dry white wine
Bouquet garni with 1 sprig tarragon or
    1 teaspoon dried
2 to 3 pinches cayenne pepper
1½ tablespoons butter
1 tablespoon flour
Minced fresh herbs

LOBSTER À L'AMÉRICAINE

Preparation and cooking time: 1 hour and 15 minutes

To stun the lobster, plunge it into a large pot of boiling water for a minute or two. Remove the claws. Cut off the head, then slice the tail in 5 to 6 pieces. Season with salt and pepper. Split the head lengthwise. Remove the coral, which will be used to thicken the sauce. Discard the sand sacs. Crack the claws with a hammer.

Heat 4 tablespoons of the oil in a large skillet. Toss in the lobster and its claws. Remove from the heat as soon as it reddens.

Sauté the carrot and shallot in a casserole with the remaining tablespoon of oil. Add the lobster and Cognac. Flame it. Add the fresh tomatoes and tomato paste, the wine, 1½ cups of water, bouquet garni, cayenne, salt, and pepper. Simmer, over medium-high heat, 20 minutes.

Let the lobster pieces drain on a platter. Keep them warm. Strain the sauce and put it back over high heat to reduce it by a third. Then stir in, in small chunks, the butter blended with the flour. Off the heat, stir in the coral. Pour over the lobster. Sprinkle with the minced fresh herbs and serve very hot, with rice.

Langouste en bellevue

[FOR 8 TO 10 PEOPLE]

1 large live lobster, about 4 to 5 pounds

COURT BOUILLON
8 cups water / ¼ cup vinegar
2 onions, chopped coarse
4 whole cloves, crushed
1 shallot, 1 carrot, sliced in rounds
Bouquet garni / Salt to taste

2 cups mayonnaise (see p. 26)
2 tablespoons (2 envelopes) unflavored
    gelatin, dissolved in cold water.

GARNISH
10 small tomatoes
4 cups mixed vegetable salad (see p. 66)
5 hard-boiled eggs
A few lettuce leaves

Remarks: The gelatin won't make your mayonnaise curdle; on the contrary, it will help keep it firm.

WHOLE COLD LOBSTER

Preparation and cooking time: 3 hours and 30 minutes

Before plunging the lobster into the court bouillon (which has been simmering 30 minutes), tie it flat with string on a cutting board. Then cook it 25 to 30 minutes. Drain and chill it.

Separate the head from the tail with a twisting motion. Cut through the underside of the shell. Lift the meat out. Cut it into slices about ½ inch thick (medallions).

To decorate the medallions, prepare the mayonnaise. Mix in ½ cup of cold but still liquid gelatin. Cover the medallions with it. Put them on a rack and chill.

To serve the lobster, reshape it, bracing the head on a firm base to keep it upright. Run a small decorative skewer through it, between the eyes. Overlap the medallions along the back of the shell (in a line from the head down). Ring the platter with the tomatoes stuffed with vegetable salad mixed with mayonnaise, hard-boiled eggs, and lettuce.

My advice: You'll save time by buying a precooked lobster.

Merlans en lorgnettes

[FOR 4 PEOPLE]

4 cleaned whiting*
Flour for dredging
1 egg / Bread crumbs
Salt and pepper to taste
1 lemon, cut in quarters
1 bunch parsley

4 skewers

Remarks: The fish cleaning will be simpler if you can ask your fish dealer to lift out the backbone without cutting off the heads. Otherwise, do it yourself as indicated in the recipe.

ROLLED BREADED WHITING FILLETS

Preparation and cooking time: 35 minutes / *Deep-frying temperature:* 350°

To fillet a fish, hold the knife blade flat and slide it along the backbone without severing the flesh. Then cut through the backbone as close as possible to the head and remove the backbone.

Dip the fillets first in flour, then in beaten egg, and finally in bread crumbs. Add salt and pepper. Roll up the breaded fillets until they meet on each side of the head. Keep them rolled up by piercing them through with a skewer.

Plunge them into hot deep fat. When the fish are golden brown, drain them well on paper towels. Taste for seasoning. Remove the skewers and serve very hot, garnished with lemon quarters and parsley.

*Trout may be prepared the same way.

Mouclade vendéenne

[FOR 4 PEOPLE]

2 shallots, chopped fine
1 tablespoon butter
2 cups dry white wine
4 quarts large mussels

SAUCE

1 egg yolk
¾ cup *crème fraîche* or whipping cream
1 teaspoon cornstarch
1 teaspoon curry powder
2 cups mussel-cooking broth

Salt (optional)
Freshly ground black pepper (optional)

MUSSELS WITH CREAM

Preparation and cooking time: 45 minutes

In a casserole, gently simmer the minced shallots with the butter and wine about 10 minutes.

Scrub and rinse the mussels. Cook them in the casserole over high heat, stirring occasionally. As soon as they open, remove them from the casserole, reserving the cooking liquid. Arrange them in a deep platter. Keep them warm over a pot of boiling water or in a very low oven. Pour the cooking broth through a metal strainer lined with paper towels to get rid of any sand.

SAUCE: In a saucepan, off the heat, whisk together the sauce ingredients with 2 cups of boiling mussel-cooking broth, poured in little by little so that the egg yolk doesn't coagulate. Add salt and pepper if needed. Return to the heat, whisking constantly. As soon as it comes to a boil, pour over the mussels and serve.

My advice: If you aren't too rushed, remove one shell from each cooked mussel before arranging it on the serving platter. Your fingers won't get as messy from the sauce while you're eating.

Moules à la crème moutardée

[FOR 4 PEOPLE]

2 shallots, chopped fine
2 tablespoons butter
1 cup dry white wine
1 stalk celery, chopped coarse
4 quarts mussels
Freshly ground black pepper to taste
½ cup *crème fraîche* or whipping cream
1 teaspoon Dijon-type mustard
2 tablespoons minced parsley

MUSSELS WITH CREAM AND MUSTARD

Preparation and cooking time: 45 minutes

In a large pot, over low heat, cook the shallots in the butter for 2 to 3 minutes. Add the wine and chopped celery. Let it almost completely evaporate over high heat.

Meanwhile clean the mussels. Toss them into the pot, over high heat, add pepper, and cover. Shake the pot frequently.

As soon as the mussels open (about 5 minutes) drain them, reserving the cooking liquid. Discard one shell from each mussel. Place the mussels in a colander and keep warm. Pour the cooking liquid through a fine strainer lined with paper towels to get rid of any sand.

Pour off one cupful of it. Reduce it by half, over high heat. Then, still over high heat, beat in, with a whisk, the *crème fraîche* and mustard. Pour immediately over the mussels. Sprinkle with parsley and serve.

Moules marinière comme aux Halles

MUSSELS IN WHITE WINE *LES HALLES* STYLE

[FOR 4 PEOPLE]

4 quarts mussels
1 tablespoon butter
2 shallots, chopped fine
1 cup dry white wine
Freshly ground black pepper to taste
1 tablespoon minced parsley
1 clove garlic (optional)

Preparation and cooking time: 45 minutes

Scrub the mussels well and wash them. Place them in a large pot with butter, minced shallots, and wine. Steam them open in the pot, covered, over high heat for a few minutes. Stir 2 to 3 times during cooking.

As soon as they open, remove them from the pot. Put them in a deep platter and keep warm. Save the cooking liquid.

Pour the mussel-cooking liquid through a fine strainer. Put it back on the heat. Let it boil for a second. Add pepper. Pour over the mussels. Sprinkle with minced parsley and serve.

Variation: Before serving, sprinkle with a finely minced garlic clove.

MUSSELS WITH TOMATO AND FRESH BASIL

Moules à la Martegale

[FOR 4 PEOPLE]

4 quarts mussels
2 tablespoons olive oil
2 cloves garlic, crushed
½ cup bread crumbs
3 tablespoons tomato sauce (fresh or canned)
Freshly ground black pepper to taste
Pinch salt
8 to 10 leaves fresh basil, minced
2 tablespoons minced parsley

Preparation and cooking time: 45 minutes

Scrub and wash the mussels. Place them in a covered pot over medium-high heat, 6 to 8 minutes. As soon as they've all opened, remove a shell from each one. Keep them warm in the pot set in a barely warm oven.

In a skillet with the olive oil, cook the minced garlic. Add the bread crumbs (pulverized in a food mill or food processor), then the tomato sauce, pepper, and a little salt. Stir over high heat a few seconds.

Pour this sauce over the mussels. Return to the heat 3 to 4 minutes, stirring from time to time. Before serving, sprinkle with basil and parsley.

SKATE WITH LEMON AND CAPERS

Raie grenobloise

[FOR 4 PEOPLE]

2 pounds skate, cut into 4 pieces
Salt to taste
6 tablespoons vinegar
2 slices firm white bread
½ lemon
5 sprigs parsley, chopped fine
1 to 2 tablespoons capers
Freshly ground black pepper to taste
8 tablespoons (1 stick) butter

Preparation and cooking time: 30 minutes

Wash the skate, then put it in a large pot. Cover with cold water mixed with salt and 5 tablespoons of the vinegar. Bring gently to a boil. Leave 15 minutes in barely simmering water.

While the skate is cooking, cut the bread into small dice. Peel the lemon "to the quick" and cut it into small dice. Mince the parsley.

Drain the skate. Remove the skin from both sides. Arrange the skate on a warm platter. Sprinkle with the capers, parsley, and lemon pieces. Add pepper. Keep warm.

Melt the butter in a skillet. Quickly brown the bread cubes in it. Pour over the skate. Put the skillet back on the heat with the remaining tablespoon of vinegar. Boil it a moment. Pour over the skate and serve.

Remarks: Don't let the bread brown too much. It's best just golden brown.

Peel the lemon by cutting slightly into the pulp so that no traces of white membrane remains.

Rougets grillés aux herbes

[FOR 4 PEOPLE]

4 whole mullet *
Salt to taste
Freshly ground black pepper to taste
½ teaspoon rosemary
½ teaspoon thyme
1 sprig fennel or ½ teaspoon dried
2 tablespoons minced parsley
Juice of ½ lemon
1 cup oil

Remarks: To scale the fish more easily, do it with the edge of a knife or a wet cheese grater. Scrape the scales moving from head to tail.

If you're using very fresh mullet, don't remove the liver, which is prized by gourmets.

BROILED WHOLE MULLET WITH HERBS

Marination time: 30 minutes / *Preparation and cooking time:* 20 minutes

Remove the insides of the mullet through the gills. Scale them. Make a few incisions in them with a very sharp knife. Place them in a deep platter with salt, pepper, rosemary, thyme, fennel, half the parsley, lemon juice, and oil. Let them marinate 30 minutes in the refrigerator.

Take the fish out of the marinade. Arrange them, on a rack, on a broiler pan. Place them under a very hot broiler. Cook, with the broiler door open, 3 to 4 minutes on each side. During cooking, baste the fish with oil from the marinade. Sprinkle with the remaining parsley before serving.

My advice: Dried thyme and rosemary leaves are better than the powdered variety. Pick some yourself in season and store your dried herbs in airtight cans or bottles.

*You can use any small whole fish for this.

Rougets en papillotes

[FOR 4 PEOPLE]

4 whole mullet*
½ pound mushrooms
1 shallot
4 tablespoons butter
Salt to taste
Freshly ground black pepper to taste
1 tablespoon minced parsley
Juice of 1 lemon

PARCHMENT PACKETS
4 sheets foil or kitchen parchment paper
Oil for brushing

1 lemon, cut in quarters (optional)

WHOLE MULLET IN PARCHMENT

Preparation and cooking time: 40 minutes

Scale and wash the fish. Remove the insides completely. Save the livers.**

Wash the mushrooms quickly. Mince them finely with the shallot. Cook them slowly, uncovered, over medium heat, with 1½ tablespoons of the butter, salt, and pepper until the juices given off by the mushrooms have evaporated. Stir occasionally with a wooden spoon.

With a fork, mash the remaining butter with the minced parsley, lemon juice, the fish livers cut into dice, salt, and pepper. Spread the mixture inside the fish.

PARCHMENT PACKETS: Cut 4 squares of foil (or parchment baking paper) much larger than the fish. Brush them with oil. On each one, place ¼ of the mushrooms and 1 fish. Fold the parchment over the filling, loosely enough for it to remain slightly inflated. Press down on the edges to seal it.

Slide the packets under a broiler for about 4 to 5 minutes on each side. Serve immediately with quartered lemon, if desired.

My advice: You can replace the mushrooms with anchovy paste mixed with a little butter. In this case, add pepper, but no salt.

*See the note on p. 84.
**Chances of getting fish with their livers in the U.S. are slim unless you've caught them yourself. Fortunately, the recipe is fine without them.

Saumon froid en bellevue

[FOR 8 TO 10 PEOPLE]

1 whole salmon, 4 to 6 pounds (fresh or frozen)

COURT BOUILLON

8 cups water
1 bottle dry white wine
2 onions, 2 carrots, sliced in rounds
Bouquet garni
Salt to taste
Freshly ground black pepper to taste

GARNISH

1 tablespoon (1 envelope) unflavored gelatin
12 small firm tomatoes
Salt to taste
2 large (16-ounce) cans mixed vegetables or two 16-ounce packages frozen mixed vegetables (about 4 cups)
A few leaves tarragon
10 hard-boiled eggs

MAYONNAISE

2 egg yolks
2 cups oil
2 teaspoons Dijon-type mustard
Salt to taste
Freshly ground black pepper to taste

1 fish poacher

Remarks: Other whole large fish may be prepared the same way.

WHOLE COLD POACHED SALMON

Preparation and cooking time the day before: 2 hours, plus defrosting

The day before, poach the fish. In a fish poacher, simmer 4 cups of water with the wine, sliced onions and carrots, bouquet garni, salt, and pepper 30 minutes. Off the heat, add 4 cups of very cold water (or even ice cubes) to hasten cooling. Place the salmon, fresh or defrosted, on the poaching rack. Lower it into the cold court bouillon. If necessary, add enough additional water to just cover the fish. Slowly bring to a boil. Continue cooking at a bare simmer 10 minutes and leave it in the fish stock overnight.

Several hours before serving, make the gelatin according to the instructions on the envelope. Cut a slice off each tomato (on the stem side). Hollow each one out with a spoon. Salt it inside and turn upside down on a rack. Drain the mixed vegetables thoroughly.

To garnish, place the fish on a large cutting board. Carefully pull the skin off the top. Brush with cold but still-liquid gelatin. Dip tarragon leaves in gelatin and arrange them on the fish. Brush them a second time with gelatin to hold them in place and make them shine.

Slide the salmon on to a large platter or a tray covered with a white kitchen towel. Refrigerate it.

Make the mayonnaise with the proportions indicated (see the recipe for Lobster Mayonnaise, p. 26, for directions). Stir in 2 spoonfuls of cold but still-liquid gelatin. Stir half into the mixed vegetables. Stuff the tomatoes with them. Arrange the tomatoes around the salmon, alternating with the hard-boiled eggs.

When the remaining gelatin has solidified, break it up with a fork and decorate the platter with it. Pass the remaining mayonnaise in a sauceboat.

Saumon meunière   SALMON SAUTÉED IN BUTTER

[FOR 4 PEOPLE]

Preparation and cooking time: 25 minutes

4 salmon steaks or fillets, about ½ pound
    each*
Milk for dipping
Flour for dredging
Salt to taste
Freshly ground black pepper to taste
2 tablespoons oil
3 tablespoons butter
1 lemon
A few sprigs parsley

Dip the salmon pieces in milk. Dredge them in lightly salted and peppered flour. Shake off any excess.

Heat the oil and butter in a large skillet (preferably nonstick). Place the salmon in it (each slice must be touching the bottom). Cook over medium-high heat at first, then lower it slightly, 5 to 6 minutes on each side. Shake the skillet frequently during cooking. Turn with a spatula.

Serve the salmon, well browned, on warmed plates garnished with lemon slices, parsley, and some steamed potatoes.

*Any other fish steak or fillet may be prepared the same way.

Saumon sauce mousseline

[FOR 10 TO 12 PEOPLE]

8 cups water
1 bottle dry white wine
2 onions, 2 carrots, sliced in rounds
Bouquet garni
Salt and pepper to taste
1 whole salmon, about 6 pounds (fresh or frozen)

MOUSSELINE SAUCE

5 egg yolks
4 tablespoons water
Salt and pepper to taste
Juice of ½ lemon
8 ounces (2 sticks) butter
5 tablespoons *crème fraîche*

1 long fish poacher

Remarks: If the salmon is frozen, defrost it completely in the refrigerator before cooking. This can take at least 10 hours.

SALMON WITH MOUSSELINE SAUCE

Preparation and cooking time: 1 hour, plus 30 minutes waiting time

In a fish poacher, simmer the 8 cups of water, white wine, sliced onions and carrots, bouquet garni, and salt and pepper for 30 minutes. Cool. Place the salmon on a rack and lower it into the court bouillon. Bring slowly to a boil and simmer 10 minutes.

MOUSSELINE SAUCE: In a heavy saucepan or double boiler, put the egg yolks, water, salt, pepper, and lemon juice. With a wire whisk, beat vigorously over low heat until the mixture is thick and clings to the whisk. Make sure the saucepan never gets hot enough to burn your hand. Remove from heat. Beat in the butter, bit by bit, whisking continuously, then add the *crème fraîche*. Keep in the saucepan over warm water or in a double boiler until ready to serve.

Serving: Carefully peel the skin from the salmon, except for the head. Arrange the fish on a platter lined with a folded white kitchen towel (to absorb water). Decorate with thin slices of lemon garnished with parsley. Serve the salmon surrounded by steamed potatoes and with a sauceboat of the mousseline sauce.

Soufflé de crabe   CRAB SOUFFLÉ

[FOR 4 PEOPLE]

About 3½ ounces canned lump crab-
    meat
2½ tablespoons butter
1 tablespoon flour
1 cup milk
Salt to taste
Freshly ground black pepper to taste
3 eggs, separated

1 soufflé mold, 8 to 10 inches in diam-
    eter

Preparation and cooking time: 1 hour / *Oven temperature:* 375°

Drain the crabmeat, reserving the juices. Chop the meat in a food mill or with a sharp knife. Preheat the oven to 375°.

Melt, over low heat, 2 tablespoons of the butter. Add the flour. Stir over heat a few seconds until the mixture foams. Add, all at once, the crab juices and cold milk. Salt and pepper it. Stir until the mixture comes to a boil. Simmer 5 minutes over very low heat.

Remove this sauce from the heat and stir in the crabmeat, egg yolks, and, finally, the egg whites, stiffly beaten.

Butter a soufflé mold with the remaining butter. Pour the mixture into the mold, which should be about ¾ full. Bake in the oven 25 to 30 minutes.

My advice: This soufflé can be very economical if you make it with about a cup of court bouillon left over from poaching a fish. Reduce it by boiling, uncovered, over high heat 15 minutes. It can be used instead of milk in your sauce. Salt and pepper it lightly.

Variation: Add a teaspoon of *anglaise* sauce to the mixture before folding in the egg whites.

Remarks: Before baking, run a knife blade all around the mold, between the sides and the soufflé, to allow it to rise more evenly.

Thon frais braisé aux tomates et aux poivrons

FRESH TUNA BRAISED WITH TOMATOES AND PEPPERS

[FOR 4 PEOPLE]

1½ to 2 pounds fresh tuna (in one or
   more pieces)
2 tablespoons oil / 1 bell pepper
1 onion, 1 carrot, 1 tomato, sliced in
   rounds
½ cup dry white wine or water
1 clove garlic, crushed
Bouquet garni (parsley, thyme, bay leaf)
Salt and pepper to taste

VEGETABLE SAUCE
1 large onion / 2 tomatoes
1 bell pepper / 2 tablespoons oil
1 clove garlic, crushed
Bouquet garni (parsley, thyme, bay leaf)
Salt and pepper to taste

Preparation and cooking time: 1 hour and 15 minutes

In a casserole, lightly brown the tuna on both sides in the oil.

Cut the bell pepper open, remove the seeds, and cut it into strips. Slice the onion, carrot, and tomato. Add them to the casserole along with the wine or water, garlic, bouquet garni, salt, and pepper. Cover and simmer 30 to 40 minutes.

VEGETABLE SAUCE: Peel the onion and tomatoes, then cut them into pieces. Cut the bell pepper open, remove the seeds, and cut it into strips. Heat the oil in a skillet. Add all the vegetables, garlic, bouquet garni, salt, and pepper. Simmer 30 minutes, over medium heat, uncovered.

Place the tuna on a very deep platter. Strain the cooking liquid. Add the vegetable sauce. Discard the bouquet garni. Pour the sauce over the fish. Serve hot for the main course, or cold as an hors d'œuvre.

Tronçons de lotte Suchet

[FOR 4 PEOPLE]

1½ to 2 pounds monkfish*
1 carrot / 1 leek (white part only)
1 stalk celery
2 tablespoons butter
1 cup dry white wine
1 cup water
Salt and pepper to taste

SUCHET SAUCE

1 tablespoon butter
1 teaspoon flour
About 2 cups fish-poaching court bouillon
½ cup *crème fraîche*
Salt and pepper to taste

Remarks: You can mix an egg yolk in the cream before adding it to the very hot sauce, whisking constantly. Do not put back on the heat.

MONKFISH WITH SUCHET SAUCE

Preparation and cooking time: 45 minutes

Cut the monkfish into chunks. Rinse and dry them with paper towels.

Cut the carrot, leek, and celery into thin strips. Cook slowly in a covered casserole with the butter, 5 minutes. Place pieces of monkfish on top. Add the wine, water, salt, and pepper. Cover and bring slowly to a boil, cooking 10 minutes with the broth barely simmering (not boiling).

Arrange pieces of monkfish on a serving platter. Keep them warm. Strain the poaching liquid, reserving the vegetables that you scatter over the fish.

SUCHET SAUCE: In a small saucepan, stir the butter and flour over low heat. Add the fish-poaching liquid, whisking until it comes to a boil. Simmer slowly 2 minutes. Then stir in the *crème fraîche*, salt, and pepper. Pour over the fish and serve.

*See the note for Monkfish with Garlic and Parsley, p. 76.

Truites aux amandes

[FOR 4 PEOPLE]

4 trout
1 cup milk
Salt to taste
Freshly ground black pepper to taste
½ cup flour
4 tablespoons butter
½ cup slivered almonds
1 lemon

TROUT WITH ALMONDS

Preparation and cooking time: 30 minutes / *Oven temperature:* 250°

Clean the fish and wipe them dry. Dip them in milk seasoned with salt and pepper, then lightly in flour.

In a large skillet, heat 2 tablespoons of the butter. Cook the fish in it until golden brown, about 7 to 8 minutes on each side. Watch the fish carefully while they are cooking, for this is a delicate operation.

Lightly brown the almonds in a small saucepan with the remaining butter. Pour over the trout just before serving. Garnish with half-slices of lemon.

My advice: If your skillet isn't large enough, make no more than two trout at a time. The first ones will keep, in a very low (250°) oven, while the next are cooking.

Truites à la crème

[FOR 4 PEOPLE]

1 tablespoon butter
1 shallot, chopped fine
4 trout
2 cups dry white wine or water
1 tablespoon minced chives
Salt to taste
Freshly ground black pepper to taste
Juice of ½ lemon
4 tablespoons *crème fraîche*

TROUT IN CREAM

Preparation and cooking time: 45 minutes / *Oven temperature:* 475°

Butter a baking dish. Sprinkle the minced shallot over the bottom. Place the cleaned and wiped trout on top. Add the wine, minced chives, salt, pepper, and lemon juice. Bake in a hot (475°) oven 10 minutes.

Drain the trout thoroughly, reserving the cooking liquid. Keep them warm on a serving platter. Return the cooking liquid to the heat, in a small saucepan. Stir in the *crème fraîche*, letting it simmer a few seconds to thicken a little. Pour over the trout and serve at once. Steamed potatoes with parsley go well with this.

My advice: Use a handsome enough baking dish (an ovenproof porcelain, for example) to serve in, after wiping the rim with a paper towel if necessary.

Remarks: Clean the trout, or have them cleaned, through the gills, and not by splitting them open. This way the fish won't get misshapen while baking.

GRILLED TURBOT WITH BÉARNAISE SAUCE

Turbot grillé béarnaise

[FOR 4 PEOPLE]

4 pieces turbot,* about 6 ounces each
Salt and pepper to taste
2 tablespoons oil

BÉARNAISE SAUCE

2 shallots, chopped fine
1 tablespoon minced fresh tarragon or
  ½ teaspoon dried, *or* tarragon vinegar
3 tablespoons vinegar / 2 egg yolks
2 tablespoons water
Salt and pepper to taste
8 tablespoons (1 stick) butter

Remarks: You can marinate the fish a few hours with ½ cup of oil, lemon juice, 1 minced onion, thyme, 1 bay leaf, and parsley. Before broiling, carefully sponge the fish dry.

For a successful béarnaise sauce, it's essential to have a wire whisk and a small saucepan with a rounded heavy bottom, such as in enameled cast iron.

In a double boiler, cooking will take longer but be less risky.

Preparation and cooking time: 30 minutes

Preheat the broiler on high. Salt and pepper the turbot pieces. Brush them with oil on both sides. Arrange them in the broiler pan. Place the pan under the broiler and cook, with the broiler door open, 10 minutes on each side.

BÉARNAISE SAUCE: Mince the shallots and tarragon finely. Place them in a small heavy saucepan with the vinegar. Simmer a few minutes until the liquid has almost completely evaporated. Cool.

In a saucepan, off the heat, add the egg yolks, water, salt, and pepper. Place over very low heat. Beat vigorously, without pausing, with a wire whisk, until the mixture is thick and clings to the whisk (watch carefully to make sure the pan never gets hot enough to burn your hand).

Remove from the heat and mix in the butter, bit by bit, stirring constantly with a wooden spoon. Serve immediately, for this sauce cannot be reheated.

My advice: Melted butter can accompany broiled fish, but I find that béarnaise sauce is even better.

*Halibut and salmon may also be prepared this way.

POULTRY
AND
GAME

Canard braisé aux navets

DUCK BRAISED WITH TURNIPS

[FOR 4 PEOPLE]

Preparation and cooking time: 1 hour and 30 minutes

DUCK STOCK
Duck neck, wingtips, and giblets
1 small onion, chopped fine
2 tablespoons butter
1 small carrot, sliced in rounds
2 cups dry white wine / 2 cups water
Bouquet garni (parsley, thyme, bay leaf)
Salt and pepper to taste

1 duck, about 3 pounds
2 tablespoons butter
Salt and pepper to taste
2 pounds small turnips
2½ pounds small white onions

Remarks: In France, ducks are usually sold with their heads on. A tender duck has a bill that can be easily bent with a finger. Its breastbone is supple.

If the onions and turnips are from a winter crop, blanch them before adding to the casserole: plunge them into boiling water. Simmer 5 minutes and drain thoroughly.

DUCK STOCK: Brown the neck, wingtips, and giblets and the minced onion in the butter. Add the sliced carrot, wine, water, bouquet garni, salt, and pepper. Simmer, uncovered, at least 1 hour.

Cook the duck in a casserole with 2 tablespoons of butter. As soon as it has browned on all sides, drain off all the cooking grease, add salt and pepper, and pour in the strained stock. Cover and simmer 10 minutes over low heat.

Peel the turnips and onions. Cut the turnips in quarters or eighths if they are large. Place the vegetables in the casserole with the duck and simmer, covered, 40 to 50 minutes.

Canard à l'estragon DUCK WITH TARRAGON

[FOR 4 PEOPLE]

2 to 3 sprigs tarragon or ½ teaspoon
   dried
1 whole duck*
Salt to taste
Freshly ground black pepper to taste
3 tablespoons butter
⅓ cup Calvados
1 cup dry white wine
4 apples
4 to 5 tablespoons *crème fraîche* or
   whipping cream

Preparation and cooking time: 1 hour and 30 minutes

Pull the leaves off the tarragon. Slip the bare stems into the cavity of the duck, or use ¼ teaspoon dried. Add salt and pepper. Brown the duck in a casserole with 1½ tablespoons of the butter. Pour off the cooking grease. Then pour the Calvados over it. As soon as it boils, flame it over the heat with a match. Cover and simmer, over low heat, 45 minutes. Stir 2 to 3 times during cooking. Add 2 to 3 spoonfuls of water during cooking if the cooking liquid gets too low.

Arrange the cooked duck on a platter. Keep it warm. Skim grease off the cooking juices, return the casserole to the heat, and pour in the wine. Boil rapidly, uncovered, over high heat, so that it reduces by half.

Peel and cut the apples into thick slices. Sauté them rapidly in a skillet with the remaining butter until they are golden brown.

Add *crème fraîche* and fresh tarragon leaves (or ¼ teaspoon dried) to the duck-cooking broth. Boil it a couple of minutes, stirring constantly with a wooden spoon. Pour it into a sauceboat. Serve it with the duck surrounded by sautéed apples.

*American ducks usually have more fat on them than French ducks, so you may wish to trim excess fat from the duck with a pair of scissors or a sharp knife before cooking it.

Canard à l'orange DUCK WITH ORANGE SAUCE

[FOR 4 PEOPLE]

Preparation and cooking time: 2 hours

DUCK STOCK
Duck neck, wingtips and giblets
1 small onion, chopped fine
2 tablespoons butter
1 small carrot, sliced in rounds
2 cups dry white wine
2 cups water
Bouquet garni (parsley, thyme, bay leaf)
Salt to taste
Freshly ground black pepper to taste

1 whole duck*
2 tablespoons butter
Salt to taste
Freshly ground black pepper to taste
3 oranges
3 tablespoons Curaçao**
Juice of ½ lemon

A good hour beforehand, make the duck stock with the neck, wingtips, and giblets, following the recipe for Duck Braised with Turnips (p. 96).

In a casserole, brown the duck on all sides in the butter over medium-high heat. Pour off all accumulated cooking grease. Add salt and pepper. Pour in the strained stock. Simmer gently 50 minutes.

Peel one of the oranges, removing only a thin layer of the outer rind (the zest). Cut the zest into very thin strips. Put them in a saucepan with cold water. Bring to a boil. Drain. Macerate in the Curaçao. Peel the 2 remaining oranges down to the pulp. Slice them.

Five minutes before the duck has finished cooking in the casserole, add the orange slices, lemon juice, orange zest, and the Curaçao in which it was macerating.

Arrange the duck on a large warmed platter. Over high heat, boil the sauce remaining in the casserole a few moments to reduce it somewhat. Pour it over the duck. Serve with orange slices arranged around the edge of the platter or on the duck itself. Because of their neutral taste, boiled potatoes or plain rice are the best accompaniments to Duck with Orange Sauce.

*See the notes about duck on pp. 96 and 97.
**Or other orange-flavored liqueur.

Coq au chambertin   CHICKEN IN RED WINE SAUCE

[FOR 6 TO 8 PEOPLE]

1 large chicken, cut into serving pieces

MARINADE
1 bottle Chambertin wine
2 tablespoons oil
1 onion, sliced in rounds
2 shallots, chopped fine
1 small carrot, sliced thin
3 cloves garlic, crushed
Bouquet garni / 1 whole clove
3 whole peppercorns, crushed

3 tablespoons butter
3 to 4 ounces bacon or salt pork, diced*
1 tbsp. flour / 3 tbsp. Cognac
1 tablespoon tomato paste
Salt and pepper to taste
½ pound sliced mushrooms
1 to 2 chicken livers
1 tablespoon minced parsley

Remarks: You can substitute another robust red wine such as Beaujolais, Côtes du Rhône, Pinot Noir, or Zinfandel for the Chambertin.

Marination: The day before / *Preparation and cooking time:* 2 hours and 30 minutes

The day before, put the chicken pieces in the marinade in a small enough bowl for them to be entirely covered. The next day, remove the chicken and drain it. Remove the onion and carrot with a slotted spoon and drain them separately. Reserve the marinade.

In a casserole, gently heat the butter and half the bacon or salt pork. Then add the chicken, browning it on all sides. Add the onion from the marinade. Sprinkle with flour and stir. Pour the Cognac over it. Bring to a boil. Flame it over the heat. Add the marinade, 1 cup of water, tomato paste, salt, and pepper. Cover and simmer 1 hour and 20 minutes.

Heat the remaining bacon or salt pork and sauté the mushrooms in it.

Arrange the chicken pieces in a serving bowl along with the mushrooms and bacon. If the sauce is too liquid, reduce it over high heat. Grind the raw chicken livers in a food processor and stir them into the sauce. Remove from the heat immediately and pour over the chicken. Correct the seasoning and sprinkle with minced parsley.

My advice: To achieve a smooth sauce, the pureed liver should be added only at the end. The heat will cause it to thicken the sauce immediately. Remove it as soon as it thickens or else the sauce will separate. Serve with potatoes or flat noodles.

*See the note about bacon on p. 54. See Miscellaneous Notes on pork fatback.

Dinde farcie aux cèpes

[FOR 10 PEOPLE]

STUFFING

1 large can boletus mushrooms *
½ cup warm milk
1 cup cubed bread
¼ pound ground pork
¼ pound ground veal
½ cup port
1 egg
1 turkey liver
Salt to taste
Freshly ground black pepper to taste

1 turkey, about 10 pounds
3 tablespoons butter
Salt to taste
Freshly ground black pepper to taste
2 tablespoons port

TURKEY STUFFED WITH MUSHROOMS

Preparation and cooking time: 3 hours, plus 30 minutes time after cooking / *Oven temperature:* 350°

STUFFING: Rinse and drain the canned mushrooms. Dice the caps and mince the stems. Pour the warm milk over the bread in a large bowl. Add the mushrooms, ground meats, port, egg, diced turkey liver, salt, and pepper. Mix thoroughly and stuff the turkey without packing it too tightly. Close up the opening by sewing it or with a wad of crumbled foil.

Rest the turkey on one thigh in a large roasting pan. Smear it with butter. Salt and pepper it. Place in a moderate (350°) oven 1 hour on each thigh, then 30 minutes on its back, basting frequently.

When the turkey is done and has rested 30 minutes in the oven with the heat turned off, arrange it on a warmed platter. Pour the cooking juices into a saucepan. Bring to a boil. With a spoon, skim off the fat that rises to the top. Continue boiling to reduce it. Add the port. Pour immediately into a sauceboat and serve with the carved turkey.

*If you can't find canned boletus or *cèpe* mushrooms in specialty food stores, look for dried. Or try using ½ pound of sautéed fresh mushrooms—the taste won't be the same, but good nonetheless.

Oie farcie de la Saint-Michel   STUFFED GOOSE WITH APPLES

[FOR 10 PEOPLE]

STUFFING

2 pounds large sweet onions
1½ cups cubed bread
½ cup milk
Salt to taste
Freshly ground black pepper to taste
¼ teaspoon nutmeg
5 sprigs sage or 2 teaspoons dried

1 goose, about 10 pounds
3 tablespoons butter
Salt to taste
Freshly ground black pepper to taste
2 pounds apples

Preparation and cooking time: 3 hours and 45 minutes / *Oven temperature:* 400° then 450° then 350°

Preheat the oven to 400°.

STUFFING: Bake the onions, with their skins on, in the oven about 45 minutes. Then peel them and chop them coarsely. Soak the bread in the warm milk. Squeeze it and mix with the chopped onions, salt, pepper, nutmeg, and the fresh minced or dried sage. Stuff the goose with this mixture. Sew the opening closed and tie it with string.

Butter the goose's legs. Add salt and pepper, and place the goose in a very hot (450°) oven. After 15 minutes, add a few spoonfuls of water to the roasting pan. Reduce the oven temperature to 350°. Bake about 2 hours and 30 minutes. With a spoon, skim off grease frequently during baking.

Peel and slice the apples. Make them into an unsweetened marmalade by simmering them, covered, 30 minutes over low heat.

Serve the goose carved, with the apple marmalade passed separately. Only steamed potatoes, or even better, deep-fried potato puffs (see p. 190) go well with this stuffed goose.

Oie rôti à la choucroute

[FOR 8 TO 10 PEOPLE]

SAUERKRAUT

6 pounds fresh sauerkraut
½ pound bacon or salt pork*
1 carrot, sliced in rounds
2 onions
3 whole cloves
30 juniper berries
Bouquet garni
20 peppercorns, crushed
Salt to taste
1 pound sausage**
10 frankfurters
10 potatoes

1 goose, 8 to 10 pounds
Salt to taste
Freshly ground black pepper to taste
8 to 10 apples
3 tablespoons butter

Remarks: Preparing goose stuffed with sauerkraut requires you to be in the kitchen because of the number of steps involved, simple though they may be. Having said that, this is still the ideal dish for family gatherings.

Canned sauerkraut, though not as good as fresh, may be used if fresh sauerkraut is unavailable.

GOOSE STUFFED WITH SAUERKRAUT

Soaking the sauerkraut: The day before / *Preparation and cooking time:* 3 hours
Oven temperature: 450° then 350°

The day before, soak the sauerkraut in a large bowl of cold water. Change the water 2 to 3 times.

The next day, drain the sauerkraut. Squeeze it thoroughly dry. Spread it out on a large kitchen towel to untangle it.

COOKING THE SAUERKRAUT: In the bottom of a large casserole, scatter the diced bacon or salt pork that has been previously blanched. On top of it, place half the sauerkraut, sliced carrot, whole onions stuck with cloves, juniper berries, bouquet garni, pepper, a little salt, and the remaining sauerkraut. Cover and simmer 2 hours and 30 minutes. Add the sausage, frankfurters, and peeled potatoes. Cover and simmer another 30 minutes.

COOKING THE GOOSE: Salt and pepper the goose inside and out and place it in a roasting pan. Bake it at 450°. When it is golden brown, lower the temperature to 350°. Bake about 2 hours and 30 minutes (20 to 25 minutes per pound). Spoon off the grease frequently during baking.

Peel the apples and hollow them out with an apple corer, leaving them whole. Slip a small chunk of butter into each one and a little salt. Arrange them in the baking dish around the goose during the last 30 minutes of cooking after pouring off all the grease.

Pile the sauerkraut on to your largest platter. Arrange the roast goose on top of it (carve it first, it will be easier), surrounded by apples, slices of sausage, frankfurters, and potatoes.

My advice: Only after thoroughly degreasing should the goose-cooking juices be poured over the sauerkraut, just before serving.

*See the note about bacon on p. 54. See Miscellaneous Notes on pork fatback.
**Use any mild-flavored sausage, or even browned pork sausage links that you'll serve whole instead of sliced.

Pigeons cocotte grand-mère

SQUAB BRAISED WITH POTATOES AND ONIONS

[FOR 4 PEOPLE]

½ pound small white onions
4 potatoes
2 large squab
Salt to taste
Freshly ground black pepper to taste
3 tablespoons butter
½ pound mushrooms
1 tablespoon minced parsley

Preparation and cooking time: 1 hour

Peel the onions and potatoes. Dice the potatoes. Plunge both, 5 minutes into boiling water. Drain.

Salt and pepper the inside of the squab.

Place the squab in a large casserole. Brown them on all sides in 2 tablespoons of the butter. Remove them from the casserole. Add the onions and potatoes, thoroughly dried. As soon as the vegetables are lightly browned, add the squab, salt, and pepper. Cover the casserole and cook 45 minutes over medium-low heat.

Wash the mushrooms. Cut them in halves or quarters. Sauté them rapidly in a skillet with the remaining butter. Season with salt and pepper. Add mushrooms to the casserole. Sprinkle with minced parsley and serve.

Variation: A few small pieces of bacon or salt pork, previously blanched 1 to 2 minutes in boiling water or sautéed in a skillet, may be added to the casserole about halfway through.

Pintade à l'estragon et aux pâtes fraîches

GUINEA HEN WITH TARRAGON AND FRESH NOODLES

Preparation and cooking time: 45 minutes / Oven temperature: 350°

[FOR 4 PEOPLE]

2 guinea hens or Cornish game hens
4 sprigs tarragon or 1 teaspoon dried
6½ tablespoons butter
1 cup dry white wine
Bouquet garni
Salt to taste
Freshly ground black pepper to taste
½ pound wide noodles, fresh or dried
1 teaspoon flour
¼ cup *crème fraîche* or whipping cream
4 slices homemade-type white bread

Slip a sprig of tarragon into each hen (or scatter about ¼ teaspoon dried in each). Brown them on all sides, in a casserole, with 2 tablespoons of the butter.

Then add the wine, ½ cup of water, bouquet garni, salt, pepper, and 2 stems of tarragon without the leaves (or ¼ teaspoon dried). Simmer a few minutes. Cover and bake in a moderate (350°) oven 30 to 35 minutes. Turn on the other side halfway through.

Plunge the noodles into a large pot of boiling salted water and stir. Simmer, uncovered, 3 to 5 minutes (or according to package instructions) until *al dente*. Taste to correct the seasoning. As soon as the noodles are done, drain them and mix with 1 tablespoon of butter so they don't stick. Keep them warm. Remove the guinea hens from the casserole. Keep warm. Strain cooking juices.

Knead the flour with 1 teaspoon of butter. Mix, in little pieces, into the cooking juices, over medium heat. Add the minced tarragon leaves (or ¼ teaspoon dried) and the *crème fraîche*. Simmer 5 minutes.

CANAPÉS: Toast the bread slices until golden brown on both sides in a skillet with the remaining butter. Cut the guinea hens in half. Arrange each piece on a canapé. Serve on well-drained and buttered noodles.

Pintade bonne-femme

GUINEA HEN WITH PEARL ONIONS AND POTATOES

[FOR 4 PEOPLE]

½ pound small white onions
4 potatoes
1 tablespoon oil
6 tablespoons butter
2 guinea hens or Cornish game hens
Salt to taste
Freshly ground black pepper to taste
½ pound mushrooms
1 tablespoon minced parsley

Preparation and cooking time: 1 hour and 15 minutes

Peel the onions and potatoes. Cut the potatoes in even slices. Plunge the onions and potato slices into boiling water 5 minutes. Drain and sponge them dry, then brown them lightly in a skillet (a *sauteuse*) or casserole with the oil and 3 tablespoons of the butter, 35 to 40 minutes. Do not cover.

Meanwhile salt and pepper the cavity of the guinea hens. Brown them on all sides in a large casserole with 2 tablespoons of butter. Then cover and cook 40 to 50 minutes, over moderate heat.

Wash the mushrooms. Slice them. Sauté them rapidly in the remaining tablespoon of butter. Add salt and pepper. Add to the guinea hens. Cook another 5 minutes. Sprinkle with minced parsley just before serving, surrounded by sautéed potatoes and onions.

Pintade farcie marinée au porto STUFFED GUINEA HEN MARINATED IN PORT

[FOR 4 PEOPLE]

Marination: The day before / Preparation and cooking time: 1 hour
Oven temperature: 475° then 375°

STUFFING

2 slices white bread / ½ cup milk
1 tablespoon minced fresh herbs (chives,
     chervil, parsley, tarragon)
1 egg / ¼ pound fresh sausage meat
2 tablespoons port
Salt and pepper to taste

1 large guinea hen / 3 tablespoons port
1 tablespoon oil / Bouquet garni
1 stalk celery, chopped coarse
Salt and pepper to taste
3 tablespoons butter
⅓ pound mushrooms
2 shallots, chopped fine
1 tablespoon minced parsley
2 tablespoons dry white wine
½ teaspoon tomato paste

STUFFING: The day before, soak the bread in the milk. Squeeze it lightly before mixing it with the minced herbs, egg, sausage meat, 2 tablespoons of port, salt, and pepper. Stuff it into the guinea hen. Place it in a bowl that will just hold it. Add another 2 tablespoons of port, the oil, bouquet garni, and celery. Marinate the guinea hen 24 hours, turning it from time to time.

The same day, drain the hen, reserving the marinating liquid. Salt and pepper the bird. Brown the hen in 2 tablespoons of the butter, in a casserole, then slide the casserole into a very hot (475°) oven, uncovered.

Slice the mushrooms. Sauté them rapidly in a skillet, over high heat, with the remaining tablespoon of butter. Add the minced shallots and parsley, white wine, tomato paste, salt, and pepper. Leave it a minute or two over high heat, then pour it into the casserole.

After 30 minutes of cooking the hen, add the marinating liquid and the last tablespoon of port. Cover the casserole. Simmer 20 to 25 minutes more in a reduced (375°) oven.

Poularde braisée au vin blanc

[FOR 6 TO 8 PEOPLE]

1 large chicken, about 4 to 5 pounds,
   cut into serving pieces
¼ pound bacon or salt pork*
1 calf's foot, split
Bouquet garni
2 carrots, 1 onion, sliced in rounds
Salt to taste
Freshly ground black pepper to taste
1 cup dry white wine
2 tablespoons Cognac

CHICKEN BRAISED IN WHITE WINE

Preparation and cooking time: 3 hours and 15 minutes

In a stockpot, place the pieces of chicken, the salt pork or bacon cut into dice, the calf's foot split by the butcher, bouquet garni, sliced carrots and onion, salt, and pepper.

Add the wine, Cognac, and enough water to cover the meat. Bring to a boil. Cover and simmer about 3 hours.

After cooking, arrange the chicken pieces in a deep platter. Pour the cooking broth over it through a strainer.

You can serve this stew hot, with steamed potatoes. If you prefer it cold, refrigerate it overnight until it gels, then serve it with lettuce and *cornichons.* **

*See the note about bacon on p. 54. See Miscellaneous Notes on pork fatback.
**Small French pickles available in specialty food stores.

Poule au pot farcie

POACHED STUFFED CHICKEN

[FOR 6 PEOPLE]

Preparation and cooking time: 4 hours

1 meaty veal shank / Salt to taste
1 whole chicken
1 onion / 2 cloves garlic
1 stalk celery, chopped coarse
Bouquet garni
Freshly ground black pepper to taste

STUFFING

1 cup stale bread crumbs / 1 cup milk
¼ pound boneless ham
¼ pound boneless veal
1 chicken liver / 5 cloves garlic
1 teaspoon minced parsley
¼ pound fresh sausage meat
1 ounce pâté de foie (optional)
1 teaspoon thyme
⅛ teaspoon nutmeg
1 egg / Salt and pepper to taste
4 carrots, 4 turnips, 6 leeks, sliced in rounds
6 slices French bread

Kitchen string

Boil a half-potful of water. Plunge the veal shank into it 5 minutes. Drain.

Rinse out the pot. Fill it with cold water. Put it back on the heat with salt, the veal shank, the chicken gizzard, heart and giblets, the onion stuck with 2 cloves, celery, bouquet garni, salt, and pepper. Skim it.

STUFFING: Put the bread crumbs in a bowl. Pour in the milk. In a food processor, chop the ham, boneless veal, chicken liver, garlic, parsley, sausage meat, pâté de foie, thyme, nutmeg, egg, salt, and pepper.

Pack this seasoned stuffing into the chicken. Sew up the opening and tie the wings and legs down with kitchen string. Plunge it into the boiling court bouillon. Simmer, over low heat, 2 hours and 30 minutes to 3 hours.

After cooking 1 hour, add the carrots, turnips, and leeks.

Just before serving, toast a few slices of bread. Put them in a soup tureen. Pour the steaming bouillon over them.

The poached chicken and veal shank pieces should be served in a large deep platter, with the stuffing and the vegetables from the broth.

CHICKEN WITH TOMATOES AND PEPPERS

Poulet basquaise

[FOR 4 PEOPLE]

2 pounds tomatoes (about 4 medium)
1 bell pepper / 2 to 3 onions
1 chicken (about 2½ to 3 pounds), cut
    into serving pieces
5 tablespoons oil or butter
2 to 3 cloves garlic, crushed
Salt and pepper to taste
1 cup rice

Remarks: This dish must be highly seasoned, with lots of pepper; a little cayenne would go well.

For an attractive serving, pack portions of rice into a buttered drinking glass and unmold it around the chicken on the platter.

Preparation and cooking time: 1 hour and 15 minutes

Plunge the tomatoes into boiling water. Peel and cut them into large pieces. Cut open the pepper and discard the seeds. Chop it and the onions into large pieces.

Brown the pieces of chicken in a casserole with half the oil or butter. Add the onions, then the tomatoes, peppers, minced garlic, salt, and pepper. Simmer 45 to 50 minutes, half covered.

Twenty minutes before serving, prepare the rice. Heat the remaining oil or butter in a saucepan. Add the rice and stir. Add 2 cups of water, salt, and pepper. Cover and simmer 17 to 20 minutes, until all the liquid is absorbed.

Put the rice in a deep warm platter. Arrange the chicken over it.

Poulet au citron vert

[FOR 4 PEOPLE]

1 whole chicken, about 3 pounds

MARINADE

Juice of ½ orange
Juice of ½ lime
1 small onion or 1 shallot, sliced in
    rounds
1 tablespoon oil
A few drops Tabasco sauce

Salt to taste
Freshly ground black pepper to taste
3 tablespoons butter
½ pound noodles or other pasta
1 to 2 cloves garlic
½ cup *crème fraîche*

CHICKEN WITH CITRUS JUICE

Marination: The day before / *Preparation and cooking time:* 1 hour / *Oven temperature:* 450°

The day before, split the chicken open down the back with a large heavy knife (it's easy to do, but you can ask your butcher to do it). Then flatten the chicken completely. Marinate it, in a large shallow bowl, in the orange and lime juice, onion or shallot slices, oil, and Tabasco sauce. Cover with a sheet of foil and let it macerate in the refrigerator overnight.

The next day, drain the chicken. Lay it out flat, skinside down in a shallow baking dish. Sprinkle with salt and pepper and smear with butter. Slide it into a hot (450°) oven about 40 minutes. Baste frequently with a little marinade.

Cook the pasta in a lot of salted water 5 to 7 minutes, or according to the directions on the package, until *al dente.*

Lay the cooked chicken flat on a cutting board. Cut it into 4 portions. Place them on the serving plates. Keep warm in the oven (heat turned off).

Preparing the noodles with cream: Rub garlic around the inside of the serving bowl (very hot), then mix in it the well-drained but steaming-hot pasta with the cream. Keep warm.

Pour off the excess fat from the baking dish. Add the remaining marinade and a little water (3 teaspoons in all) and stir over high heat. Boil a few seconds. Pour it over the chicken in the plates. Serve the pasta separately.

Poulet au curry CURRIED CHICKEN

[For 4 to 5 people]

2 carrots
1 clove garlic
1 apple
2 onions
4 small stalks celery
1 chicken, about 2⅓ to 3 pounds, cut into 8 pieces
3 tablespoons butter
Salt to taste
Freshly ground black pepper to taste
1 to 2 tablespoons curry powder
1 tablespoon flour
3 tomatoes

RICE PILAF

1 onion, chopped fine
2 tablespoons butter
3 cups rice
6 cups water
Salt and pepper to taste
Bouquet garni

½ cup *crème fraîche*
Grated coconut, mango chutney, 2 bananas

Preparation and cooking time: 1 hour and 15 minutes / *Cooking the rice:* 20 minutes

Peel the carrots, garlic, apple, and onions. Trim the celery. Cut everything into dice.

Brown the chicken in the butter in a casserole. Halfway, add the diced vegetables and salt and pepper.

Sprinkle with curry powder and flour. Stir it in well. Add 1 cup of water and the tomatoes, cut into quarters and squeezed lightly in your hand. Stir, over high heat, a minute or two. Cover the casserole. Simmer, over low heat, about 1 hour.

RICE PILAF: Meanwhile, in a saucepan, cook the onion in butter until it is golden. Stir in the dry rice to coat it with fat. Pour in 6 cups of water. Add salt and pepper and the bouquet garni. Cover and simmer slowly about 18 minutes.

Remove the cooked chicken from the casserole. Let the sauce simmer while you skim off, with a spoon, as much grease as possible from the top. Then stir *crème fraîche* into this degreased sauce. Simmer 1 minute.

Arrange the chicken pieces in a deep platter. Pour the sauce over it. Serve the rice pilaf separately and, if possible, with grated coconut, chutney, and banana slices to enhance the curry's flavors.

Poulet en gelée   COLD JELLIED CHICKEN

[FOR 4 PEOPLE]

Preparation time: 45 minutes, plus 1 hour refrigeration

1 roasted chicken, about 2⅓ to 3 pounds
1 tablespoon (1 envelope) unflavored gelatin
1 tablespoon port
1 bunch fresh tarragon
4 tomatoes
A few leaf lettuce leaves

Carve the cold chicken. Place the pieces on a rack.

Prepare the gelatin according to package instructions.* Flavor it with the port. As soon as it takes on the consistency of thick oil, spoon a little of it over the chicken. Let it set in the refrigerator.

Garnish: Dip the tarragon leaves in gelatin and arrange them over the chicken. Cover with a little gelatin. Let set again in the refrigerator a few minutes.

Pour the rest of the gelatin into the bottom of a serving platter. Let it set in the refrigerator.

Arrange the pieces of chicken on the layer of jelly in the bottom of the platter. Garnish with quartered tomatoes and lettuce leaves (or with artichoke bottoms, potato chips, asparagus tips, stuffed eggs, or fish roe).

*See the notes about gelatin on pp. 23 and 78.

Poulet sauté provençale au basilic   CHICKEN WITH OLIVES AND BASIL

[FOR 4 PEOPLE]

Preparation and cooking time: 1 hour

1 chicken, about 2⅓ to 3 pounds, cut into serving pieces
2 tablespoons butter / 1 tablespoon flour
3 tomatoes / 1 clove garlic, crushed
8 to 10 basil leaves, minced, or ½ teaspoon dried
½ bottle dry white wine / Bouquet garni
Salt and pepper to taste
½ pound mushrooms / 20 black olives
2 tablespoons minced parsley

Brown the chicken on all sides in the butter in a casserole. Sprinkle with the flour. Stir. Add the tomatoes, cut in eighths, garlic, basil, wine, bouquet garni, salt, and pepper. Simmer 30 minutes.

Wash the mushrooms and wipe them dry. Slice and add them to the casserole with the olives. Cook another 15 minutes. Remove the bouquet garni. Transfer the chicken and sauce to a deep serving dish. Sprinkle with minced parsley before serving.

Poulet sauté Vallée d'Auge

[FOR 4 PEOPLE]

1 chicken, about 2⅓ to 3 pounds, cut
   into serving pieces
2 tablespoons butter
Salt to taste
Freshly ground black pepper to taste
3 tablespoons Calvados
2 egg yolks
1 cup *crème fraîche*

CHICKEN WITH CALVADOS AND CREAM

Preparation and cooking time: 1 hour and 15 minutes

Cook the chicken pieces in a casserole in the butter over medium heat without letting them brown. Add salt and pepper. Cover and simmer over low heat, in its own juices, about 1 hour. Then skim as much grease as possible off these juices with a spoon.

Pour the Calvados over the chicken. Bring to a boil. Flame over the heat. Immediately place the chicken on a warm platter.

Stir the egg yolks into the *crème fraîche*. Mix this into the cooking juices still over heat, without letting it boil, beating continuously with a wire whisk. Pour part of this rich sauce over the chicken, the rest in a warm sauceboat. Rice or boiled potatoes are the best accompaniment to this chicken.

My advice: The cooking juices should be thoroughly degreased before adding the egg yolks and *crème fraîche*. Otherwise, the mixture, being too greasy, will separate instead of emulsifying. To avoid this last-minute annoyance, remove with a spoon, almost all of the chicken grease floating on top of the juices.

Cailles aux raisins sur canapés   QUAIL WITH GRAPES ON TOAST

[FOR 4 PEOPLE]

Preparation and cooking time: 30 minutes

GARNISH

4 slices homemade-type white bread
5 tablespoons butter

8 quail, trussed and larded*
3 tablespoons butter
Quail livers
¼ cup Cognac
Salt to taste
Freshly ground black pepper to taste
½ pound seedless grapes

Cut each slice of bread into 2 triangles. Sauté them in a skillet in butter until golden brown.

Brown the quail in a casserole with 1 tablespoon of the butter. Then cover and simmer gently 10 minutes.

Rapidly sauté the quail livers in another tablespoon of butter. Pour in half the Cognac. Flame it. Mash the livers with the remaining butter, salt, and pepper. Place them in a dish and keep warm.

Remove the bacon from the quail. Degrease the sauce with a spoon. Put the quail back in the casserole. Pour in the remaining Cognac. Flame it. Add the grapes. Cover and simmer 2 minutes over low heat. Serve the quail on the toast points, with the cooking juices poured over them, and the grapes.

Variation: Partridge or game hens may be prepared the same way. The proportions would be the same for 4 small partridges, but the cooking time would be 25 to 30 minutes in the casserole.

*To lard the birds, wrap each one in slices of bacon that have been previously simmered in water 10 minutes.

Côtelettes de chevreuil au genièvre   VENISON CHOPS WITH JUNIPER

[FOR 4 PEOPLE]

8 venison chops or cutlets

GAME SAUCE WITH JUNIPER

1 tablespoon oil
1 small onion, chopped fine
1 small carrot, chopped fine
1 clove garlic, crushed
1½ tablespoons butter
10 juniper berries, crushed
1 tablespoon tomato paste
2 tablespoons flour
⅓ cup gin
2 tablespoons vinegar
½ cup red wine
Salt to taste
Freshly ground black pepper to taste
Bouquet garni

1½ tablespoons butter
¼ cup *crème fraîche* or whipping cream

Preparation and cooking time: 1 hour and 30 minutes

GAME SAUCE WITH JUNIPER: Trim and debone the chops or cutlets. Brown them in a pot, over high heat, in the oil. Drain off the fat. Add the minced onion and carrot, garlic, and the butter, reducing the heat. As soon as they are lightly browned, add the crushed juniper berries and tomato paste. Sprinkle with flour. Stir. Pour in half the gin. Flame it. Add the vinegar, red wine, salt, pepper, and bouquet garni. Boil rapidly 1 to 2 minutes, then cover. Simmer gently 1 hour. Strain the very reduced sauce.

Just before serving, rapidly sauté the chops in a skillet with a little butter, 1 to 2 minutes on each side (they should remain rare). Keep them warm on a serving platter. Pour the rest of the gin into the skillet, over heat, then add the sauce. Simmer 1 minute. Off the heat, stir in the cream. Serve this sauce over the meat or in a warmed sauceboat.

My advice: To save time, make the sauce in advance. You can reheat the sauce and cook the chops 15 minutes before serving.

Gigue de chevreuil Grand Veneur LEG OF VENISON WITH CLASSIC BROWN GAME SAUCE

Marination: 2 days before / *Preparation and cooking time:* 3 hours / *Oven temperature:* 475°

[FOR 8 PEOPLE]

1 venison leg, about 4½ pounds

MARINADE
2 cups dry white wine
¼ cup oil
1 onion, 1 carrot, sliced in rounds
2 shallots, chopped fine
1 clove garlic, crushed
Bouquet garni
5 peppercorns, crushed

GAME SAUCE
2 ounces bacon or salt pork*
Trimmings from the venison
1 split veal bone (or soup bone)
1 onion, 1 carrot, chopped fine
2 tablespoons flour
1 clove garlic, crushed
2 cups strong beef stock
Salt to taste
Bouquet garni
2 teaspoons freshly ground black pepper

2 tablespoons oil
2 tablespoons *crème fraîche*
1 tablespoon currant jelly

At least 48 hours before, bone the leg. Trim it, removing gristle and the thin skin covering the leg. Marinate the leg in all the marinade ingredients. Turn occasionally.

GAME SAUCE: In a pot, gently melt the bacon or salt pork. Add the trimmings from the venison, the veal bone (split by the butcher), minced onion and carrot. Sprinkle with flour. Stir over the heat until it starts to color. Add the garlic, 2 cups of the marinade, 2 cups of stock, salt, and bouquet garni. Cook on low heat, uncovered, 2 hours. Add the pepper 30 minutes before the end of cooking.

Cook the venison over high heat in oil. Meanwhile place a roasting pan in a very hot (475°) oven. Put the venison in it. Cook 40 to 50 minutes, according to the desired degree of doneness.

Strain the sauce. Add the *crème fraîche*. Simmer an instant. Mix in the currant jelly and pour it into a warmed sauceboat.

My advice: Game sauces, in order to be smooth, should reduce during a long period of simmering uncovered over low heat. Split veal bones are indispensable to achieving the desirable rich texture.

Deep-fried potato puffs (p. 190) and toasted French bread slices, spread with huckleberry or blueberry jam, go well with venison.

*See the note about bacon on p. 54. See Miscellaneous Notes on pork fatback.

Faisan farci aux noix

[For 4 people]

STUFFING

⅓ cup raisins
¼ cup Cognac
1 cup cubed bread
½ cup milk
8 ounces shelled walnuts
Pheasant liver and heart
1 egg
Salt to taste
Freshly ground black pepper to taste

1 pheasant
Salt to taste
Freshly ground black pepper to taste
Bacon strips or thin sheet lard
6 tablespoons butter
1 carrot, 1 onion, chopped coarse
Bouquet garni
4 slices homemade-type bread

Kitchen string

PHEASANT STUFFED WITH NUTS

Macerating the raisins: 2 hours before / *Preparation and cooking time:* 1 hour and 30 minutes
Oven temperature: 350°

Two hours in advance, put the raisins in the Cognac and soak the bread in the milk.

STUFFING: Reserve 10 walnut halves and chop the rest with the pheasant liver and heart. Stir in the egg, bread, and raisins (reserving the Cognac). Add salt and pepper. Pack the stuffing into the pheasant. Salt and pepper it. Wrap in bacon strips or lard. Tie up with string.

Brown the pheasant in a casserole with 2 tablespoons of the butter. Add coarsely chopped carrot and onion, and bouquet garni. Put the casserole, uncovered, in a moderate (350°) oven 10 minutes. Then cover it and bake for 1 hour.

Meanwhile cut each slice of bread into 2 triangles. Brown them in a skillet with the remaining butter.

Remove the bacon from the pheasant. Place the bird on a warm platter. Surround with toasted bread and reserved nuts. With a spoon, degrease the sauce left in the casserole. Add the Cognac the raisins soaked in. Bring to a boil and flame. Pour over the pheasant and serve.

Variation: Partridge or game hens may be prepared the same way. The proportions in this recipe could apply to 4 partridges. Cut the baking time back to 30 minutes.

Perdreaux rôtis sur canapés

[FOR 4 PEOPLE]

2 young partridges
5 tablespoons butter
Salt to taste
Freshly ground black pepper to taste
2 grape leaves
2 thin sheets lard or blanched bacon
2 slices homemade-type bread
½ teaspoon thyme

ROAST PARTRIDGES ON TOAST

Preparation and cooking time: 30 minutes / *Oven temperature:* 375°

Reserve the partridge livers. Smear the partridges with 1½ tablespoons of the butter. Salt and pepper them. On each breast, lay a grape leaf, then a sheet of lard or strip of bacon. Tie in place with string. Place in a hot (375°) oven 20 minutes. Baste frequently during cooking.

Brown the bread in a skillet with 2 tablespoons of butter. Dice the livers. Brown them rapidly in the remaining butter. Add salt, pepper, and thyme. Mash with a fork and spread on the browned bread. Arrange these canapés on a platter.

Remove the lard and grape leaves from the partridges. Reserve the leaves. Put the partridges back in the oven 5 minutes to brown the bare surfaces. Before arranging them on the canapés, place a grape leaf on each one. Serve with a sauceboat filled with the cooking juices.

Perdrix en chartreuse

[FOR 4 PEOPLE]

1 head green cabbage, about 2 pounds
½ pound bacon*
2 tablespoons butter
2 partridges
2 carrots, sliced in rounds
1 onion, chopped fine
1 mild French or Polish sausage
Salt to taste
Freshly ground black pepper to taste

PARTRIDGES WITH CABBAGE

Preparation and cooking time: 2 hours and 30 minutes to 3 hours / *Oven temperature:* 350°

Bring a large pot of water to a boil. Cut the cabbage in eighths. Trim away the large cores. Plunge the cabbage into boiling water and cook 10 minutes. Drain.

Slowly melt the diced bacon in a pot with the butter. Then add the partridges to brown.

Next add the cabbage, carrots, onion, sliced sausage, salt, and pepper. Cover and simmer, over very low heat, 1 hour and 30 minutes to 2 hours (even better: put the pot, covered, into a 350° oven and bake the same amount of time). Butter the inside of a flat-bottomed bowl. Press the carrot and sausage slices against this flat surface before packing the cabbage in. Then unmold it and arrange the partridges over it before serving.

Variation: Pheasant can be prepared the same way, using the same proportions.

*See the note about bacon on p. 54.

Lapereau à l'oseille

[FOR 4 PEOPLE]

1 rabbit, cut into serving pieces
2 tablespoons oil
2 ounces bacon or salt pork *
15 small white onions
4 tablespoons butter
Salt to taste
Freshly ground black pepper to taste
½ pound fresh sorrel
¾ cup *crème fraîche* or whipping cream
1 egg yolk

RABBIT WITH SORREL

Preparation and cooking time: 1 hour and 30 minutes

In a casserole, brown the rabbit pieces on all sides, in the oil. Add the diced bacon or salt pork and the onions with 3 tablespoons of the butter. Season with salt and pepper. Cover and simmer 45 minutes to 1 hour.

Rinse the sorrel. Chop it and cook a few minutes, over high heat, with the remaining tablespoon of butter. Drain it thoroughly.

When the rabbit is done, arrange it on a warm platter. Put the sorrel and *crème fraîche* in the casserole. Simmer, stirring, 1 minute. Then, off the heat, mix in the egg yolk, stirring rapidly so that it doesn't cook. Pour over the pieces of rabbit and serve immediately with boiled potatoes or pasta.

*See the note about bacon on p. 54. See Miscellaneous Notes on pork fatback.

Lapin farci à la normande

[FOR 4 PEOPLE]

1 rabbit, about 3 pounds

MARINADE

1 teaspoon thyme
1 bay leaf
½ teaspoon rosemary
Freshly ground black pepper to taste
1 tablespoon oil

STUFFING

8 ounces lean ham
2 rabbit livers
½ cup bread crumbs
⅓ cup minced chives
¼ teaspoon allspice
1 egg
1 tablespoon Cognac, brandy, or Calvados
Salt and pepper to taste

¼ pound mushrooms
1½ tablespoons butter
12 small onions
1 large sheet fatback*
1½ cups dry white wine
2 tablespoons Cognac, brandy, or Calvados
Salt and pepper to taste

String or skewers

STUFFED RABBIT WITH CALVADOS

Marination: The day before / *Preparation and cooking time:* 2 hours and 30 minutes
Oven temperature: 350°

The day before, rub the rabbit with the marinade. Wrap it in foil. Refrigerate overnight.

STUFFING: In a food mill or food processor, combine the ham, livers, breadcrumbs, chives, allspice, egg, Cognac, salt, and pepper. You should have a fairly smooth stuffing. Spread it along the inside of the rabbit. To keep the stuffing in place, pull down the thin thoraxic skin and bring the thighs close together. Sew up with string, or pin the edges together with small skewers (the stuffing holds together well in cooking).

Trim the sandy bases off the mushrooms. Wash the mushrooms, then slice them thinly and cook 10 minutes in the butter, over low heat. Peel the onions. Brown them lightly.

Line the inside of a large casserole with pieces of fatback. Spread ⅔ of the mushroom-onion mixture over it. Put in the rabbit folded up on itself. Add the remaining mushrooms, the wine, the Cognac, salt, and pepper.

Begin the cooking on top of the stove. As soon as it comes to a boil, flame it. Cover tightly. Place the casserole in a moderate (350°) oven. Bake slowly about 1 hour and 30 minutes. Serve the rabbit cut into pieces.

My advice: If you don't have a second rabbit's liver, a slice of lamb or pork liver will do. If the cooking juices evaporate quickly, add a little boiling water. In any event, remember that the more concentrated the sauce, the better it will be.

*See Miscellaneous Notes on pork fatback.

Lapin sauté à la moutarde

[FOR 4 PEOPLE]

1 rabbit, cut into pieces
1 tablespoon oil
3 tablespoons butter
1 tablespoon flour
1 onion
3 whole cloves
Bouquet garni
Salt to taste
Freshly ground black pepper to taste
2 tablespoons *crème fraîche* or whipping cream
1 tablespoon Dijon-style mustard

RABBIT WITH MUSTARD

Preparation and cooking time: 1 hour

Sauté the rabbit pieces over high heat, in very hot oil, in a deep skillet or *sauteuse*.

When the meat is golden brown, transfer it to a casserole over high heat. Add the butter. Sprinkle with flour. Stir with a wooden spoon to lightly brown the flour.

Add the onion stuck with 3 cloves, the bouquet garni, salt, and pepper. Cover tightly and simmer over low heat about 45 minutes. When the rabbit is done, arrange the pieces in a deep serving platter. Keep them warm.

In a bowl, mix the *crème fraîche* with the strong Dijon-type mustard (add it to taste). Beat it into the cooking juices with a wire whisk. Pour over the rabbit immediately. Serve with boiled potatoes or pasta.

My advice: Sauce with mustard should never boil or it might separate. It's best to mix the mustard into the very hot sauce, off the heat. However, if it is mixed in with a significant amount of cold *crème fraîche*, as in this recipe, the mixture can be prepared over heat but be careful: no boiling!

Lapin aux pruneaux mariné au vin RABBIT WITH PRUNES MARINATED IN WINE

Marination: The day before / *Preparation and cooking time:* 2 hours / *Oven temperature:* 350°

[FOR 4 TO 6 PEOPLE]

1 rabbit, about 4½ pounds, cut into serving pieces

MARINADE
1 bottle full-bodied red wine
¼ cup Cognac
2 carrots, 2 large onions, sliced in rounds
Bouquet garni
Freshly ground black pepper to taste

3 ounces bacon or salt pork *
½ pound small white onions
3 tablespoons butter
1 tablespoon flour
Salt to taste
Freshly ground black pepper to taste
½ pound prunes

The day before, cover the rabbit with the marinade.

The same day, pat the rabbit completely dry. Cook the diced bacon or salt pork and the small onions in a casserole with the butter until lightly browned. Remove this mixture from the casserole and set aside. In its place, put the rabbit pieces. As soon as they are golden brown, sprinkle with flour. Stir. Add salt and pepper. Pour in enough strained marinade to just cover. Cover the casserole. Simmer over low heat or in the oven (350°). All this should take about 1 hour. Add diced bacon, onions, and prunes. Simmer 45 minutes, in the covered casserole.

My advice: Hare may be prepared the same way, but you'll have to increase the cooking time according to the size of the animal. It's up to you to judge. The tradition in northern France is to serve this hare with unsweetened baked apples, along with steamed potatoes.

*See the note about bacon on p. 54. See Miscellaneous Notes on pork fatback.

Lièvre en civet JUGGED HARE

[FOR 6 PEOPLE]

Marination: 2 to 3 days before / *Preparation and cooking time:* 2 hours and 30 minutes
Oven temperature: 350°

1 hare or rabbit (with its blood if possible)
2 tablespoons vinegar

MARINADE
1 bottle full-bodied red wine
1 tablespoon vinegar
1 carrot, sliced in rounds
2 shallots, 1 onion, chopped coarse
1 clove garlic, crushed
Bouquet garni
½ teaspoon tarragon
6 peppercorns, crushed
2 whole cloves

2 tablespoons oil
6 tablespoons butter
1 tablespoon flour
2 tablespoons Cognac
1 tablespoon tomato paste
Salt to taste
Freshly ground black pepper to taste
4 ounces lean bacon or salt pork*
12 small white onions
¾ pound mushrooms

LIAISON (THICKENER)
2 tablespoons Cognac
½ cup *crème fraîche*

Remove the insides from the hare. Catch the blood in a bowl with the vinegar added to keep it from coagulating.** Discard the bile from the liver. Put the pieces of hare into a bowl with the liver and the marinating ingredients. Refrigerate 2 to 3 days.

In a casserole, brown the hare pieces (but not the liver) in hot oil. Discard the cooking fat. Add 3 tablespoons of the butter and the vegetables from the marinade. Sprinkle with flour. Pour in the Cognac. Flame over heat. Add the tomato paste, salt, pepper, and just enough marinade to cover the hare. Simmer over low heat about 2 hours (or in the oven, at 350°).

Mince the bacon or salt pork. Put it in a saucepan with cold water. Simmer about 10 minutes. Drain. Brown it lightly with 1 tablespoon of the butter and the onions. Cover halfway through cooking.

Keep the pieces of hare warm. Strain the sauce. Put it back on the heat with bacon bits and onions. Simmer a few minutes.

Meanwhile rapidly sauté the mushrooms in a skillet with the remaining 2 tablespoons of butter. Add to the sauce.

LIAISON: Puree the liver and blood in a food mill or food processor. Add Cognac, *crème fraîche*, and a spoonful of hot sauce. Pour this into the sauce, stirring continuously over low heat without letting it come to a boil; otherwise the blood will coagulate. Pour over the hare and serve immediately.

My advice: If the hare is frozen, it should defrost in the marinade. Afterward, make it like fresh game, with one small difference: cook it rapidly in very hot oil to tighten up the meat fibers that have slackened in freezing. Once the meat has browned, lower the heat and proceed to follow the recipe.

*See the note about bacon on p. 54. See Miscellaneous Notes on pork fatback.
**Although less authentic, the recipe is good even without the blood.

MEATS

Carré d'agneau persillade

[FOR 4 PEOPLE]

1 rack of lamb (cracked at the base of
  each rib)
2 tablespoons butter
Salt to taste
Freshly ground black pepper to taste
1 clove garlic, crushed
About 10 sprigs parsley, chopped fine
2 tablespoons bread crumbs

RACK OF LAMB WITH PARSLEY AND GARLIC

Preparation and cooking time: 30 minutes / Oven temperature: 500°

Preheat the oven to 500°.

Brown the rack in a skillet over high heat in 1 tablespoon of the butter (or oil if
you prefer). Then put it in a large roasting pan in the oven 15 minutes. Halfway
through cooking, season with salt and pepper and turn it on the other side.

Mince the garlic and parsley. Mix with bread crumbs, salt, and pepper. Spread
this over the fatty side of the meat. Press it down with a spatula to make it stick.
Scatter the remaining butter, cut into tiny pieces, over it. Put it back in the oven a
few minutes.

My advice: The rack may be cooked ahead of time (15 to 20 minutes) and kept
warm in 2 to 3 thicknesses of foil. At the last minute, cover it with the parsley
mixture and put it back in the hot oven 5 minutes, to heat it and brown the top.

Following the same principles as for leg of lamb, carve the rack with a sturdy
knife. When you reach the bone, search with the knife blade for the articulation or
crack in the bone made by the butcher.

Cassoulet HEARTY BEAN AND LAMB STEW

[FOR 6 PEOPLE]

1 pound dry white beans
¼ pound bacon or salt pork *
2 carrots
4 medium onions
2 whole cloves
3 cloves garlic
Bouquet garni
Salt to taste
Freshly ground black pepper to taste
1 pound lean lamb shoulder
¾ pound pork loin
2 tablespoons goose fat or lard
2 shallots, chopped fine
2 to 3 tomatoes, chopped coarse
1 tablespoon tomato paste
1 large garlic sausage
¼ *confit d'oie* **
¼ cup bread crumbs

Preparation and cooking time: 3 hours and 30 minutes / Oven temperature: 300°

In a large pot, cover the beans with cold unsalted water. Simmer 15 minutes. Drain.

Put the beans back in the pot with the diced bacon or salt pork, carrots split in half, 1 onion stuck with 2 cloves, 1 clove of garlic, and bouquet garni. Cover the pot and simmer just until the beans are done, about 1 hour. Add salt and pepper halfway through the cooking.

Brown the lamb and pork in another pot with 2 tablespoons of goose fat or lard. Add the remaining 3 onions, the shallots, and the garlic, all minced. Finally, add the tomatoes, peeled, seeded and chopped, the tomato paste, salt, and pepper. Add enough liquid from the bean-cooking to just cover the meats. Cover and cook for 1 hour.

Remove all the meat and slice it. Skin and slice the sausage. In a casserole or baking dish, preferably earthenware, arrange successive layers of beans, meats, the *confit d'oie* cut in pieces, etc., ending with a layer of bacon or sausage. Sprinkle with bread crumbs and pieces of goose grease or lard. Bake in a slow (300°) oven 1 hour.

My advice: When the first golden crust forms on the surface, break it and stir it in with a spoon until another crust forms. And so on until the seventh . . .

*See the note about bacon on p. 54. See Miscellaneous Notes on pork fatback.
**Confit d'oie*, preserved goose, can be purchased or ordered from any specialty food store. If you can't find it, you may leave it out, although the dish won't be quite the same.

Couscous COUSCOUS WITH LAMB

[For 8 people]

Preparation and cooking time: 3 hours

BROTH

4 pounds lamb (neck or ribs)
4 onions
2 pinches saffron
¼ cup olive oil
4 tablespoons tomato paste
2 cloves garlic
Salt to taste
Freshly ground black pepper to taste
1 tablespoon *arissa* (hot sauce)

2 pounds couscous
½ cup oil
2 carrots, sliced in rounds
2 turnips, cut in eighths
1 whole chicken
4 zucchini, sliced
2 tomatoes, chopped coarse
1 to 2 teaspoons *ras-el-hanout*
1 teaspoon Arab cumin

SPICY BROTH SAUCE

1 small (8½-ounce) can peas
16-ounce can chick-peas
½ cup raisins
4½-ounce jar sweet red peppers (packed
    in water or oil)
8 tablespoons (1 stick) butter

1 *couscoussier* (couscous cooker)

Remarks: There are many variations of couscous. For this one, get a fairly tough chicken if possible or else it will fall apart in the broth during the long cooking period.

The spices: *ras-el-hanout*, Arab cumin, and *arissa* (or harissa) can be found in specialty food stores. Arab cumin can, if necessary, be replaced by ordinary cumin.

Don't drink too much with couscous! It is traditionally accompanied by fresh mint tea, or by a glass of cool rosé or light red wine.

BROTH: In the pot of the *couscoussier*, simmer 8 cups of water with the lamb, whole onions, saffron, olive oil, tomato paste, garlic, salt, pepper, and *arissa*. Cover.

Pour the couscous into a large bowl. Flood it with enough cold salted water to saturate it (about 10 to 12 cups). Pour ½ cup of oil over it. Fluff it up with a fork. Let it swell up the amount of time indicated on the package.

When the broth has cooked for 30 minutes, add the carrots, turnips, and chicken.

Transfer the couscous to the strainer of the *couscoussier*. Set it over the broth. Cover with a kitchen towel. Simmer about 30 minutes. Then flood the couscous with cold salted water. Aerate it with a fork.

To the broth still on the heat, add zucchini, tomatoes, *ras-el-hanout*, and cumin. Put the couscous back into the strainer over the broth. Simmer it, covered with a kitchen towel, another 30 minutes.

SPICY BROTH SAUCE: In a saucepan, pour in about 1 cup of broth, the drained peas and chick-peas, raisins, red peppers, and more or less *arissa* for flavor. Place over low heat just until it reaches a boil.

Finally, pour the cooked couscous into a deep platter. With a fork, beat in the butter cut into small pieces. Pile the couscous into a dome. Arrange the meat and vegetables around it. Separately, serve the spicy broth sauce and *arissa*.

Épaule d'agneau mitonnée à la champenoise

SHOULDER OF LAMB SIMMERED IN WINE

[FOR 4 TO 6 PEOPLE]

1 lamb shoulder, 3 to 4 pounds

MARINADE

2 onions, 2 carrots, 2 shallots, sliced in rounds
2 tablespoons oil
½ bottle dry white or red wine
1 tablespoon vinegar
1 stalk celery, chopped coarse
2 cloves garlic, crushed
Bouquet garni
2 whole cloves
3 whole peppercorns, crushed
1 sprig rosemary or ½ teaspoon dried

1 calf's foot, split
1 tablespoon butter
1 tablespoon oil
1 tablespoon flour
2 tomatoes, seeded and chopped coarse
2 cloves garlic, crushed
Salt and pepper to taste
1 pound large flat noodles or macaroni

Preparation and marination time: 1 to 2 days before / *Cooking time:* 2 hours

Ask the butcher to bone the lamb shoulder, leaving the shank on.

MARINADE: Slice the onions, carrots, and shallots. Cook them until golden brown, in a large pot, with oil. Add the wine, vinegar, chopped celery and garlic, bouquet garni, whole cloves, peppercorns, and rosemary. Simmer slowly, uncovered, 30 minutes. Cool thoroughly before pouring over the lamb in a deep dish. Refrigerate a day or two. Turn the meat each morning and evening to prevent it from darkening.

About 1 hour before serving, simmer the calf's foot halves about 10 minutes.

Sponge the lamb dry with paper towels. Brown it in a casserole in very hot butter and oil. Sprinkle it with flour. Simmer about 10 minutes with the well-drained vegetables from the marinade.

Add the drained calf's foot, the seeded and coarsely chopped tomatoes, minced garlic, salt, pepper, marinade, and 1½ cups of water. Cover and simmer over low heat or in the oven (350°) about 1 hour and 30 minutes.

Serve the shoulder sliced, with noodles cooked separately, bathed in a generous amount of meat-cooking juices.

Épaule braisée farcie d'aromates

BRAISED SHOULDER OF LAMB STUFFED WITH HERBS

[FOR 4 TO 6 PEOPLE]

STUFFING

3 tablespoons butter
2 tablespoons minced parsley
2 cloves garlic, crushed
1 egg
Salt and pepper to taste
½ teaspoon tarragon
1 teaspoon each: thyme, rosemary, oregano, basil, bay leaf, etc.

1 boned shoulder of lamb, about 3½ pounds
5 to 6 sprigs thyme, or ½ teaspoon dried
1 tablespoon oil
½ cup dry white wine

Kitchen string

Preparation and cooking time: 1 hour and 15 minutes / *Oven temperature:* 475° then 350°

STUFFING: With a fork, work the butter into the minced parsley and garlic, the egg, salt, pepper, and herbs.

Spread this stuffing over the inside surface of the lamb shoulder. Roll it up and fold the edges in to enclose the stuffing. Wrap a string around it lengthwise, then around the width at 1-inch intervals. Place it in a roasting pan garnished with thyme sprigs, or with dried thyme rubbed into the surface. Sprinkle with oil.

Bake in a hot (475°) oven about 10 minutes. Turn the meat occasionally. When it is well colored, drain off and discard all the cooking grease. Return the meat to the oven. Pour the wine over it. Bake in a moderate (350°) oven about 45 minutes.

Serve the lamb sliced, with the cooking juices.

My advice: Lamb shoulder prepared this way may be either braised or cooked on a skewer. If made on a skewer, baste the lamb frequently with a pastry brush dipped in white wine.

Gigot mariné en chevreuil

[FOR 8 PEOPLE]

MARINADE

2 onions, 2 carrots, 2 shallots, sliced in rounds
2 tablespoons oil
3 cups white or red wine
1 tablespoon vinegar
1 stalk celery, chopped coarse
2 cloves garlic, crushed
Bouquet garni
2 whole cloves
3 peppercorns, crushed
1 sprig rosemary or 1 teaspoon dried

1 leg of lamb, about 5½ pounds
8 apples
2 tablespoons butter
Salt to taste
Freshly ground black pepper to taste

LEG OF LAMB MARINATED VENISON STYLE

Marination time: 2 days / Preparation and cooking time: 1 hour / Oven temperature: 475° then 400°

MARINADE: Slice the onions, carrots, and shallots 48 hours ahead of time. Brown them in a pot with the oil. Add the remaining marinade ingredients. Simmer slowly, uncovered, 30 to 40 minutes. Cool thoroughly before pouring over the lamb in a deep platter.

Marinate in the refrigerator 2 days. Turn the meat over each morning and evening.

An hour before serving, remove the vegetables from the marinade with a slotted spoon. Put them in a roasting pan. Place the lamb on top. Bake in a very hot (475°) oven long enough to brown the lamb on each side. Peel the apples, whole, and remove the cores and seeds. Place a dab of butter in each one and arrange them around the lamb roast. Finish roasting in a hot (400°) oven 35 to 45 minutes. Season with salt and pepper.

My advice: The marinade gives lamb the flavor of venison. For greater efficiency, if the skin on the leg of lamb can be removed by the butcher (ask if he'll do it), the marinade can penetrate the meat fibers better.

Gigot Richelieu   LEG OF LAMB WITH MUSHROOM-STUFFED TOMATOES

[FOR 8 PEOPLE]

Preparation and cooking time: 1 hour / *Oven temperature:* 400°

2 pounds small potatoes
4 tablespoons butter
Salt to taste
Freshly ground black pepper to taste
2 cloves garlic
1 leg of lamb, about 5½ pounds

STUFFING

2 tablespoons butter
2 shallots, chopped fine
½ pound mushrooms, chopped coarse
2 tablespoons dry white wine
Salt to taste
Freshly ground black pepper to taste

2 tomatoes
1 tablespoon oil
8 cooked artichoke bottoms

Peel the potatoes. Plunge them into a pot of water. Drain them and blot dry. Heat 3 tablespoons of the butter in a skillet or *sauteuse.* Brown the potatoes lightly. Add salt and pepper, then cover them partially and cook until tender (30 to 40 minutes).

Slip garlic between the bone and the meat. Season with salt and pepper. Roast in a hot (400°) oven about 10 to 12 minutes per pound.

STUFFING: In a saucepan, place 2 tablespoons of butter with the minced shallots and mushrooms. Cook until lightly browned. Add the wine, salt, and pepper. Simmer, uncovered, until the mixture is almost completely reduced.

Cut the tomatoes in half. Brown them in oil, 5 minutes on the cut side, 5 minutes on the other side. Reheat the artichoke bottoms in the remaining tablespoon of butter.

Arrange the lamb, with a few slices already cut, on a large platter with potatoes, artichoke bottoms, and tomatoes topped with mushroom stuffing.

My advice: Choose a very large platter. Arrange the vegetable garnish around the edges. Keep it warm. Cut a few slices off the lamb. Arrange it and its slices in the center of the platter already garnished with vegetables.

Navarin d'agneau   LAMB STEW

[FOR 4 PEOPLE]

Preparation and cooking time: 1 hour and 30 minutes

About 2 pounds lamb stew meat with bones
1 tablespoon oil / 2 tablespoons butter
4 onions, cut in quarters
1 tablespoon flour
1 tablespoon tomato paste
Bouquet garni
Salt and pepper to taste
6 carrots, sliced in rounds
4 medium turnips
1 pound peas (fresh or frozen)
1 pound new potatoes

In a large pot, brown the meat in a little oil. Then drain off the accumulated fat. Add the butter and quartered onions. Brown lightly. Sprinkle with flour. Stir over the heat. Add tomato paste, bouquet garni, salt, pepper, and enough water to just cover the meat. Cover and simmer 40 minutes.

Add to the pot sliced carrots, turnips cut in quarters or eighths, and peas. After simmering 15 minutes, add the peeled potatoes, whole or cut in quarters if they're large. Simmer everything together 25 to 30 minutes.

Sauté d'agneau   SAUTÉED LAMB

[FOR 4 PEOPLE]

About 4 pounds lean lamb stew meat
3 tablespoons butter
1 onion, cut in quarters
1 carrot, sliced in rounds
2 cloves garlic, crushed
1 tablespoon flour
1 cup dry white wine
2 tablespoons tomato paste
Bouquet garni
Salt to taste
Freshly ground black pepper to taste
2 to 3 fennel bulbs

Preparation and cooking time: About 1 hour

In a pot, brown the meat in the butter over high heat. Add the onion, sliced carrot, and minced garlic. Sprinkle with flour. Stir over high heat to brown.

Add the wine, tomato paste, bouquet garni, salt, and pepper. Cover and simmer over low heat about 1 hour.

Meanwhile prepare the fennel. Scrape the bulbs, cut them in half, and plunge them into boiling salted water 20 minutes. Drain thoroughly and add to the lamb halfway through cooking.

My advice: With the palm of your hand, gently squeeze the fennel bulbs when they've finished simmering in the water. Otherwise, they may water down the lamb-cooking juices too much.

Bœuf à la ficelle   BEEF ON A STRING

[For 6 people]

Preparation and cooking time: 45 minutes

4½ pounds beef fillet or tenderloin
1 onion
1 whole clove
1 carrot, sliced in rounds
Bouquet garni
Salt to taste
Freshly ground black pepper to taste
Kosher salt to taste
*Cornichons**
Selection of mustards

Ask the butcher to tie up a roast, leaving at least 15 inches of string hanging from it.

Boil a deep potful of water with the onion stuck with a clove, the sliced carrot, bouquet garni, salt, and pepper about 20 minutes.

Lower the meat into this boiling water without letting go of the string. Tie it to the handle of the pot. Cover and simmer 20 minutes for rare beef.

Remove the meat by pulling the string up. Place it on a platter. Slice it. Serve it simply, with kosher salt, *cornichons*, and different mustards. Boiled or steamed potatoes are the ideal accompaniment.

My advice: The beef, to be cooked just right, is placed in boiling court bouillon for as short a time as if it were being roasted in the oven. Don't be alarmed by its grayish appearance as it comes out of the court bouillon. From its first slice it will be perfectly rare, with a delicious flavor.

*Small French pickles available in specialty food stores.

Bœuf à la mode aux carottes

[For 4 PEOPLE]

3 tablespoons butter
2½ pound-piece of braising beef, larded*
1 onion, 1 pound carrots, sliced thin
1 veal knuckle, split
1 tablespoon tomato paste
2 cups dry white wine
1 clove garlic, chopped coarse
Bouquet garni
Salt to taste
Freshly ground black pepper to taste

Remarks: Beef is larded by having strips of fresh pork fat inserted into it to make it more tender. The butcher does this for you, along with splitting the veal knuckle.

You can add a few slices of mushrooms 15 minutes before the cooking has finished.

BEEF BRAISED WITH CARROTS

Preparation and cooking time: 3 hours

Melt the butter in a casserole. Brown the meat in it, on all sides, over high heat. Then add the onion and 1 carrot, split veal knuckle, tomato paste, wine, 2 cups of water, garlic, bouquet garni, salt, and pepper. Simmer 1 hour and 30 minutes over low heat.

Scrape and cut the remaining carrots in thin slices. Add them to the casserole. Simmer at least another hour.

Place the sliced beef and pieces of veal knuckle surrounded by carrots in a deep serving platter. Pour cooking juices over it.

*Because of its relatively high fat content, American beef seldom requires larding.

Bourguignon RED WINE BEEF STEW

[FOR 4 PEOPLE]

3 pounds lean stewing beef

MARINADE

1 bottle full-bodied red wine
1 tablespoon oil
1 small carrot, sliced in rounds
1 onion, 2 shallots, chopped coarse
1 clove garlic, crushed
1 teaspoon minced parsley
1 teaspoon thyme
1 bay leaf
5 peppercorns, crushed
1 whole clove

2 tablespoons oil
2 tablespoons butter
1 tablespoon flour
Salt to taste
Freshly ground black pepper to taste
1 tablespoon tomato paste
2 cloves garlic, crushed
Bouquet garni
2 pounds potatoes
2 tablespoons minced parsley

Remarks: *Bourgignon* takes a long time to prepare and cook. Make enough for 2 meals. It keeps for several days in the refrigerator and is excellent reheated.

Marination: The day before / *Preparation and cooking time:* 2 hours and 30 minutes

The day before, put the meat, cut in large cubes, into a bowl with all the marinating ingredients.

Drain and sponge the meat dry with paper towels before browning it over high heat in oil. Next add the vegetables from the marinade (carrots, onions, and shallots) and the butter. Cook 15 minutes, uncovered. Sprinkle with flour. Stir over high heat until the flour browns lightly.

Cover the meat with the marinade. Bring to a boil. Add salt, pepper, ½ cup of water, tomato paste, garlic, and bouquet garni. Cover and simmer slowly 2 hours.

Thirty minutes before the end of cooking, boil the potatoes in water. Serve the meat in a bowl, covered with sauce. Serve the potatoes separately, peeled and sprinkled with minced parsley.

For a more elegant *Bourgignon*, add, just toward the end of cooking, small onions cooked separately (in boiling water 2 minutes, drained, then lightly browned with a little blanched bacon and butter about 5 minutes) and mushrooms previously sautéed in butter 5 minutes and 2 tablespoons of Cognac.

Côte de bœuf beaujolaise

[FOR 4 PEOPLE]

1 rib roast, 3 to 4 pounds
A little oil
Salt to taste
Freshly ground black pepper to taste

RED WINE SAUCE
2 to 3 shallots, chopped fine
6 tablespoons butter
2 cups Beaujolais wine
Salt to taste
Freshly ground black pepper to taste
1 teaspoon flour

Remarks: You can keep the sauce warm over a container of warm (not hot) water, but never reheat it or it will separate.

RIB ROAST WITH BEAUJOLAIS SAUCE

Preparation and cooking time: 40 minutes / Oven temperature: 425° then 375°

Rub the beef lightly with oil. Place it on a rack over a roasting pan. Slip it into the middle of a very hot (425°) oven 10 minutes per pound, about 30 to 40 minutes in all for rare beef. Halfway through the cooking, turn it and lower the oven temperature to 375°. Salt and pepper it at the end.

Place the meat on a serving platter. Let it sit in the still-warm but turned-off oven.

RED WINE SAUCE: Slowly cook the minced shallots in 1 tablespoon of the butter, without browning them. Then add the wine, salt, and pepper. Let simmer slowly, uncovered, until reduced by about half. Add the degreased meat juices left in the roasting pan. Stir over heat.

Work the flour into 1 teaspoon of softened butter. Piece by piece, beat it into the sauce still on the heat, using a wire whisk. Then, off the heat, whisk in the remaining butter, beating it, as if making mayonnaise, to obtain a creamy sauce. Pour into a warmed sauceboat and serve it along with the sliced roast beef.

My advice: To ensure that the roast is properly done, press it with your finger: it should be browned, slightly crusty, and a little resistant. Before slicing it, you must let it rest at least 10 minutes in the turned-off oven.

Daube de bœuf béarnaise

[For 8 people]

5 pounds braising beef, cut into large
  cubes (rump or bottom round)

MARINADE

1 bottle red wine
2 tablespoons oil
1 teaspoon thyme
1 bay leaf
Freshly ground black pepper to taste
2 onions, sliced in rounds
2 whole cloves
2 cloves garlic, crushed
1 small hot pepper

4 ounces bacon or salt pork*
1 to 2 tablespoons flour
4 ounces ham
Bouquet garni

BEEF BRAISED IN SPICY RED WINE

Marination: The day before / *Cooking time:* 4 to 5 hours

The day before, marinate the meat overnight in the marinating ingredients.

Spread the diced blanched bacon or salt pork in the bottom of a casserole. Drain and blot the beef dry. Roll it in flour. Put it in the casserole with the diced ham and the marinade. Add the bouquet garni. Cover and simmer slowly 4 to 5 hours.

Serve with boiled potatoes or pasta, which will heighten appreciation of the sauce.

My advice: It is very disagreeable to bite down on a hot pepper lost in the sauce! Tie it on to a piece of long string in order to fish it out easily.

Slow, even cooking makes this dish tender and juicy. This can be accomplished even better in a 300° oven, with no danger of sticking on the bottom.

*See the note about bacon on p. 54. See Miscellaneous Notes on pork fatback.

Daube du gardian

BEEF BRAISED WITH TOMATOES AND OLIVES

[FOR 4 PEOPLE]

4 ounces bacon or salt pork*
1 tablespoon oil
3 pounds braising beef
3 onions, cut in quarters
2 tablespoons flour
1 cup dry white wine
1 cup water
3 cloves garlic
Bouquet garni
Freshly ground black pepper to taste
Pinch salt
4 to 5 tomatoes
⅓ cup black olives
2 tablespoons minced parsley

Preparation time: 15 minutes / *Cooking time:* 2 hours plus 1 hour

Blanch the bacon or salt pork to extract saltiness. Sponge it dry and dice it. Brown it lightly in a casserole with the oil over medium heat. With a slotted spoon, remove the bacon. Save the cooking oil.

Cut the meat into large cubes. Brown them in the oil left in the casserole over high heat, along with the quartered onions.

Sprinkle with flour. Stir over the heat to brown the flour. Then add the wine, water, garlic, bouquet garni, pepper, and a very little salt because of the olives that will be added later. Bring to a boil. Cover and simmer slowly 2 hours.

Add the tomatoes peeled, chopped and lightly squeezed dry, the bacon pieces, and the olives. Put back over very low heat for 1 hour. Serve this dish sprinkled with minced parsley, accompanied by pasta or steamed potatoes.

*See the note about bacon on p. 54. See Miscellaneous Notes on pork fatback.

STEAK WITH MARROW SAUCE

Entrecôte à la moelle

[FOR 4 PEOPLE]

Preparation and cooking time: 30 minutes

BORDELAISE SAUCE

2 shallots, chopped fine
1½ tablespoons butter / 1 cup red wine
¼ teaspoon thyme / 1 small bay leaf
1 tablespoon tomato paste
Salt and pepper to taste
1 teaspoon flour

2 ounces beef marrow
2 tablespoons butter / 1 tablespoon oil
2 sirloin or rib steaks, 1 to 1½ pounds
Salt and pepper to taste
2 tablespoons minced parsley

BORDELAISE SAUCE: Cook the shallots in half the butter until they are golden. Add ¼ cup of the wine, the thyme, and bay leaf. Simmer over low heat until the liquid has completely evaporated. Then add the rest of the wine, the tomato paste, ½ cup of water, salt, and pepper. Work the flour into the remaining butter. Whisk it into the sauce, little by little, and let it simmer over low heat.

Meanwhile cut the marrow into 4 thick slices. Plunge them, in a metal strainer, into boiling salted water. Simmer 1 minute over low heat. Remove from the heat but wait 2 minutes before draining. Keep warm.

Heat the butter and oil in a large skillet. Brown the steaks rapidly 2 to 3 minutes on each side. Salt and pepper them. Remove from the skillet.

Boil the sauce in the skillet, stirring up the meat scraps stuck on the bottom. Pour it over the steaks garnished with marrow slices and sprinkle with minced parsley.

Remarks: The shallots should cook very slowly without browning at all. In browning they lose all their flavor, and can even acquire a bitter taste.

Filet de bœuf des gastronomes au madère   BEEF FILLET WITH MADEIRA

[FOR 4 PEOPLE]

1 piece beef fillet, about 2½ pounds
2 small truffles, fresh or canned
⅓ bottle Madeira
Enough strips of fresh pork fat or beef
    suet to wrap around beef
2 tablespoons oil
Salt to taste
Freshly ground black pepper to taste

MADEIRA SAUCE

1 onion, chopped fine
3½ tablespoons butter
1 tablespoon flour
2 cups beef bouillon (homemade, canned,
    or in cubes) plus liquid from canned
    mushrooms
1 small can mushrooms
Salt to taste (optional)
Freshly ground black pepper to taste

Kitchen string

Marination time: 4 hours / *Preparation and cooking time:* 1 hour / *Oven temperature:* 450°

Cut slits in the beef here and there with a small sharp knife and slip in slivers of truffles. Save a few truffle scraps for the sauce. Put the meat in a medium-sized bowl. Pour in the Madeira reserving ½ cup for the sauce). Marinate in the refrigerator 4 hours.

Drain the meat and wipe it dry. Wrap it partially in fat strips (they shouldn't cover the meat completely). Hold fat in place with several loops of string.

Brown the meat on all sides in a *sauteuse* or large skillet in the oil. Drain it and place it on a buttered roasting pan. Add 2 to 3 spoonfuls of marinade.

Bake in the middle of a very hot (450°) oven 12 to 15 minutes per pound, according to the thickness of the meat and individual tastes. Add salt and pepper at the end of cooking.

MADEIRA SAUCE: Meanwhile prepare the sauce. Lightly brown the minced onion in butter. Sprinkle it with flour. Stir a few moments over the heat. Pour in the beef bouillon and liquid from the can of mushrooms. Stir just until it boils, then simmer about 10 minutes. Add salt if necessary, and pepper. Five minutes before the end, add the sliced mushrooms, the tiny scraps of truffles, and the ½ cup Madeira (adding this at the end reinforces the flavor of the sauce).

On a large warm platter, serve the roast unwrapped from its strips of fat, cut in slices and covered with a few spoonfuls of sauce. Serve the rest of the sauce in a sauceboat.

Remarks: If you use fresh mushrooms, sauté them separately in 1 tablespoon of butter 2 to 3 minutes before adding them to the sauce.

Pot-au-feu BOILED BEEF

[FOR 4 TO 6 PEOPLE]

4 carrots
2 turnips
4 leeks
1 onion stuck with 3 cloves
1 clove garlic, cut in half
1 small stalk celery
Bouquet garni
Salt to taste
3 to 4 ½ pounds assorted meats (chuck,
    short ribs, brisket)
1 marrow bone
Kosher salt
*Cornichons**
Dijon-type mustard

Remarks: To keep the marrow from separating from the bone during cooking, rub it
on both ends with lemon before lowering it
into the boiling stock, at the end of cooking
only.

Preparation and cooking time: 3 hours and 30 minutes / *Oven temperature:* 250°

Peel the vegetables. Put them in a large pot with 12 cups of cold water, the onion stuck with cloves, the garlic, celery stalk, bouquet garni, and salt. As soon as the water boils, lower the meat into it. Simmer 2 hours and 30 minutes. Skim occasionally.

Thirty minutes before the end of cooking, add the marrow bone. Serve the meat, drained, with the vegetables, on a warm platter. Separately, serve kosher salt, *cornichons*, mustard, and the marrow extracted from the bone.

My advice: For a good *pot-au-feu*, combine two or three different pieces of meat: fat, lean, and tender. I'm very fond of a piece of oxtail, which lends flavor and body. Do you want an excellent bouillon?** Start the meat in cold water. If you put the beef in boiling water, the bouillon will not be as good, but the meat will be better. And simmer it a long time, but slowly.

For an enormous *pot-au-feu* worthy of an informal feast, add veal shank, a small piece of lamb neck, and even a chicken to the beef. Take out each piece of meat as it's done and keep it warm in a warm (250°) oven. But put the pieces back into the bouillon toward the end to reheat them.

*Small French pickles available in specialty food stores.
**The bouillon from a *pot-au-feu* is often served separately, in soup bowls.

Steak au poivre vert

[FOR 4 PEOPLE]

4 steaks, 6 to 8 ounces each (fillet, rib steak)
2 tablespoons crushed green peppercorns
1½ tablespoons butter
1 tablespoon oil
2 tablespoons Cognac or rum
2 tablespoons *crème fraîche*
Salt to taste

Remarks: Green peppercorns are preserved in brine, freeze-dried, or frozen. Their flavor is much milder than dried pepper.

STEAK WITH GREEN PEPPERCORN SAUCE

Preparation and cooking time: 15 minutes

Cover the steaks with lightly crushed green peppercorns. Place them in a skillet with butter and oil. Brown them rapidly, 1 to 2 minutes on each side, or according to taste. Remove the steaks from the pan and keep them warm.

Drain the grease from the skillet. Add the Cognac (or even rum). Flame over the heat. Stir in the *crème fraîche*, a few more crushed green peppercorns, and salt. Stir with a wooden spoon while it simmers for a minute or two.

Pour over the steaks before serving with such accompaniments as fried potatoes or french fries and grilled tomatoes.

Tournedos grillés aux baies de poivre rose — BEEF FILLET GRILLED WITH PINK PEPPERCORNS

[FOR 4 PEOPLE]

Preparation and cooking time: 20 minutes

PINK PEPPERCORN SAUCE
1 to 2 tablespoons pink peppercorns (freeze-dried)
1 cup dry white wine
½ cup *crème fraîche*
¼ teaspoon cornstarch
Salt to taste

4 tournedos (beef fillet), 6 to 8 ounces each
Oil

PINK PEPPERCORN SAUCE: Place the peppercorns and wine in a small saucepan. Cover and simmer slowly to rehydrate the peppercorns.

In a bowl, mix the *crème fraîche* with cornstarch and salt. When the pepper and wine have been reduced by a good half, stir in the cream, over heat. Cook for a few moments until the sauce is light but smooth. Keep warm.

Lightly oil both sides of the tournedos. Place them on a very hot grill (or under a very hot broiler). Cook a minute or two, according to taste and the thickness of the steaks.

Remove the strip of fat around the steaks before arranging them on warm plates. Pour pink peppercorn sauce over them and serve.

Tournedos Rossini

[For 4 people]

STOCK
1 veal bone, split
1 carrot, 1 onion, chopped fine
1 tablespoon oil
1 tablespoon flour
½ cup dry white wine
½ teaspoon tomato paste
Bouquet garni
Salt to taste
Freshly ground black pepper to taste

4 slices homemade-type white bread
4½ tablespoons butter
4 thick tournedos (beef fillets)
Salt to taste
Freshly ground black pepper to taste
4 slices foie gras or mousse*
4 slices truffle**
½ cup port

BEEF FILLET WITH FOIE GRAS

Preparation and cooking time: 1 hour (15 minutes, if you don't make the stock)
Oven temperature: 250°

STOCK: In a pot, over high heat, brown the split veal bone with the diced carrot and onion in oil. Sprinkle with flour. Stir until it browns. Add the wine, 1 cup of water, tomato paste, bouquet garni, salt, and pepper. Stir until it comes to a boil. Simmer over very low heat, uncovered, at least 45 minutes.

Meanwhile, in a skillet, sauté the slices of bread on both sides in 2½ tablespoons of the butter until golden brown. Keep warm.

Cook the tournedos in the remaining butter, over high heat, about 2 minutes on each side. Salt and pepper them.

Arrange them on the toasted bread. Top them with a thin slice of foie gras and a sliver of truffle. Keep them hot in a warm (250°) oven.

Pour the port in the skillet, over heat. Scrape the pan with a wooden spoon to stir in meat scraps stuck on the bottom. Add the strained stock. Taste for seasoning. Pour a little sauce over the tournedos and serve the rest in a warmed sauceboat.

*Foie gras, or goose liver mousse, may be ordered from specialty food stores. You can also use canned mousse or pâté.
**Truffles may be bought in cans, or you can use truffled mousse or pâté.

Carré de porc braisé à l'orange

[FOR 4 PEOPLE]

3 pounds pork roast
2 tablespoons butter
1 onion, 1 carrot, sliced in rounds
1 teaspoon tomato paste
2 cloves garlic, crushed
1 cup dry white wine
Bouquet garni
Salt to taste
Freshly ground black pepper to taste
2 oranges
2 tablespoons Curaçao

Remarks: A few minutes of boiling will rid the orange zest of some of its bitterness. Boiled next in orange juice, its natural flavors are reinforced.

PORK ROAST WITH ORANGE SAUCE

Preparation and cooking time: 2 hours

In a very large casserole, over high heat, brown the unboned roast in the butter. Add the sliced onion and carrot. Let them brown lightly. Then add the tomato paste, minced garlic, wine, bouquet garni, salt, and pepper. Cover and simmer, over low heat, 1 hour to 1 hour and 15 minutes.

Peel the zest (colored rind) from the oranges with a small sharp knife. Cut into thin strips. Plunge them in boiling water 3 minutes. Drain them and simmer a few minutes in the juice from the oranges.

Remove the meat from the casserole. Keep it warm. Strain the sauce, then put it back over the heat with the drained orange zest, uncovered, until reduced by half. Pour the Curaçao in at the last moment.

Serve the roast sliced and covered with sauce.

SAUERKRAUT WITH SAUSAGES

Choucroute alsacienne

[FOR 6 TO 8 PEOPLE]

3 pounds sauerkraut, raw if possible,
  fresh or canned
1 pound bacon, diced*
1 veal knuckle, split
1 pound smoked pork shoulder
1 pound smoked pork butt
1 garlic sausage
1 onion, 1 carrot, sliced in rounds
1 whole clove
20 juniper berries
Bouquet garni
Salt to taste
Freshly ground black pepper to taste
2 cups dry white wine
1 pound potatoes
12 frankfurters

Remarks: Frankfurters, which burst easily (unless skinless), are added just at the end. Prick them beforehand with a pin.

Preparation and cooking time: 2 hours and 30 minutes

Place the sauerkraut in a large colander and rinse under running water. If the sauerkraut isn't fresh, let it soak a few hours. Rinse in fresh water. Then squeeze it hard and untangle it.

Place the diced bacon and the split veal knuckle in a large pot. Bring to a boil, then drain.

Spread the bacon in the bottom of a large casserole, cover with half the sauerkraut, the pork shoulder and butt, veal knuckle, sausage, sliced onions and carrot, clove, juniper berries, bouquet garni, salt, pepper, and the remaining sauerkraut. Add wine and enough water to cover. Cover tightly and simmer 2 hours.

After the first 30 minutes, remove the sausage. Remove the meats 45 minutes before the end. Add the peeled potatoes (quartered if large) to the sauerkraut. Cook together 30 minutes. Then put the sausage back in along with the meats and the frankfurters about 20 minutes to reheat them.

My advice: Put the meat garnish (bacon, shoulder, butt, sausage) in from the beginning to flavor the sauerkraut, but since they take less time to cook, don't forget to take them out as indicated in the recipe. By the end of the cooking time, the liquid (white wine and water) should be mostly evaporated.

*See the note about bacon on p. 54.

Enchaud périgourdin

[For 4 to 6 people]

3 pounds pork loin or fillet, boned but
   untied
½ teaspoon thyme
6 to 7 cloves garlic, crushed
Salt to taste
Freshly ground black pepper to taste
4 ounces fresh pork fat, sliced
½ bay leaf

Remarks: If the roast remains unsliced,
it will keep in the refrigerator 2 to 3 days.
But if you want to eat part of it right away
and save the rest, it's best to divide it up into
two different containers as soon as it has
cooked.

COLD PORK ROAST WITH THYME AND GARLIC

Maceration: The day before / *Preparation and cooking time:* 2 hours and 45 minutes
Oven temperature: 325°

The day before, spread the loin or fillet out (untie it if necessary). Sprinkle thyme and minced garlic over it. Add salt and pepper. Roll up the meat to keep the seasonings in and tie it together fairly tightly. Cover it and let it macerate overnight.

In a casserole, over low heat, brown the meat lightly in no other grease than the sliced pork fat. Add salt, pepper, and the bay leaf. Cover and simmer very slowly about 2 hours and 30 minutes over low heat or in a 325° oven.

Place the well-done meat in a container that just holds it (a bowl or loaf pan). Pour the cooking juices over it, strained if possible to eliminate the seasonings. Let chill completely overnight.

Serve the roast sliced, with *crudités* (an assortment of raw vegetables), green salad, and *cornichons.**

*Small French pickles available in specialty food stores.

Grillades de porc farcies au céleri

[FOR 4 PEOPLE]

1 celery heart (or white part of 4 stalks)
1 cup fresh bread crumbs
3 tablespoons milk
Salt to taste
Freshly ground black pepper to taste
3½ tablespoons butter
4 thin boneless pork chops
Flour for dredging

Toothpicks

PORK CHOPS STUFFED WITH CELERY

Preparation and cooking time: 45 minutes / *Oven temperature:* 350°

Mince the celery until you have about 2 tablespoons. Mix it in a bowl with the bread crumbs, milk, salt, pepper, and 1 tablespoon of the butter.

Spread this stuffing over half of each piece of meat. Fold it over and keep closed with a toothpick. Season with salt and pepper and dredge in flour.

Brown on both sides in a skillet with the remaining butter. Arrange in a shallow baking dish. Cover with foil. Slip into a moderate (350°) oven about 20 minutes.

Paupiettes de porc au fenouil

PORK STUFFED WITH FENNEL

[For 4 people]

Preparation and cooking time: 1 hour and 30 minutes / *Oven temperature:* 350°

4 large, thin boneless pork chops
8 slices Gruyère or Swiss cheese
1 fennel bulb, sliced in rounds
Salt to taste
Freshly ground black pepper to taste
3 tablespoons butter
1 onion, 1 carrot, sliced in rounds
1 clove garlic, crushed
1 teaspoon flour
1 tomato, peeled and chopped coarse
1 teaspoon tomato paste
Bouquet garni
⅓ cup dry white wine
1 cup water

Kitchen string

On each pork chop place 1 slice of cheese, a 1½-inch slice of fennel, another slice of cheese, salt, and pepper. Roll up and tie closed with a piece of string looped across the length and width.

Brown the pork in a pot with the butter. Add the sliced onion and carrot, minced garlic, flour, tomato, tomato paste, bouquet garni, salt, pepper, wine, and water. Cover and simmer 1 hour, over low heat, or in a moderate (350°) oven.

Serve with buttered lasagne noodles or steamed potatoes.

Variation: You might find it easier to prepare 2 large pieces of meat and then cut them in half to serve.

My advice: For a very rich sauce, slip a piece of salt pork, previously blanched in boiling water, in the bottom of the pot under the meat.

Potée lorraine VEGETABLE STEW WITH POTATOES AND SAUSAGE

[For 4 to 6 people]

Preparation and cooking time: 3 hours and 30 minutes

4 carrots, sliced in rounds
2 turnips, 4 leeks, chopped coarse
2 onions / 3 whole cloves
1 clove garlic, crushed / 1 bay leaf
1 tablespoon minced parsley
1 teaspoon chervil / 1 teaspoon thyme
1 stalk celery
1 pound smoked pork shoulder
½ cup dried white beans
4 ounces bacon or salt pork *
1 green cabbage, chopped coarse
¼ pound wax beans or green beans
1 large mild sausage / 6 potatoes
Salt and pepper to taste

In a large pot, place the sliced carrots, chopped turnips and leeks, 1 sliced onion and 1 whole onion stuck with 3 cloves, minced garlic, bay leaf, parsley, chervil, thyme, celery, and pork shoulder. Cover with water and simmer 1 hour.

Meanwhile simmer the dried beans 45 minutes in unsalted water.

Then add to the pot the bacon or salt pork, cabbage, wax beans, and cooked dried beans. Simmer together 1 hour.

Finally add the sausage and potatoes. Add salt and pepper to taste. Cook another 30 minutes over low heat.

*See the note about bacon on p. 54. See Miscellaneous Notes on pork fatback.

Remarks: If the bacon or salt pork is very salty, soak it in cold water for a while. Change the water as necessary.

Rôti de porc boulangère

[FOR 4 PEOPLE]

1 pork roast, about 3 pounds

MARINADE

1 onion, sliced in rounds
4 whole cloves
1 tablespoon oil
1 teaspoon thyme
1 bay leaf
1 cup white wine
Freshly ground black pepper to taste

1 pound potatoes (about 4)
3 onions
1½ tablespoons butter
Salt to taste
Freshly ground black pepper to taste
½ bay leaf
2 whole cloves

PORK ROAST WITH POTATOES AND ONIONS

Marination time: 12 hours / *Preparation and cooking time:* 2 hours / *Oven temperature:* 375°

The day before, marinate the roast (as in Pork Roast with Sage, p. 153).

Peel and thinly slice the potatoes and onions. Butter the inside of a fairly large casserole with half the butter. In the bottom, put half the potatoes and onions. Salt lightly. Put the roast on top of them. Cover with the rest of the potatoes and onions. Season with salt and pepper. Add the bay leaf and cloves.

Pour the strained marinade into the casserole. Dot with small pieces of the remaining butter. Cover the casserole and simmer about 1 hour and 30 minutes over low heat or in a moderate (375°) oven.

Rôti de porc à la sauge

[FOR 4 PEOPLE]

1 pork roast, about 2 pounds

MARINADE
1 onion, sliced in rounds
2 whole cloves
1 tablespoon oil
½ teaspoon thyme
1 bay leaf
1 cup white wine
Freshly ground black pepper to taste

12 leaves fresh sage
1½ tablespoons butter
Salt and pepper to taste

PORK ROAST WITH SAGE

Marination time: 12 hours / *Preparation and cooking time:* 1 hour and 45 minutes
Oven temperature: 375°

The day before, marinate the meat with the sliced onion and all the marinade ingredients. Turn it occasionally.

Drain the meat. With your finger, poke sage leaves inside the roast (cut slits in the meat if necessary). Rub the roast with the butter, salt and pepper it, and cook in a moderate (375°) oven. Baste frequently with the strained marinade. Roast another 45 minutes. When ¾ done, protect the top of the roast with a piece of foil to prevent it from drying out.

Serve the roast with boiled or scalloped potatoes, or pasta, and fresh green vegetables first cooked in water then braised in butter.

Rouelle de jambon braisée en gelée COLD JELLIED HAM SLICES

[FOR 4 TO 6 PEOPLE]

1 slice fresh ham, 2 to 4 pounds
1 tablespoon oil
2 tablespoons butter
¼ pound salt pork or fatback*
½ pound split veal bone
2 carrots, 4 large onions, sliced in rounds
1 small stalk celery
2 to 3 cloves garlic, crushed
Bouquet garni
2 whole cloves
Salt to taste
Freshly ground black pepper to taste
1 cup white wine

Remarks: A *rouelle* is a fairly thick round slice cut from a fresh ham or from the meatiest part of the leg.

Preparation and cooking time the day before: 2 hours and 30 minutes

Brown the ham slice on both sides, in a large skillet, with oil and butter, over high heat.

Place the diced salt pork or fatback and veal bones in a pot of cold water. Bring to a boil and cook 5 minutes. Drain and rinse in cold water.

Cover the bottom of a casserole with salt pork. Scatter sliced carrots and onions over it, then add the ham slice. Surround it with: veal bones, celery, minced garlic, bouquet garni, and cloves. Season with salt and pepper.

Add the wine. Bring to a boil. After a few seconds, add 2 cups of water. Cover and simmer slowly about 2 hours.

Arrange the boneless meat, cut into pieces, in a fairly deep and not-too-large serving dish. Cover it with the strained cooking juices and sliced carrots. Let it set overnight. Serve with *cornichons*** and a green salad.

*See Miscellaneous Notes on pork fatback.
**Small French pickles available in specialty food stores.

Blanquette à l'ancienne

[FOR 4 PEOPLE]

2 pounds veal shoulder, cut into large
    cubes
3 tablespoons butter
1 onion, 1 carrot, chopped coarse
2 tablespoons flour
Bouquet garni
2 whole cloves
Salt and pepper to taste

LIAISON (THICKENER)

1 egg yolk
2 tablespoons *crème fraîche* or whipping
    cream
Juice of ¼ lemon

1 tablespoon minced parsley

Remarks: At the last minute, you can
add to the sauce whole small mushrooms
sautéed with a little butter and lemon juice.

VEAL STEW WITH CREAM

Preparation and cooking time: 1 hour and 45 minutes

Lightly brown the meat in a casserole with the butter. Then add the chopped onion and carrot and stir. Sprinkle with flour. Stir over heat a few minutes.

Add 2 cups of hot water, bouquet garni, cloves, salt, and pepper. Cover and simmer about 1 hour and 15 minutes.

When the meat is cooked, drain it carefully, and keep it warm in a serving bowl. Leave the casserole uncovered over high heat to reduce the cooking sauce. Remove the bouquet garni and carrot.

LIAISON: In a large bowl, mix the egg yolk, *crème fraîche*, and lemon juice. Then, little by little, beat in the sauce with a whisk. Pour over the meat. Sprinkle with parsley and serve immediately, with steamed potatoes or rice.

My advice: To keep a thickened stew waiting, there's only one solution: a bain-marie (see Miscellaneous Notes at end of book).

Côtes de veau aux girolles en papillotes

VEAL CHOPS WITH WILD MUSHROOMS IN PARCHMENT

Preparation and cooking time: 1 hour / Oven temperature: 375°

[FOR 4 PEOPLE]

1 pound canned *girolle* or *chanterelle* mushrooms (available in specialty food stores), or fresh cultivated mushrooms, sliced and sprinkled with lemon juice
1 tablespoon oil
4 thin veal chops
4 tablespoons butter
Salt to taste
Freshly ground black pepper to taste
4 tablespoons dry white wine

Cut off the sandy base of the mushroom stems. Wash mushrooms in several batches of water with a little vinegar added. Drain them by squeezing with your hands. Put them in a large skillet with the oil. Cook, over medium heat, 5 minutes, so that they render their juices. Drain them.

Brown the chops on both sides over high heat in half the butter. Remove them from the skillet before they're completely cooked. In their place, sauté the mushrooms with salt, pepper, and wine, over fairly high heat, 5 to 6 minutes.

Cut 4 large hearts out of a sheet of foil or kitchen parchment paper. On one half of the sheet, place a veal chop covered with ¼ of the mushrooms and dotted with 2 pieces of the remaining butter. Seal it by rolling the edges together tightly. Cook in a hot (375°) oven 20 minutes. Serve in the foil or parchment packets, which the guests open on their plate.

My advice: Think big when cutting out the packet. Picture the piece of meat on half the sheet (the other half will be folded over to enclose it). Also, you'll have to leave a margin of 1½ inches all around the meat since the packet will puff up in the oven.

VEAL CHOPS WITH CREAM AND CALVADOS

Côtes de veau Vallée d'Auge

[For 4 people]

6 to 8 small onions
½ pound mushrooms
4 veal chops
Salt to taste
Freshly ground black pepper to taste
Flour for dredging
2 tablespoons butter
¼ cup Calvados
4 tablespoons *crème fraîche* or whipping cream

Preparation and cooking time: 30 minutes

Peel the onions. Plunge them into boiling water 5 minutes and drain. Clean the mushrooms and slice them.

Salt, pepper, and flour the veal chops. In a very large skillet, brown them lightly on both sides in the hot butter. Then add the onions and mushrooms. Simmer about 20 minutes. Cover halfway through cooking.

At the end of cooking, add the Calvados. Flame it over the heat. Remove the meat. Pour the cream into the cooking juices left in the pan. Simmer a few seconds, stirring constantly. Add more salt and pepper if necessary. Pour over the chops and serve with potatoes, pasta, or plain rice, all of which go well with cream sauces.

VEAL SCALLOPS WITH TARRAGON AND CREAM

Escalopes normandes

[For 4 people]

4 veal scallops
2 tablespoons butter
½ cup dry white wine
4 sprigs tarragon or 1 teaspoon dried
3 tablespoons *crème fraîche*
Salt to taste
Freshly ground pepper to taste

Preparation and cooking time: 25 minutes

Brown the veal in a skillet in the hot butter, 3 to 4 minutes on each side. Add the wine and stems from the fresh tarragon (the leaves will be added later) or ½ teaspoon dried. Cover and cook over low heat 10 minutes.

Place the cooked veal on a platter and keep warm. Leave the cooking juices in the skillet. Stir in 1 to 2 tablespoons of water. Boil 1 minute. Remove the tarragon stems. Add the *crème fraîche* and dried minced tarragon leaves. Salt and pepper to taste. Simmer another minute. Pour over the meat.

Serve with peeled, unsweetened baked apples, or quartered apples rapidly sautéed in the skillet with a little butter along with, or just before, the veal.

Variation: All recipes for veal scallops can be used for veal chops. One slight difference: the cooking time is somewhat longer since chops are generally thicker, especially around the bone.

Escalopes Lucullus

BROILED VEAL CHOPS WITH GRUYÈRE AND HAM

[FOR 4 PEOPLE]

Preparation and cooking time: 15 minutes/*Oven temperature:* 550°

4 veal chops
1 tablespoon flour
2 tablespoons butter
Juice of ½ lemon
2 thin slices ham
4 slices Gruyère cheese

Lightly flour the veal chops. Brown them in a skillet with the hot butter, 4 minutes on each side.

When the chops are done, sprinkle them with lemon juice. Cover each one with a half-slice of ham and a slice of Gruyère.

Arrange them in a shallow baking dish, with their cooking juices. Brown them under a broiler or in the top of a very hot (550°) oven 5 to 10 minutes.

Serve with pasta or a fresh green vegetable: spinach, peas, green beans, or braised endive.

Grenadins de veau chasseur VEAL FILLET WITH MUSHROOMS

[FOR 4 PEOPLE]

Preparation and cooking time: 20 minutes

WINE SAUCE
5 ounces mushrooms
1 shallot, chopped fine
1½ tablespoons butter
1 cup dry white wine
1 teaspoon tomato paste
Salt to taste
Freshly ground black pepper to taste
1 tablespoon minced parsley

2 veal fillets, about ½ pound each*
Flour for dredging
3 tablespoons butter
Salt to taste
Freshly ground black pepper to taste

WINE SAUCE: Remove the sandy base from the mushroom stems. Wash and slice the mushrooms. Mince the shallot. In a *sauteuse* or wide-bottomed saucepan, melt the butter. Add the sliced mushrooms and minced shallot. Stir, over fairly high heat, 2 to 3 minutes. Add the wine, tomato paste, salt, pepper, and half the minced parsley. Simmer very slowly, uncovered, while the fillets cook.

Cut each veal fillet into 4 to 6 pieces (making 8 to 12). Flatten the fillets with the side of a large knife blade. Flour them lightly. Place them in a skillet with very hot butter, then lower the heat a little and cook 4 to 5 minutes on each side. Salt and pepper them. Then arrange them on a warm platter.

Transfer the wine sauce to the skillet placed back on the heat. Bring to a boil, scraping up meat particles stuck to the bottom. Pour over the veal. Sprinkle with the remaining parsley before serving.

*Veal *grenadins* are small fillets cut from the leg, loin, or rib-eye. Veal scallops or chops may also be served with this sauce.

Osso-buco milanaise

[FOR 4 PEOPLE]

2 to 3 pounds veal shin, cut into pieces
Flour for dredging
5 tablespoons butter
1 onion, chopped fine
1 tablespoon tomato paste
1 cup dry white wine
3 cups water
Bouquet garni
1 clove garlic, crushed
Salt to taste
Freshly ground black pepper to taste
3 fresh tomatoes, peeled, seeded, and
    chopped coarse
½ lemon
½ pound spaghetti
Grated Parmesan or Gruyère cheese

OSSO BUCO WITH FRESH TOMATO SAUCE

Preparation and cooking time: 1 hour and 45 minutes

Dredge the pieces of meat in flour. Brown them on all sides in a pot with 1½ tablespoons of the butter, over moderately high heat. Then add the minced onion.

Add the tomato paste and wine. Boil a few seconds. Then add the water, bouquet garni, minced garlic, salt, and pepper. Cover and simmer slowly 1 hour. Add the tomatoes to the meat along with the lemon zest (yellow rind only, in one piece or cut in half). Simmer another 15 minutes.

Cook the spaghetti in a generous amount of salted boiling water 5 to 7 minutes, or according to package directions, until *al dente*. Drain immediately to keep it firm. Mix with the remaining butter to prevent the spaghetti from sticking.

Discard the bouquet garni and lemon zest. Mince the zest. Arrange the spaghetti in a large deep serving dish and, on top of it, the meat covered with sauce and minced zest. Serve grated cheese separately.

My advice: As soon as the meat has browned, pour ¼ cup of Cognac over it and flame it before adding the remaining ingredients. The sauce will be even tastier. And to make the osso buco look even more appetizing, sprinkle it liberally with grated cheese and brown it under a broiler.

Paupiettes cordon-bleu

[FOR 4 PEOPLE]

4 large thin veal scallops
Freshly ground black pepper to taste
2 thin slices boiled ham
1 tablespoon Dijon-type mustard
4 slices Gruyère cheese

BREADING

2 eggs / ½ cup flour
½ cup bread crumbs
3 tablespoons butter

Kitchen string

ROLLED STUFFED VEAL SCALLOPS

Preparation and cooking time: 1 hour / *Oven temperature:* 350°

Season the veal scallops with pepper. On each one, place ½ slice of ham spread with mustard and 1 slice of Gruyère. Roll up the veal and fold the edges in to hold the stuffing. Tie the roll closed with a piece of string looped across the width and length.

Dip the veal, successively, in beaten egg, flour, and bread crumbs, covering them completely.

Brown lightly in a casserole with very hot butter. Then cover and cook slowly over low heat—or better yet, in a moderate (350°) oven. Serve with Deep-Fried Potato Puffs (p. 190) or, even simpler, pasta.

Paupiettes provençale

[For 4 people]

STUFFING

1 cup stale cubed bread
4 tablespoons milk
3 ounces mushrooms
1 tablespoon minced parsley
1 clove garlic
Salt to taste
Freshly ground black pepper to taste

4 large, thin veal scallops
1 thin sheet larding fat*
3 tablespoons butter
Salt to taste
Freshly ground black pepper to taste
¼ pound black olives, pitted**

Kitchen string

STUFFED VEAL SCALLOPS WITH OLIVES

Preparation and cooking time: 1 hour / *Oven temperature:* 375°

STUFFING: Crumble the bread into a bowl. Pour the milk over it. Wash the mushrooms. Chop them with the parsley and garlic. Drain and squeeze the moisture from the bread. Stir it into the mushroom mixture along with salt and pepper.

Spread the stuffing over the veal scallops. Fold them in quarters. Wrap them in larding fat and tie them with string to keep the stuffing in. Brown on all sides in a casserole with very hot butter. Add salt and pepper. Cover and simmer over low heat or in a moderate (375°) oven 30 minutes.

Meanwhile simmer the olives in water 5 minutes. Drain them and rinse in cold water. Add them to the casserole. Simmer 10 to 15 minutes longer. Remove the string and larding from each scallop. Serve with Tomatoes Baked with Garlic and Parsley (p. 195) and spaghetti.

My advice: Scallops are easy to stuff if they are extremely thin and very large. Ask your butcher to flatten them as much as possible.

* Use fresh pork fatback, fat from a loin roast, salt pork, or bacon, blanched in water 5 minutes, or beef suet.
** Preferably Mediterranean-type.

Poitrine de veau farcie

[For 8 to 10 people]

1 boneless veal breast, about 4½ pounds

STUFFING

1½ cups bread crumbs
1 cup milk
1 egg
¼ pound sausage meat
1 tablespoon minced parsley
Salt to taste
Freshly ground black black pepper to
   taste
⅛ teaspoon nutmeg
2 hard-boiled eggs

3 tablespoons butter
1 onion, cut in quarters
1 carrot, sliced in rounds
Bouquet garni
Salt to taste
Freshly ground black pepper to taste

MORNAY SAUCE

2 tablespoons butter
1 tablespoon flour
1 cup milk
Salt to taste
Freshly ground black pepper to taste
1 egg yolk
½ cup grated Gruyère or Parmesan
   cheese

STUFFED BREAST OF VEAL

Preparation and cooking time: 2 hours and 30 minutes

Slit an opening at one end of the veal breast. Form a pocket going almost to the other end.

STUFFING: In a bowl, combine the bread crumbs, milk, egg, sausage meat, parsley, salt, pepper, and nutmeg. Mix thoroughly. Pack the stuffing as evenly as possible to the edges of the pocket, with the hard-boiled eggs in the middle. Sew up the opening with a large needle.

Heat the butter in a casserole. Brown the meat in it. Add a quartered onion, sliced carrot, bouquet garni, salt, and pepper. Cover and simmer, over low heat, 1 hour and 30 minutes to 2 hours.

MORNAY SAUCE: Stir 2 tablespoons of butter and 1 tablespoon of flour together over medium heat until it foams. Pour the cold milk in all at once. Add salt and pepper. Stir until thick and simmer about 10 minutes. Off the heat, stir in the egg yolk and grated cheese.

When the breast of veal is done, let it rest a moment before slicing. Arrange slices on a serving platter. Cover with Mornay sauce and serve.

Variation: Stuffed veal breast is much appreciated at picnics, buffet suppers, and cold meals. You can replace the Mornay sauce with spicier accompaniments: *cornichons,** pickles, and various mustards.

*Small French pickles available in specialty food stores.

Potée de jarret de veau

[FOR 4 PEOPLE]

2 to 3 carrots
1 to 2 turnips
½ celery root
1 veal shank, 2 to 3 pounds
Salt to taste
Freshly ground black pepper to taste
1 onion
2 while cloves
Bouquet garni
4 leeks (white part only), sliced
1 cup baby lima beans
1½ pounds potatoes

STEWED VEAL SHANK

Preparation and cooking time: 2 hours

Peel and scrub the carrots, turnips, and celery root. Cut them in large chunks.

Place the veal shank in a stockpot. Add enough cold water to just cover. Bring to a boil slowly. Add salt and pepper.

Skim when it reaches a boil. Add the onion stuck with 2 cloves, bouquet garni, and the vegetables (except the potatoes).

Cover and simmer slowly 1 hour and 15 minutes to 1 hour and 30 minutes.

Meanwhile peel the potatoes. Rinse and cut them in half if they're large. Add them to the pot 30 to 45 minutes before the end of cooking.

Serve the veal shank and vegetables covered with a little broth from the cooking. Serve, separately, kosher salt, *cornichons*,* and mild mustard.

*Small French pickles available in specialty food stores.

VEAL STEAK WITH PRUNES

Rouelle de veau aux pruneaux

[FOR 4 PEOPLE]

⅓ cup raisins
½ pound prunes
Salt to taste
Freshly ground black pepper to taste
1 tablespoon flour
1 thick slice veal, 2 to 3 pounds
3 tablespoons butter
2 onions, cut in quarters
2 cups water
2 carrots, sliced in rounds
Bouquet garni

Preparation and cooking time: 1 hour and 45 minutes

Soak the raisins and prunes in warm water for 1 hour.

Salt, pepper, and lightly flour the veal. In a casserole, brown it on all sides in the butter, along with the quartered onions. Then add the water, carrots, bouquet garni, salt, and pepper. Cover and simmer 1 hour over low heat.

Drain the raisins. Add them to the casserole and simmer another 30 minutes. Serve the meat in a deep serving dish, covered with sauce, prunes, and raisins.

My advice: You must order your meat from the butcher ahead of time, because there is not much demand these days for this cut, which is a rather thick slice from the leg.

Sauté de veau printanier à l'oseille

[FOR 4 PEOPLE]

3 tablespoons butter
2 pounds veal shoulder, cut into pieces
2 onions, chopped fine
1 tablespoon flour
1 cup dry white wine
Bouquet garni
2 cloves garlic, crushed
Salt to taste
Freshly ground black pepper to taste
1 bunch sorrel
2 tablespoons *crème fraîche*

VEAL SAUTÉED WITH SORREL

Preparation and cooking time: 1 hour and 30 minutes

Heat 1½ tablespoons of the butter in a casserole. Brown pieces of meat in it on all sides. Then add the minced onions and flour. Stir over moderately high heat. Add the wine, 1 cup of water, bouquet garni, minced garlic, salt, and pepper. Stir. Cover and simmer 1 hour over low heat.

Remove the tough stems from the sorrel. Rinse it and chop coarsely. Put it in a saucepan with the remaining butter, salt, and pepper. Simmer slowly 8 to 10 minutes, until it has given off most of its juice. Drain it.

When the meat is almost done, stir in the sorrel puree and *crème fraîche*. Add salt and pepper if necessary. Serve with small shell pasta, plain rice, or potatoes.

Veau Orloff VEAL ROAST WITH MUSHROOM-ONION STUFFING

[FOR 8 PEOPLE]

2 carrots, 2 onions, cut into dice
4 pounds veal leg, center roast
1 tablespoon butter
2 veal bones
Salt to taste
Freshly ground black pepper to taste

STUFFING
3 onions, chopped fine
1½ tablespoons butter
1 pound mushrooms

THICK BÉCHAMEL SAUCE
2 tablespoons butter
1 tablespoon flour
3 cups milk
Salt to taste
Freshly ground black pepper to taste

2 egg yolks

Preparation and cooking time: 1 hour and 15 minutes / *Oven temperature:* 425° then 350°

Preheat the oven to 425°.

In a baking dish, place the diced carrots and onions, the roast smeared with butter, the bones (split by the butcher), salt, and pepper. Brown them in the oven 30 minutes. Pour 2 cups of boiling water into the bottom of the baking dish. Lower the oven temperature to 350° and continue baking 1 hour.

STUFFING: Mince the onions. Cook them, covered, over low heat, 30 minutes with the butter. Do not let them brown. Wash and slice the mushrooms. Add to the onions. Stir frequently to prevent burning. Mince the mixture finely in a blender or food processor after the mushrooms have cooked about 5 minutes.

THICK BÉCHAMEL SAUCE: Mix, over low heat, the butter, flour, 2 cups of the milk, salt, and pepper. Stir until it reaches a boil.

Mix ¾ of the stuffing with 3 tablespoons of the béchamel sauce. Slice the roast. Spread each slice with a layer of stuffing-sauce mixture (overlapping slices down the length of the serving platter).

Off the heat, mix the rest of the sauce with the remaining stuffing and about 1 cup of milk. Then, off the heat, whisk in the egg yolks. Pour over the roast. Serve cooking juices separately.

My advice: This roast can be completely cooked and stuffed 1 hour ahead of time. Wrap it while it's still very hot in several thicknesses of foil and keep it in a warm (250°) oven. Before serving, unwrap it and place it in a hot (550°) oven 10 minutes, or under a broiler.

Remarks: Before serving, you can put the roast under a broiler to glaze the top of it.

Andouillettes braisées au vouvray

[FOR 4 PEOPLE]

2 shallots, chopped fine
3 to 4 cups dry Vouvray wine*
4 *andouillettes***
Pinch salt
Liberal seasoning freshly ground pepper

Remarks: To keep the sausages from bursting during baking, prick them all over with a thin needle before cooking.

SAUSAGES BRAISED IN WHITE WINE

Preparation and cooking time: 1 hour / Oven temperature: 350°

Preheat the oven to 350°.

Mince the shallots. Scatter them over the bottom of a baking dish. Pour Vouvray over them. Heat until the mixture comes to a boil.

Remove the baking dish from the heat. Arrange the sausages in it. Add a pinch of salt. Season generously with pepper. Place in the middle of the oven until the juices are almost completely absorbed (about 45 minutes). Cover the sausages with a sheet of foil if they start browning too rapidly.

Serve the sausages warm, in their baking dish, with, separately, sautéed, steamed or mashed potatoes, or even with unsweetened baked apples.

*Some Vouvray is very sweet. Ask your wine dealer to recommend one on the dry side.
**See *Andouillettes* in Miscellaneous Notes.

BEEF TONGUE WITH MADEIRA

Langue de bœuf madère

[For 10 people]

1 beef tongue
Salt to taste
2 carrots, 1 small turnip, 2 leeks, 1 on-
    ion, chopped coarse
3 cloves garlic
Freshly ground black pepper to taste
1 whole clove

MADEIRA SAUCE
2 cups tongue-cooking broth
3 tablespoons butter
2 tablespoons flour
1 small can tomato paste
½ cup Madeira

Preparation and cooking time: 3 hours

Plunge the tongue into boiling salted water in a stockpot. Simmer 5 minutes, then drain. Place it back in the pot. Cut all the vegetables into large pieces and add to the pot with the garlic, salt, pepper, and clove. Cover with cold water. Simmer 2 hours and 30 minutes over medium-low heat.

MADEIRA SAUCE: Thirty minutes before the tongue has finished cooking, pour off 2 cups of its broth. Over low heat, mix the butter and flour. Whisk in the tomato paste, Madeira, and the broth. Stir until it comes to a boil. Simmer 30 minutes over very low heat, half covered.

Drain the tongue. Trim off any fatty parts, loose scraps, or bones. Peel it by slitting the skin—without piercing the flesh—and pulling it off. Cut several thin slices on the bias. Arrange them on a warm platter. Pour sauce over them, serving the rest in a sauceboat.

BRAISED CALF'S TONGUE

Langue de veau braisée

[For 4 people]

1 calf's tongue
3 tablespoons butter
10 small onions
2 medium carrots, cut into dice
1 tablespoon flour
1 small (6-ounce) can tomato paste
Salt to taste
Freshly ground black pepper to taste
Bouquet garni
1 clove garlic, crushed

Preparation and cooking time: 2 hours

Wash the tongue in running water, then place it in a stockpot covered with cold water. Simmer 30 minutes. Drain, and rinse in cold water. Scrape the tongue with a pointed knife to remove the skin. Dry it thoroughly.

Heat half the butter in a casserole. Add the tongue. As soon as it has browned on all sides, remove it. Discard the cooking grease.

In the empty pot, place the remaining butter, small onions, and diced carrots. Brown lightly. Sprinkle with flour and stir. Add tomato paste mixed with 3 cups of water, the tongue, salt, pepper, bouquet garni, and minced garlic. Cover and simmer about 1 hour. Discard the bouquet garni just before serving.

My advice: I often add about 20 olives to this dish, 15 minutes before serving. I pit them beforehand, then simmer a few minutes in a large saucepan of water. They're less bitter and salty.

Ris de veau en cocotte

[For 4 people]

BRAISING STOCK

1 carrot, 2 onions, cut into dice
1 tablespoon butter
1 tablespoon flour
1 beef bouillon cube
1 teaspoon tomato paste
Salt to taste
Freshly ground black pepper to taste

1 to 2 sweetbreads
1 tablespoon flour
2 tablespoons butter

BRAISED SWEETBREADS

Preparation and cooking time: 1 hour and 30 minutes

BRAISING STOCK: Dice the carrot and onions. Brown them lightly in a casserole in the butter. Sprinkle with flour and stir. Add 1 cup of boiling water mixed with the bouillon cube, tomato paste, salt, and pepper. Simmer, uncovered, about 1 hour.

To make the sweetbreads, plunge them into a panful of cold salted water. Bring slowly to a boil and simmer 5 minutes without letting them actually boil. Drain them and rinse in cold water. Trim the sweetbreads, then flatten them under a weight, about 1 hour.

Lightly flour the sweetbreads. Cook them in a skillet, over moderately high heat, in 2 tablespoons of butter, until lightly browned. Drain them. Simmer them 30 minutes with the strained stock.

Braised sweetbreads go well with peas or fried potatoes sprinkled with parsley.

My advice: To obtain firm sweetbreads, place them under a weight (not too heavy) after briefly simmering in water. They will firm up while cooling and, if you wish, you can cut them in very neat slices.

Ris de veau panés aux raisins frais

SWEETBREADS PAN-FRIED WITH GRAPES

[FOR 4 PEOPLE]

2 sweetbreads
1 cup flour
2 eggs
Salt to taste
Freshly ground black pepper to taste
2 cups bread crumbs
1 tablespoon oil
8 tablespoons (1 stick) butter
20 large seedless green grapes
2 tablespoons Madeira

Preparation and cooking time: 1 hour and 30 minutes

To make the sweetbreads, plunge them into a panful of cold salted water. Bring slowly to a boil and simmer 5 minutes without letting them actually boil. Drain them and rinse in cold water. Trim the sweetbreads, then flatten them under a weight, about 1 hour.

Cut the sweetbreads in slices about ½ inch thick. In 3 deep dishes, place separately the flour, beaten eggs seasoned with salt and pepper, and the bread crumbs. Dip the sweetbreads in them in the order of flour, eggs, and bread crumbs.

Brown the sweetbreads on both sides in a *sauteuse* or skillet in the oil and 3 tablespoons of the butter. Then let them cook slowly 15 to 20 minutes. Turn them halfway through cooking.

Meanwhile peel the grapes. Heat them with the Madeira in a small saucepan. At the last minute, blend into their very reduced juices the remaining butter, cut into small pieces, stirring briskly with a wooden spoon, over very low heat. Remove from the heat at once. Serve the sweetbreads on warm plates with the grapes and their concentrated sauce.

Remarks: Once the butter liaison has been achieved, the grapes should not be put back on the heat.

Rognons d'agneau grillés vert pré

GRILLED LAMB KIDNEYS WITH WATERCRESS AND FRIED POTATOES

[FOR 4 PEOPLE]

8 lamb kidneys
Oil
Salt and pepper to taste

MAITRE D'HÔTEL BUTTER
3 tablespoons soft butter
1 tablespoon minced parsley
Juice of 1¼ lemon
Salt and pepper to taste

4 to 8 skewers

Preparation and cooking time: 20 minutes

Peel off the thin filament surrounding the kidneys and cut out the button of fat on the underside. Then cut the kidneys open with a sharp knife. Pierce them in a few places with a skewer so they stay opened out flat.

Brush them with a little oil. Place under a very hot broiler 5 to 6 minutes (3 to 4 minutes if there are heating elements above and underneath). Turn them halfway through cooking. Salt and pepper them at the end.

MAITRE D'HÔTEL BUTTER: Meanwhile mash together with a fork the softened butter, minced parsley, lemon juice, salt, and pepper.

Place a knob of butter on each kidney and serve on a warm platter garnished with small bunches of unseasoned watercress and fried potatoes.

Rognons sautés au porto

KIDNEYS SAUTÉED WITH PORT WINE

[FOR 4 PEOPLE]

2 to 3 veal or pork kidneys
3 tablespoons butter
Salt to taste
Freshly ground black pepper to taste
Juice of ¼ lemon
1 cup port
1 small can truffle pieces
½ tablespoon flour

Preparation and cooking time: 15 minutes

Dice the kidneys. Sauté them over high heat in a skillet with 2 tablespoons of the butter. Salt and pepper them. After 3 to 4 minutes, sprinkle with lemon juice. Remove the kidneys from the skillet, but leave the browned cooking scraps. Keep the kidneys warm, placed on a rack so they'll drain.

Add the port and truffle pieces and their juices to the skillet. Boil 2 minutes. Meanwhile mash together with a fork the remaining butter, softened, and the flour. Incorporate this mixture in little pieces into the sauce, whisking until it comes to a boil.

Put the kidneys back in the skillet just long enough to coat them with sauce, and serve immediately with steamed potatoes, rice, or fried potatoes.

Rognons de veau flambés Baugé

FLAMED VEAL KIDNEYS WITH MUSHROOM GARNISH

[FOR 4 PEOPLE]

4 ounces mushrooms
1 thick slice ham
3 tablespoons butter
Freshly ground black pepper to taste
½ cup *crème fraîche* or whipping cream
2 veal kidneys
2 tablespoons Cognac
Small toasted slices of French bread
(optional)

Preparation and cooking time: 20 minutes

Clean the mushrooms. Dice them and cut the ham in match-sized strips. Sauté both rapidly in 1 tablespoon of the butter, over moderately high heat, in a skillet. Add pepper and *crème fraîche*. Simmer 2 minutes. Pour into a bowl and keep warm.

Dice the kidneys. Sauté them quickly in the skillet with the remaining butter over high heat. Add Cognac, and more pepper if desired. Flame over the heat. Transfer the kidneys to a warm platter.

Place the mushroom garnish back in the skillet over high heat for a few moments to reheat it.

Pour over the kidneys and serve over toasted rounds of bread, if desired.

VEGETABLES
PASTA
RICE

Aligot MASHED POTATOES WITH CHEESE AND GARLIC

[FOR 4 PEOPLE]

Preparation and cooking time: 1 hour

2 pounds potatoes / Salt to taste
1 clove garlic, crushed
½ pound *tomme de Cantal* cheese*
5 tablespoons butter
⅓ cup *crème fraîche* or whipping cream

Remarks: The cheese won't run properly if the mashed potatoes aren't hot enough. Keep it over low heat during the entire process. But be careful: overcooked *aligot* won't be runny either!

Scrub the potatoes without peeling them. Boil them in salted water about 30 minutes. Peel and mash them with the minced garlic. You should have a very dry puree.

Cut the cheese in thin slivers. Distribute them over the mashed potatoes, along with the butter and *crème fraîche*, in a casserole.

Place the mashed potatoes over low heat. Beat vigorously with a wooden spoon until the *aligot* becomes smooth and no longer sticks to the sides of the pan. Bring to the table immediately and serve.

*See *Tomme de Cantal* in Miscellaneous Notes.

Artichauts de Provence à la barigoule BRAISED ARTICHOKES WITH TOMATOES

[FOR 4 PEOPLE]

Preparation and cooking time: 1 hour and 15 minutes

4 to 6 small artichokes
3 tablespoons butter
Salt to taste
Freshly ground black pepper to taste
4 ounces bacon or salt pork*
1 onion, chopped coarse
2 tomatoes, chopped coarse, or 1 tablespoon tomato paste
1 cup dry white wine

Wash the artichokes. With a serrated knife, cut them in half lengthwise. Remove the purplish leaves and "chokes" with a pointed knife.

Brown the artichoke halves lightly in a casserole with 2 tablespoons of the butter. Salt and pepper them lightly.

Dice the bacon or salt pork. Chop the onion. Brown both in a skillet with the remaining tablespoon of butter. Add the tomatoes or, if unavailable, the tomato paste. Salt lightly but pepper generously. Stuff the artichoke halves with this mixture. Pour wine over them. Cover and simmer about 1 hour.

My advice: Before cooking the artichokes, trim their leaves with scissors as close as possible to the base, leaving only the fleshy part. That way they'll be easier to eat.

*See the note about bacon on p. 54. See Miscellaneous Notes on pork fatback.

ASPARAGUS WITH ORANGE SAUCE

Asperges maltaise

[FOR 4 PEOPLE]

2 pounds asparagus

MALTAISE SAUCE
2 egg yolks
2 tablespoons cold water
Salt to taste
Freshly ground black pepper to taste
1 tablespoon lemon juice
8 tablespoons (1 stick) soft butter
2 tablespoons fresh orange juice
1 teaspoon grated orange rind

Kitchen string

Preparation and cooking time: 45 minutes

To cook the asparagus, break the asparagus spears 3 to 4 inches down from the tip. Peel the stem with a small sharp knife. Rinse them rapidly. Tie them up with string in small bunches of 5 to 6 and plunge them into boiling salted water. Simmer 12 to 15 minutes. As soon as they're done, drain them. Cut off the string and arrange the asparagus on a long platter.

MALTAISE SAUCE: In a heavy saucepan, place the egg yolks, cold water, a little salt, pepper, and lemon juice. Over very low heat, or in a double boiler, beat with an electric mixer until the sauce thickens and clings to the beater. Make sure the saucepan never gets too hot to touch.

Off the heat, stir in very soft butter, piece by piece, then, when the mixture has thickened, add the orange juice and the grated orange rind (orange part only). Pour into a barely warm sauceboat. Serve immediately with warm asparagus.

My advice: If you use a blood orange, you'll get a lovely rosy sauce. Maltaise sauce cannot be reheated. If it must wait, there's only one solution: a warm bain-marie or double boiler.

Remarks: Break the asparagus stems rather than cutting them because they snap off automatically at the point where they stop being tender.

Don't overcook them. Prick them with a fork, at the base of the stem. If the fork pierces through easily, they're done. Drain them right away, otherwise they'll get waterlogged and lose their flavor.

Aubergines farcies   STUFFED EGGPLANT

[FOR 4 PEOPLE]

4 small eggplants or 2 medium
Oil
4 tablespoons butter
¼ pound boiled or smoked ham
1 bell pepper, cut into dice
2 tomatoes, peeled, seeded, and chopped
    coarse
1 clove garlic, crushed
Salt to taste
Freshly ground black pepper to taste

Preparation and cooking time: 50 minutes / *Oven temperature:* 375°

Wipe the eggplants carefully. Cut off the stems. Cut them in half lengthwise. Then, with a pointed knife, cut through the flesh without piercing the skin, ¼ inch from the edges, all around the eggplant. Cut clear through to the bottom. Lower the eggplants into hot deep-frying oil 2 minutes to soften the flesh. Drain them.

With a small spoon, lift out the flesh without piercing the skin.

In a skillet, in 1½ tablespoons of the butter, brown the diced ham and pepper, the tomatoes, and the minced garlic. Stir. Simmer 10 minutes over medium heat. Add the eggplant flesh, coarsely chopped with a sharp knife. Season with salt and pepper. Simmer 5 minutes. Fill the eggplant skins with this stuffing. Arrange them on a buttered shallow baking pan. Dot with pieces of the remaining butter and bake 20 minutes in a hot (375°) oven.

Champignons farcis aux herbes

MUSHROOMS STUFFED WITH FRESH HERBS

[FOR 4 PEOPLE]

16 tightly closed mushrooms
2 large soda crackers (or ¼ cup fresh cracker crumbs or bread crumbs)
⅓ cup warm milk
2 to 3 cloves garlic
2 tablespoons minced fresh parsley
2 tablespoons minced fresh chives
Salt to taste
Freshly ground black pepper to taste
4 tablespoons butter

Preparation and cooking time: 1 hour / *Oven temperature:* 350°

Cut the sandy base from the mushroom stems. Wash the mushrooms quickly. Remove the caps. Soak the crackers or bread crumbs in warm milk.

Chop together, in a food mill or food processor, the mushroom stems, garlic, parsley, and chives. Add the crackers or bread crumbs, lightly squeezed, along with salt and pepper. Beat together a few seconds.

Mound this mixture into the mushroom caps. Arrange them, side by side, on a shallow buttered baking dish. Place a dab of butter on each one and bake in a moderate (350°) oven 30 to 40 minutes.

My advice: This flavorful mixture may be used equally well to stuff zucchini, eggplant, artichoke bottoms, tomatoes, and even whole fish or fish fillets with the stuffing rolled up in them.

Champignons farcis de mousseline

STUFFED MUSHROOMS

[FOR 4 PEOPLE]

1¼ pounds large mushrooms
2 cups milk
Salt to taste
Freshly ground black pepper to taste
⅛ teaspoon nutmeg
1 tablespoon lemon juice
1 tablespoon cornstarch
1 tablespoon *crème fraîche* or whipping cream (optional)

Preparation and cooking time: 20 minutes

Trim the mushrooms but don't peel them. Rinse them quickly and wipe dry. Remove the caps from the 8 largest ones to stuff them. Place all the mushrooms (including the 8 large ones) in a saucepan with the milk, salt, pepper, and nutmeg. Simmer slowly 10 minutes, uncovered.

Drain the cooked mushrooms (reserve the milk mixture for a soup or a béchamel sauce, if you wish). Keep the 8 caps warm, separately. Put the rest in a blender or food processor with lemon juice and cornstarch. Cover and process until you have a smooth puree into which you can beat *crème fraîche*, if desired.

Spread the puree in the warm mushroom caps. Serve immediately, by themselves or as a garnish for fish or meat.

My advice: If you puree all the mushrooms you'll have a smooth stuffing for artichokes, crêpes, an omelette, or stuffed and rolled veal scallops or chicken breasts.

Charlotte de chou-fleur en soufflé

[FOR 4 PEOPLE]

1 cauliflower

THICK BÉCHAMEL SAUCE
3 tablespoons butter
2 tablespoons flour
2 cups milk
Salt to taste
Freshly ground black pepper to taste

3 eggs
½ cup grated Gruyère or Parmesan
cheese

1 soufflé mold

CAULIFLOWER SOUFFLÉ

Preparation and cooking time: 1 hour and 20 minutes / *Oven temperature:* 350°

Bring a large potful of water to a boil. Break the cauliflower into flowerets. Rinse them. Drop them into boiling water. Drain. Bring another potful of salted water to a boil for a second cooking of the cauliflower (about 10 minutes). Drain.

THICK BÉCHAMEL SAUCE: Melt, over low heat, 2 tablespoons of the butter. Add the flour. Stir over the heat a few seconds until the mixture foams. Pour in the cold milk all at once. Add salt and pepper. Stir until the mixture comes to a boil. Simmer over very low heat 5 minutes.

Preheat the oven to 350°. Separate the eggs. Whip the whites until stiff peaks form.

Puree the cauliflower. Stir in the béchamel sauce, the grated cheese, the 3 egg yolks, and, last of all, the beaten egg whites.

Butter a soufflé mold. Pour in the mixture. Bake in a moderate (350°) oven for 40 minutes. Serve as soon as it comes out of the oven, in the soufflé mold.

Croquettes de pommes de terre   POTATO CROQUETTES

[FOR 20 CROQUETTES]

1 pound potatoes
1 tablespoon butter
2 egg yolks
Salt to taste
Freshly ground black pepper to taste

FOR COOKING THE CROQUETTES
1 cup flour
1 egg plus 2 egg whites
1 cup bread crumbs
3 tablespoons butter

Preparation time the day before: 30 minutes / *Cooking time:* 30 minutes

The day before, boil the potatoes with their skins on. Peel and mash them, with no added liquid (if necessary, dry them out even further in the oven). Combine with the butter, egg yolks, salt, and pepper. With a wooden spoon, stir the mixture over low heat, as for puff pastry, until it no longer sticks to the sides of the pan. Spread it out on a platter in a layer no thicker than the width of a finger. Cover tightly with foil and refrigerate overnight.

To make the croquettes, shape the mashed potatoes into 1-inch balls or ovals. Bread them by rolling them in 3 dishes containing the flour, lightly beaten eggs, and bread crumbs. Brown 4 to 5 croquettes at a time, in a skillet with warm butter. Turn them carefully with a spoon without breaking them. You may also deep-fry them in oil.

My advice: To make croquettes that don't fall apart in cooking, pay careful attention to the dryness of the mashed potatoes; the resting period (it is advisable to leave the mashed potatoes in the refrigerator for several hours at least); and, careful breading.

Endives au jambon gratinées

[FOR 4 PEOPLE]

2 pounds Belgian endives
4 tablespoons butter
1 onion, sliced in rounds
Juice of ½ lemon
Salt to taste
Freshly ground black pepper to taste

MORNAY SAUCE

1 tablespoon flour
2 tablespoons butter
1½ cups milk
Salt to taste
Freshly ground black pepper to taste
⅛ teaspoon nutmeg
½ cup grated Gruyère or Swiss cheese

Remarks: Wash the endives quickly. If they soak up water, they become bitter.

BAKED ENDIVES

Preparation and cooking time: 1 hour and 15 minutes / *Oven temperature:* 500°

Remove the limp endive leaves. With a pointed knife, hollow out the base of the stem, which is frequently bitter. Wash the endives in running water and wipe dry immediately.

Melt 2 tablespoons of the butter in a casserole. Add the sliced onion and the endives. Sprinkle with lemon juice. Add salt and pepper. Cover and simmer 1 hour. Turn during the cooking, which must be slow.

MORNAY SAUCE: Over low heat, mix the flour with the butter. Let them cook a second. Pour cold milk in all at once. Stir until it comes to a boil. Add salt, pepper, and nutmeg. Simmer 5 minutes. Off the heat, stir in the grated cheese.

Arrange the endives in a shallow baking dish. Cover with Mornay sauce. Dot with the remaining butter and brown 5 minutes in the top of a very hot (500°) oven or under the broiler.

Variation: Simmer the endives in salted water for 30 minutes. Cooking in water is better for large and aged endives. Don't forget to add the lemon juice. Then put them in to brown, covered with Mornay sauce. Be careful: Drain thoroughly—squeeze them by hand—before covering with sauce, otherwise they'll lose too much water.

My advice: In my house, Baked Endives become a main course when, before putting them in the baking dish, I wrap each endive in a very thin slice of ham. Even children, who seldom like endives, appreciate them this way.

Fenouil à l'orientale

[For 4 people]

3 to 4 fennel bulbs
2 onions, 2 shallots, sliced in rounds
2 tomatoes
1 tablespoon oil
2 teaspoons sugar
1 cup dry white wine
⅓ teaspoon saffron
1-inch piece lemon peel
Salt to taste
Liberal seasoning freshly ground black
   pepper

FENNEL WITH SAFFRON

Preparation and cooking time: 1 hour

Scrape the fennel bulbs. Cut them in quarters. Plunge them 5 minutes in boiling salted water. Drain them immediately.

Peel and slice the onions and shallots. Peel and quarter the tomatoes. Seed them by squeezing them lightly. Cook the onions, shallots, and tomatoes, over moderately high heat, for a few moments in a casserole in hot oil.

Add the fennel, sugar, wine, saffron, lemon peel, salt, and a generous amount of pepper. Cover and simmer over low heat 45 minutes. Chill before serving.

SCALLOPED POTATOES

Gratin dauphinois

[FOR 4 PEOPLE]

1 clove garlic
2 tablespoons butter
2 pounds potatoes
½ cup grated Gruyère or Swiss cheese
About 2 cups milk
Salt to taste
Freshly ground black pepper to taste
1 egg

Remarks: There are several different versions of these potatoes: with or without cheese, with milk or with cream, or half cream half milk, with or without garlic, etc. The following recipe at least has the advantage of guaranteeing success.

Preparation and cooking time: 1 hour and 15 minutes / *Oven temperature:* 375° then 350°

Rub a large baking dish with the crushed garlic. Smear it with half the butter. Place a not-too-thick layer of potatoes cut in thin slices in the bottom. Sprinkle with half the cheese. Pour ¾ of the boiling milk over it. Add salt and pepper. Bake in a hot (375°) oven about 50 minutes.

Ten minutes before the end of cooking, beat the egg with salt, pepper, and the remaining milk. Pour over the potatoes.

Sprinkle with the remaining cheese and dot with butter. Put back in a moderate (350°) oven a few minutes, long enough for the mixture to "set." Serve as soon as it comes out of the oven with grilled or roast red meat.

My advice: For Scalloped Potatoes to be cooked clear through, the potatoes must be cut in very thin, even slices, by hand or with a food processor slicing attachment (easier than using a knife).

The milk in a gratin sometimes looks as if it had curdled during baking: it's just that the potatoes have juiced up in cooking. To correct this, pour, over the cooked potatoes, an egg beaten with salt, pepper, and 2 to 3 tablespoons of milk. The juice from the potatoes will blend into the beaten egg and become creamy during the last few minutes of baking.

Jardinière de légumes printaniers   SPRING VEGETABLE STEW

[FOR 4 PEOPLE]

Preparation and cooking time: 1 hour and 15 minutes

1 bunch small carrots, sliced in rounds
3 to 4 small turnips
2 tablespoons butter
4 ounces green beans
1 pound green peas
1 head leaf lettuce (Boston or Bibb, e.g.)
1 bunch parsley or fresh chervil
Salt to taste
Freshly ground black pepper to taste
½ pound new potatoes
1 tablespoon thick *crème fraîche*

Slice the carrots and dice the turnips.

Melt the butter in a large pot. Add the carrots, turnips, green beans, peas, lettuce leaves, 2 tablespoons of water, parsley or chervil (tied together with string), salt, and pepper. Stir. Cover with a deep plate filled with cold water. Simmer 20 minutes.

Then add the potatoes, cut into dice. Cook another 30 minutes. Add more water to the plate during cooking. Before serving, discard the parsley, then stir in the *crème fraîche*.

Légumes à la grecque

BASIC COURT BOUILLON
10 small onions
1 clove garlic
Juice of 2 lemons
1 cup dry white wine
½ cup oil
12 coriander seeds
6 peppercorns
1 sprig fennel or 1 teaspoon dried
Bouquet garni
½ cup water

COLD MARINATED VEGETABLES

Variation: Add to this classic combination 1 tablespoon of tomato paste (or 1 fresh minced tomato) to get the tomato-ey *grecque* currently in vogue.

BASIC COURT BOUILLON: Simmer the court bouillon ingredients slowly 15 minutes, then add the vegetables of your choice. Simmer for the amount of time indicated below:

ARTICHOKES: 10 to 12 fresh bottoms. Cut into 4 to 8 pieces after removing their leaves and "chokes," and rubbing them with lemon to prevent darkening. Cooking time: 30 minutes.

BEETS: 2 pounds. Stems and leaves removed. Then peeled sparingly, cut into 1- to 2-inch chunks, simmered in boiling water 2 minutes and drained. Cooking time *à la grecque:* 45 minutes.

CAULIFLOWER: 1 small. Broken into flowerets, 5 minutes in boiling water. Drained. Cooking time *à la grecque:* 45 minutes.

FENNEL: 4 bulbs. Scraped sparingly, cut into quarters, plunged 10 minutes into boiling water and drained. Cooking time *à la grecque:* 45 minutes.

MUSHROOMS: 1 pound. Washed (but not peeled), whole, or quartered if they're large. Cooking time: 6 to 8 minutes.

ONIONS: Small. 1 pound. Peeled, whole. If the little onions are old, simmer them a few minutes before cooking them *à la grecque:* 45 minutes.

Mousse de cresson de fontaine   WATERCRESS MOUSSE

[FOR 4 PEOPLE]

Preparation and cooking time: 15 minutes

4 bunches watercress
Pinch salt
1 lemon, all peel removed
1 tablespoon cornstarch
2 tablespoons thick *crème fraîche*
Dash freshly ground black pepper

Bring a pot of water to a boil.

Use watercress leaves only (save the stems for soup). Wash the leaves in running water. Reserve about 20 leaves. Plunge the others into the pot of boiling salted water, uncovered so that they stay green.

After boiling for 2 minutes, drain them thoroughly. Squeeze moisture out of them in a kitchen towel. Place them, still hot, in a food processor work bowl. Add the reserved raw leaves, the chopped lemon (with no trace of skin), the cornstarch, and the *crème fraîche*. Pepper lightly. Cover and process to obtain a thick puree. Serve watercress puree immediately with white meats, fish fillets, or even hard-boiled or poached eggs.

My advice: Slice through untied bunches of watercress, just at the base of the leaves, before washing them. This is a quick way to prepare them for this recipe.

Mousseline de haricots blancs   CREAMY WHITE BEAN PUREE

[FOR 4 PEOPLE]

Preparation and cooking time: 5 to 10 minutes

3 cups milk
Salt to taste
Freshly ground black pepper to taste
⅛ teaspoon nutmeg or allspice
1 tablespoon cornstarch
3 cups cooked white beans (canned or leftover)
2 tablespoons *crème fraîche* or whipping cream

Heat the milk with salt, pepper, nutmeg or allspice, and cornstarch. Stir. Add the beans, cooked and well drained.

Pour the mixture, very hot, into the work bowl of a food processor, along with the *crème fraîche*. Turn the food processor on and off several times, 4 to 5 seconds each time, on high speed. Serve this bean mousse with lamb or pork.

Variation: Use half lima beans mixed with white beans.

My advice: The beans may be cooked the day before and reheated to make the mousse. If you're cooking beans especially for this recipe (about 8 ounces), remember that dried beans must be cooked first for 15 minutes in unsalted boiling water, then for 2 full hours in boiling water with bouquet garni, onion, and whole cloves. Salt them halfway through only.

Paillassons de pommes de terre POTATO PANCAKES

[FOR 4 PEOPLE]

Preparation and cooking time: 15 minutes

1 pound potatoes
2 eggs
Salt to taste
Freshly ground black pepper to taste
1 tablespoon flour
Oil

Peel the potatoes. Grate them with a food processor grating attachment or a vegetable grater. Rinse them in running water to remove the starch. Squeeze them in a kitchen towel to wring out as much moisture as possible.

Place the potatoes in a bowl. Add the eggs, salt, pepper, and flour. Mix well with a fork.

Heat ½ inch of oil in a large skillet. When it is very hot, drop in 3 to 4 tablespoons of grated potatoes. Flatten them into thin pancakes. Brown them quickly on one side. Turn them over with a spatula and brown on the other side. Serve very hot.

My advice: To keep them hot, slide the pancakes into a warm (250°) oven or between two plates set over a pan of boiling water. You can add minced garlic and fresh herbs, or grated cheese flavored with a pinch of nutmeg, to the raw grated potatoes.

Petits navets glacés

[FOR 4 PEOPLE]

2 pounds small turnips
3 tablespoons butter
Salt to taste
Freshly ground black pepper to taste
½ teaspoon sugar

SMALL GLAZED TURNIPS

Preparation and cooking time: 1 hour

Peel the turnips. Leave them whole or, if they are large, dice them. Plunge them 5 minutes into boiling water. Drain them and rinse in cold water.

In a casserole, heat 2 tablespoons of the butter with the turnips, 2 cups of water, salt, and pepper. Cover partially and simmer until the water has almost entirely evaporated (about 45 minutes). Then add the remaining butter and the sugar. Cook over medium heat, uncovered, until the turnips are lightly browned on all sides.

Variation: Small whole glazed carrots may be prepared exactly the same way.

My advice: For glazed vegetables that don't fall apart in cooking, don't stir them too much. Shake the casserole occasionally.

Pommes Dauphine

[FOR 4 PEOPLE]

1 pound potatoes

PUFF PASTRY

1 cup water
½ teaspoon salt
5 tablespoons butter
1 cup flour
4 eggs

Salt to taste
Freshly ground black pepper to taste
Oil

DEEP-FRIED POTATO PUFFS

Preparation and cooking time: 1 hour and 15 minutes / *Deep-frying temperature:* 340°

Cook the potatoes (with their skins on) 30 minutes in boiling salted water in a large pot.

PUFF PASTRY: Over the heat, place a large pot containing water, salt, and butter cut into pieces. As soon as the butter melts, pour the flour in all at once. Stir, over low heat, until the batter no longer sticks to the spoon or to the sides of the pan. Off the heat, add the eggs one by one, beating the batter vigorously with a wooden spoon.

Peel the potatoes. Mash them (without adding any liquid). Salt and pepper them. Mix with the puff pastry.

To make the potatoes, scoop up a teaspoonful of the mixture. Scrape if off with a second spoon, into the hot (340°) oil. The potatoes should float to the surface, turning themselves over as soon as they are evenly browned. Drain them immediately, salt them lightly, and serve.

My advice: The potato batter can be prepared the day before. Tightly covered with a piece of aluminum to prevent it from drying out on top, it can keep overnight in the refrigerator. But these potatoes can be made only just before serving, because they must be eaten very hot, and not reheated.

Purée de pois cassés Saint-Germain   SPLIT PEA PUREE

[FOR 4 PEOPLE]

1 pound split peas
2 ounces bacon or salt pork*
2 tablespoons butter
1 carrot, 1 onion, sliced in rounds
A few lettuce leaves
½ teaspoon sugar
Bouquet garni
Salt to taste
Freshly ground black pepper to taste

Remarks: Pureed split peas stick easily to the bottom of the pan, so the best way to keep them warm is in a bain-marie or double boiler, rather than directly over the heat.

Cooking time: 1 hour and 30 minutes

Place the peas in a large pot of cold unsalted water. Bring slowly to a boil. Simmer 15 minutes. Drain them and rinse in cold water.

Dice the bacon or salt pork. Brown it in a casserole with half the butter. Add the sliced carrot and onion, split peas, lettuce leaves, sugar, bouquet garni, and boiling water to cover. Cover the casserole. Simmer slowly 1 hour to 1 hour and 30 minutes, depending on the quality of the peas. Salt only halfway through cooking. Add a little more water if it evaporates too fast.

Drain the peas. Puree them in a food processor or food mill. Add pepper. Stir in the remaining butter. This puree should be fairly thick.

*See the note about bacon on p. 54. See Miscellaneous Notes on pork fatback.

Ratatouille cordon bleu

[FOR 4 PEOPLE]

3 onions
4 small eggplants or 1 large
2 small, firm zucchini
3 tomatoes
2 bell peppers
1 fennel bulb
1 cup olive oil
2 cloves garlic, crushed
Bouquet garni
Salt to taste
Freshly ground black pepper to taste
1 can artichoke hearts

Remarks: Eggplant and zucchini do not have to be peeled.

RATATOUILLE

Preparation and cooking time: 1 hour and 45 minutes

Peel and cut the onions into strips. Cut the eggplant, zucchini, tomatoes, bell peppers, and fennel into bite-sized pieces.

Heat ½ cup of the olive oil in a large skillet. Lightly brown the eggplant and zucchini in it, separately. Start with the eggplant. Then transfer it to a large casserole. Add a little more oil to the skillet. Sauté the zucchini in it. Add it to the casserole without stirring. Then cook together the tomatoes, bell peppers, and onions. Transfer them to the casserole. On top, put the cut-up fennel, minced garlic, bouquet garni, salt, and pepper. Cover and simmer over very low heat 1 hour to 1 hour and 30 minutes. If the ratatouille juices up too much, uncover halfway through cooking.

When the ratatouille is done, discard bouquet garni and place the quartered artichoke hearts on top of the ratatouille, just long enough to heat them through. Serve warm to accompany meat. Cold, it makes an excellent main course.

My advice: To keep the ratatouille from sticking on the bottom—which happens frequently because of the eggplant—slide a metal grill between the casserole and the burner or, better yet, place the casserole in a moderate (350°) oven so that the ratatouille simmers evenly on the top and the bottom.

Salade de lentilles à ma façon   MY LENTIL SALAD

Preparation and cooking time: 45 minutes

[FOR 4 PEOPLE]

2 cups lentils
1 onion
2 whole cloves
1 small carrot
Bouquet garni
Freshly ground black pepper to taste
1 small stalk celery
1 pimiento (optional)
Salt to taste

VINAIGRETTE

4 to 5 tablespoons oil
1 to 2 tablespoons vinegar
1 teaspoon Dijon-type mustard
Salt to taste (optional)
Freshly ground black pepper to taste
   (optional)
1 tablespoon minced parsley
1 small shallot, chopped fine

Rinse the lentils. Place them in a large pot with a generous amount of cold water. Simmer 5 minutes. Drain. Put them back in the pot along with boiling water, 1 onion stuck with 2 cloves, the carrot cut into 4 pieces, bouquet garni, pepper, celery stalk, and, if desired, pimiento. Simmer slowly 20 to 30 minutes, according to the quality of the lentils. Do not salt them until the end of cooking to keep them from toughening. Drain them as soon as they are tender. Remove the onion, carrot, and celery pieces, the cloves, bouquet garni, and pimiento.

VINAIGRETTE: In a bowl, mix together the oil, vinegar, and mustard. Stir into the still-warm lentils. Taste for seasoning. Sprinkle with minced parsley and shallot. Serve warm or cold.

Variation: Serve as a summer salad with fresh vegetables (peppers, tomatoes, radish slices, celery, cucumber, and fresh herbs).

My advice: The secret of a flavorful lentil salad is the dressing: good-quality oil, poured generously over still-warm lentils, and, to spice it up, vinegar, mustard, and whatever fresh herbs and seasonings are available (parsley, chives, tarragon, finely minced onion, shallot or garlic, according to taste).

Tomates farcis charcutière

[FOR 4 PEOPLE]

4 large tomatoes
Salt to taste
½ cup milk
1 cup stale bread cubes
½ pound cooked chopped meat or sausage meat
1 egg
1 tablespoon minced parsley
1 onion, chopped fine
1 clove garlic, crushed
Freshly ground black pepper to taste
1½ teaspoons butter
¼ cup bread crumbs

TOMATOES STUFFED WITH MEAT

Preparation and cooking time: 1 hour / *Oven temperature:* 350°

Cut (and reserve) a slice off each tomato from the end opposite the stem. Hollow the tomatoes out with a teaspoon. Salt them inside and turn them upside down on a plate to drain. Pour the warm milk over the cubed bread.

In a bowl, place the chopped meat, egg, parsley, onion, garlic, salt, and pepper. Add the soaked bread and mix. Stuff it into the emptied tomatoes (use the juice from the tomatoes if the stuffing needs further moistening).

Grease a not-too-large baking dish with half the butter. Arrange the tomatoes in it. Sprinkle them with bread crumbs and dot with the remaining butter. Bake in a moderate (350°) oven 30 minutes. Place the cut-off pieces on each tomato and bake another 10 minutes.

My advice: Cutting a slice off each tomato from the end opposite the stem prevents the stuffed tomato from bursting in the oven. The tomatoes will be stronger that way. Once stuffed, they can be arranged, closely together, in a baking dish.

Tomates provençale

[FOR 4 PEOPLE]

6 very firm tomatoes
Salt to taste
3 teaspoons oil
5 tablespoons butter
Freshly ground black pepper to taste
4 cloves garlic
1 bunch parsley
2 to 3 tablespoons bread or cracker
   crumbs

Remarks: To make cracker crumbs, crush 2 crackers with a rolling pin.

TOMATOES BAKED WITH GARLIC AND PARSLEY

Preparation and cooking time: 15 minutes / *Oven temperature:* 400°

Cut the tomatoes in half. Salt them and turn upside down on a plate to drain.

Heat about 1 teaspoon of the oil and 1 tablespoon of the butter in a skillet. Add the tomatoes, cut side down. Fry, over high heat, 2 minutes on the cut side, 2 minutes on the other. Salt and pepper them.

Mince the garlic and parsley together. Mix with the bread or cracker crumbs. Spread over the tomatoes with a lump of butter on each one. Cover and cook over moderate heat or in a hot (400°) oven 10 minutes.

Arrange the cooked tomatoes on a platter; keep them warm and cook the rest of them in the same manner.

Zéphire d'aubergines

[FOR 4 PEOPLE]

1 eggplant, about ½ pound
1 tablespoon vinegar
3½ tablespoons butter
1 tablespoon flour
1 cup milk
Salt to taste
Freshly ground black pepper to taste
⅔ cup grated Gruyère or Swiss cheese
2 eggs, separated

EGGPLANT CUSTARD

Preparation and cooking time: 45 minutes / *Oven temperature:* 375°

Peel the eggplant and cut it into 2-inch pieces. Simmer them 2 minutes in boiling water with vinegar. Drain carefully and chop finely with a knife.

Brown the mixture in a large casserole, over high heat, with 3 tablespoons of the butter. Shake frequently. Sprinkle with flour, then mix well. Blend in the milk, little by little, stirring until thick. Add salt and pepper.

Off the heat, add the grated cheese and egg yolks. Beat the egg whites until stiff peaks form. Fold them in last.

Pour the mixture into a soufflé mold greased with the remaining butter. Bake in a medium hot (375°) oven about 25 minutes.

My advice: Instead of using a large soufflé mold, divide the eggplant among fairly large individual ramekins. They will be attractive—and easier to serve.

Gratin de macaronis

[FOR 4 PEOPLE]

½ pound macaroni

LIGHT BÉCHAMEL SAUCE
3 tablespoons butter
1 tablespoon flour
2 cups milk
Salt and pepper to taste
⅛ teaspoon nutmeg

1 cup grated Gruyère cheese
1½ tablespoons butter

Remarks: The macaroni will bake in the oven with the sauce, so it's best to shorten the cooking time in water. Drain it while it's still fairly firm.

BAKED MACARONI AND CHEESE

Preparation and cooking time: 30 minutes / Oven temperature: 550°

Toss the macaroni or other pasta into a generous amount of boiling salted water. Stir. Continue boiling, uncovered, 5 to 7 minutes, or the amount of time indicated on the package, until the pasta is cooked *al dente*. Drain immediately.

LIGHT BÉCHAMEL SAUCE: Stir the butter and flour together over low heat. Then add the cold milk all at once, whisking until it comes to a boil (the sauce should be fairly fluid. If necessary, thin it out with a little milk.) Add salt, pepper, and nutmeg. Then, off the heat, stir in ⅔ of the grated cheese.

In the bottom of a deep baking dish, spread a thin layer of sauce, then add the pasta. Cover with the remaining sauce. Sprinkle with the remaining cheese and dot with butter. Brown under a broiler or in a very hot (550°) oven about 15 minutes.

My advice: This dish may be prepared entirely ahead of time and reheated and browned just before serving.

Salade de torsades au crabe

[FOR 4 TO 6 PEOPLE]

1 can hearts of palm
1 cup vinaigrette*
3 ounces Roquefort cheese
½ clove garlic, crushed
⅛ teaspoon cayenne pepper
6 to 8 ounces pasta spirals or tortiglioni
1 tablespoon oil
1 small (6-ounce) can lump crabmeat

SPICY MAYONNAISE

½ cup mayonnaise
1 tablespoon vinegar
Freshly ground black pepper to taste
A few drops Tabasco sauce or pinches
   cayenne pepper

GARNISH

1 lemon, 1 hard-boiled egg, cut into
   slices
4 black olives

PASTA SALAD WITH CRAB

Preparation and cooking time: 30 minutes / *Chilling time:* 1 hour

Macerate the hearts of palm, sliced, in the vinaigrette seasoned with finely crumbled Roquefort, minced garlic, and cayenne.

Cook the pasta in a large pot of boiling salted water 5 to 7 minutes, or according to the instructions on the package, until it is cooked *al dente*. Drain it well. Rinse in cold water and mix with the oil. Add the crab, with cartilage and pieces of shell removed (reserve the liquid).

SPICY MAYONNAISE: Dilute 4 tablespoons of mayonnaise with the vinegar and a little bit of the crab liquid. Season with pepper and Tabasco sauce or cayenne pepper.

Just before serving, blend the two mixtures together in a bowl. Garnish with thinly sliced lemon and slices of hard-boiled egg decorated with a piece of olive.

My advice: Pasta spirals are fairly thick so they stay firm after cooking. They can be tossed in a salad without falling apart, and the dressing soaks into the folds. For the same reason, shell pasta also works well in salad.

*See the recipe for vinaigrette on p. 24.

Tagliatelles à la crème et au basilic

[FOR 4 PEOPLE]

8 ounces tagliatelle (flat noodles)
Salt to taste
½ cup *crème fraîche*
1 to 2 cloves garlic
15 to 20 basil leaves
½ cup grated Parmesan cheese
Freshly ground black pepper to taste

TAGLIATELLE WITH CREAM AND BASIL

Preparation and cooking time: 25 minutes

Plunge the tagliatelle into a large pot of boiling salted water. Stir. Continue boiling, uncovered, 5 to 7 minutes, or the amount of time indicated on the package, until the pasta is cooked *al dente*. Drain it well. Mix it with the *crème fraîche* immediately. Keep warm.

Rub the inside of a deep dish (such as a soufflé mold) with garlic. Pour in the pasta and cream. Shred the basil leaves over it. Add Parmesan and pepper. Stir and serve immediately, very hot.

Timbale de pâtes fraîches aux Saint-Jacques   SCALLOPS WITH FRESH PASTA

[FOR 4 PEOPLE]

Preparation and cooking time: 45 minutes

6 to 8 sea scallops
1 cup dry white wine
Salt to taste
Freshly ground black pepper to taste
Bouquet garni
8 ounces fresh or dried pasta
1½ tablespoons butter
½ pound mushrooms
Juice of ¼ lemon

WHITE WINE SAUCE WITH SAFFRON
2 egg yolks
2 to 3 tablespoons *crème fraîche* or
    whipping cream
3 pinches saffron
1 cup scallop-cooking broth

Rinse the scallops and their coral.* Place them in a saucepan with the wine and enough water to just cover, salt, pepper, and bouquet garni. Heat slowly. Remove from the heat as soon as it comes to a boil. Leave the scallops in their broth.

Toss the pasta into a large potful of boiling water. Stir. Continue boiling, uncovered, 5 to 7 minutes, or according to the instructions on the package, until the pasta is cooked *al dente*.

Drain immediately and stir in half the butter.

Trim the sandy base from the mushrooms, then wash and slice them. Cook them in a saucepan with the remaining butter and lemon juice. Cover and simmer 5 to 6 minutes. Add to the pasta.

WHITE WINE SAUCE WITH SAFFRON: Mix the egg yolks, *crème fraîche*, and saffron in a bowl. Stir in the scallop-cooking broth. Place back over low heat, beating constantly with a whisk until the sauce takes on the consistency of light custard (do not let it boil).

Transfer the pasta to a deep serving dish. Cut the scallops across their width into 2 to 3 slices. Arrange them on very hot serving plates. Cover with sauce and serve.

*See the note about scallops on p. 59.

Curry à l'indienne

INDIAN CURRY

[FOR 4 PEOPLE]

2 pounds lamb shoulder, plus a few bones
3 tomatoes
2 onions
2 cloves garlic
2 tablespoons butter
4 whole cloves
1 tablespoon curry powder
¼ teaspoon cinnamon
⅓ teaspoon cayenne pepper
1 teaspoon turmeric
2 teaspoons ground coriander
Kosher salt to taste
1 cup rice
3 pinches saffron
3 tomatoes

Preparation and cooking time: 1 hour and 15 minutes

Cut the meat into cubes. Coarsely chop the peeled tomatoes, onions, and garlic. Heat the butter in a casserole. Add the meat, meat bones, and 2 whole cloves. As soon as it browns, pour in ½ cup of hot water. Simmer 5 minutes over high heat.

Add the curry powder, cinnamon, cayenne, turmeric, coriander, tomatoes, onions, garlic, 2 remaining cloves, salt, and 2 cups of hot water. Cover and simmer 45 minutes.

To cook the rice, in a large saucepan, bring 2 cups of lightly salted water to a boil. Rinse the rice. Drop it into the boiling water. Simmer 15 to 17 minutes.

Drain the rice. Sprinkle the saffron over it and stir lightly.

Transfer the rice to a deep serving platter. Arrange the meat and sauce over it. Serve with quartered tomatoes to diffuse the hot curry.

RICE PILAF WITH CLAMS OR MUSSELS

Pilaf de coques

[For 4 people]

Preparation and cooking time: 1 hour

2 quarts clams or mussels
1 cup rice
1 onion, chopped fine
3 tablespoons butter
Bouquet garni (parsley, thyme, bay leaf)
Salt to taste
Freshly ground black pepper to taste
1 small (2-ounce) can mushrooms

BÂTARDE SAUCE

2 tablespoons butter
1 tablespoon flour
1 cup liquid: shellfish-cooking broth plus
    water
Freshly ground black pepper to taste
1 egg yolk
1 teaspoon lemon juice

Remarks: Bâtarde sauce can also be
prepared with plain water or meat stock.

Wash the clams or mussels and let them soak 30 minutes in heavily salted cold water. Rinse the rice under running water until the water is translucent. Drain the rice in a colander.

PILAF: Mince the onion. Cook it until golden in a saucepan with 2 tablespoons of the butter. Add the rice. Stir, then add 2 cups of water, bouquet garni, salt, and pepper. Cover and simmer slowly until the liquid is completely absorbed (17 to 20 minutes).

Let the clams or mussels open over high heat without adding anything else to the pan. Take them out of their shells. Strain the cooking broth through a fine strainer lined with paper towels to remove any sand.

Mix the clams or mussels, rice, and mushrooms cut into dice. Pile the mixture into a buttered mold. Keep warm.

BÂTARD SAUCE: Melt the butter in a small saucepan; stir in the flour, then 1 cup of cold liquid (shellfish-cooking broth, mushroom juices, or water). Do not salt, but add pepper. Bring to a boil and simmer slowly 10 minutes. Remove from the heat. Mix in the egg yolk and lemon juice. Unmold the pilaf on a platter. Cover with sauce and serve.

Risotto du pêcheur   RICE WITH MUSSELS AND CRAB

[FOR 4 PEOPLE]

2 quarts mussels
Salt to taste
Freshly ground black pepper to taste
1 onion, chopped fine
2 tablespoons butter
1 cup rice
2 cups water
1 cube chicken bouillon
⅓ cup grated Gruyère or Swiss cheese

VELOUTÉ SAUCE

1 tablespoon flour
2 tablespoons butter
¼ pound mushrooms
2 pinches saffron

1 small (6-ounce) can lump crabmeat
1 tablespoon *crème fraîche* or whipping
   cream

Preparation and cooking time: 45 minutes

Let the cleaned mussels steam open in a large pot, with salt and pepper, about 5 minutes. Strain the cooking liquid carefully and reserve it.

In a large casserole, cook the minced onion in the butter. As soon as it is golden, add the rice. Stir. Then add the water, chicken bouillon cube, salt, and pepper. Cover. Simmer 17 to 20 minutes, until the liquid is completely absorbed. Off the heat, stir in the grated cheese.

VELOUTÉ SAUCE: Over low heat, combine the flour and butter. Stir in 1½ cups of mussel-cooking liquid, bring to a boil, and simmer a minute or two. Slice the mushrooms. Add them to the sauce. Stir in the saffron. Simmer 10 minutes.

Take the mussels out of their shells, and remove the cartilage from the crab. Add the mussels and crab to the sauce. Simmer over very low heat. Stir in the *crème fraîche* at the last minute.

Pack the warm rice into a ring mold. Unmold it. Fill the center with the seafood mixture.

DESSERTS

Ananas Belle de Meaux

[FOR 6 PEOPLE]

1 pineapple, 3 to 4 pounds
1 pint strawberries
4 to 5 tablespoons sugar
⅓ cup kirsch

CRÈME CHANTILLY (WHIPPED CREAM)
1 cup *crème fraîche* or whipping cream
  (very cold)
2 to 3 tablespoons milk
1 ice cube
1 envelope vanilla sugar or 1 teaspoon
  vanilla extract

PINEAPPLE WITH STRAWBERRIES AND CREAM

Preparation time: 20 minutes / *Chilling time:* 1 hour / *Decoration time:* 10 minutes

Cut the pineapple in half below the base of the stem. Remove the flesh with a pointed knife slid along inside the skin, but ½ inch above it to avoid the eyes. Remove the flesh and dice it.

Let it macerate in a bowl with the strawberries (reserving a few for garnish), the sugar, and the kirsch 30 minutes, in the refrigerator. Before serving, fill the hollowed-out skins with this mixture.

CRÈME CHANTILLY: In a deep bowl, stir the *crème fraîche* with milk or a little cold water to dilute it to a custardy consistency. (Do not dilute whipping cream.) Add an ice cube (unless you use an electric mixer—the beaters might break). Begin beating with a slow, wide motion to whip as much air as possible into the cream, then more rapidly at the end. As soon as the cream thickens and clings to the beaters or whisk, stop beating immediately, for *crème fraîche* separates quickly. Remove the ice cube. Add the vanilla, whisking slowly a few seconds.

Decorate the pineapple with crème Chantilly and the reserved strawberries.

My advice: This pineapple, fully decorated, can be kept 1 to 2 hours as long as it's refrigerated until serving. Out of season, frozen strawberries can be substituted. Macerate them separately in kirsch. Mix with the pineapple at the last minute when they're barely defrosted: they are better slightly frozen and firm.

Bavarois praliné BAVARIAN CREAM WITH PRALINE

[FOR 6 TO 8 PEOPLE]

Preparation and cooking time the day before: 45 minutes / *Chilling time:* 12 hours

BAVARIAN CREAM

2 cups milk

⅛ teaspoon salt

½ envelope vanilla sugar or ½ teaspoon vanilla extract

6 egg yolks

3 tablespoons sugar

½ cup pralines*

1½ tablespoons (1½ envelopes) unflavored gelatin

WHIPPED CREAM

½ cup chilled whipping cream or 1 cup *crème fraîche*

1 soufflé mold or charlotte mold, about 10 inches in diameter

BAVARIAN CREAM WITH PRALINE: In a saucepan, bring the milk, salt, and vanilla to a boil. With an electric mixer, beat the egg yolks and sugar. When the mixture lightens, add boiling water, stirring continuously. Add the mixture to the saucepan and stir. Place the saucepan back over low heat just until the mixture begins to thicken. Remove from the heat without letting it boil. Add the pralines.

Dissolve the gelatin in ½ cup of cold water. Stir it into the Bavarian cream. Let it cool completely before mixing in whipped cream.

WHIPPED CREAM: Beat the cream until it is firm enough to cling solidly to the beaters. Blend it thoroughly into the cold Bavarian cream, which is starting to jell (if it has firmed up, beat it again first).

Rinse the inside of the mold in cold water. Sprinkle lightly with sugar. Pour in the mixture. Cover and refrigerate 12 hours.

Just before serving, dip the bottom of the mold in warm water a few seconds, then unmold. Decorate with pralines or small macaroons, if desired.

My advice: Making Bavarian cream intimidates beginners because of the number of different steps. But that is the extent of the problem. If you spend an hour the day before preparing the recipe and following it step by step, you will be successful. A dessert of this quality is well worth that hour.

*See the note about pralines on p. 227.

Beignets aux pommes

[FOR 4 PEOPLE]

FRITTER BATTER

5 tablespoons flour
1 whole egg plus 2 egg whites
1 tablespoon oil
⅛ tablespoon salt
¾ cup milk, water, or beer

3 to 4 apples
Oil
Powdered (confectioners') sugar

Remarks: With a food processor or electric mixer, combine all the ingredients for the batter and beat them a few seconds until they are lump-free.

APPLE FRITTERS

Preparation and cooking time: 30 minutes / *Deep-frying temperature:* 330°

FRITTER BATTER: In a bowl, place the flour, egg, oil, and salt. Mix with a wooden spoon. Add the milk or other liquid, little by little, to get a thicker batter than for crêpes. Let it rest 1 hour if possible.

Meanwhile peel the apples and slice them in rounds or quarters about ¼ inch thick.

Heat the deep-frying oil. Beat the egg whites until they are very stiff. Fold them delicately into the batter. Use it immediately: beaten whites collapse quickly.

Plunge the apples into the batter to coat them completely, then into the fairly hot (330°) oil. Put only a few fritters in at one time so that they don't cool off the oil too much. As soon as they rise back up to the surface, golden brown, drain them, sprinkle with powdered sugar, and serve.

My advice: Fritters may be flavored, either by macerating the apples in rum or Calvados, or by adding the liquor directly to the batter. The beaten egg whites make the batter lighter and crisper. Other fruit, such as pears, apricots, and bananas, can be made into fritters.

Beignets soufflés (ou pets-de-nonne)

[FOR 20 TO 30 FRITTERS]

PUFF PASTRY

1 cup water
½ teaspoon salt
5 tablespoons butter
1 cup flour
4 eggs

Oil
Powdered (confectioners') sugar

Remarks: Puff pastry may be prepared the day before. Keep it in the refrigerator, sealed in a plastic bowl, to prevent it from drying out and puffing poorly in cooking.

SUGAR FRITTERS

Preparation and cooking time: 45 minutes / *Deep-frying temperature:* 330°

PUFF PASTRY: In a saucepan, heat the water, salt, and pieces of butter. When the butter is melted, pour in the flour all at once. Stir vigorously with a wooden spoon until the batter no longer sticks to the pan. Remove from the heat. Add the eggs, one by one, beating vigorously after each egg to mix it in. The finished batter should be supple but firm. (This last step may be done with a kneading attachment.)

Heat the deep-frying oil to 330°. Drop in balls of batter shaped with a teaspoon. With dampened fingers (keep a glass of water next to you), slip the balls into the hot oil.

Put in only a few fritters at a time because they puff up considerably. The fritters will turn themselves over in the hot oil as soon as they have browned and puffed up sufficiently on one side. Let them brown on the other side before draining them on paper towels. Sprinkle them with sugar and serve immediately. Keep them warm by the oven door because they aren't as good reheated.

Bourdelots normands

[FOR 4 PEOPLE]

PASTRY DOUGH

2 cups flour
½ teaspoon salt
8 tablespoons (1 stick) butter
About ½ cup water

4 medium apples
4 teaspoons apricot jam
4 teaspoons butter
1 tablespoon Calvados (optional)
1 beaten egg (for basting the pastry dough)

1 apple corer

Remarks: Prepared with pears, this dish, also a specialty of Normandy, is called *douillon* (from *douillette*, a priest's overcoat) or *rabotte*. It's also good.

APPLE DUMPLINGS

Preparation and baking time: 1 hour / *Oven temperature:* 400°

PASTRY DOUGH: Mix the flour, salt, and butter, cut into pieces, by pressing and rubbing the palms of your hands together. Add water. Knead the dough vigorously, then form it into a ball. Do this 3 times. Wrap the dough in foil and let it rest in the refrigerator a few moments.

Preheat the oven to 400°. Roll the dough into a thin sheet. Cut out 4 squares large enough to wrap the apples in. Peel the apples whole. Hollow them out with an apple corer.

Place each apple on a square of pastry dough. In their cavities, put a little jam, some butter, and, if desired, a few drops of Calvados. Gather up the edges of the dough and fold them together at the top to enclose the apples. On the top, put a circle of dough moistened with a beaten egg. Place these dumplings on a buttered baking sheet. Press to make sure they stick. Brush with beaten egg.

Bake 35 to 40 minutes. Serve warm.

Cake aux fruits confits

[FOR 14 TO 16 SLICES]

⅓ cup raisins
1 tablespoon rum
1 cup mixed glacéed fruit
½ cup sugar
8 tablespoons (1 stick) very soft butter
 or margarine
3 eggs
1½ cups flour
½ teaspoon baking powder
½ teaspoon salt

1 loaf pan, about 12 inches long
Foil or brown kitchen paper

Remarks: There is no magic formula for keeping the fruit from sinking to the bottom of the cake. Just follow the recipe:
• the batter should be very firm (important);
• the oven should be very hot.
 When the cake has puffed and browned, reduce the oven temperature and continue baking for about 1 hour.

FRUIT CAKE

Preparation and baking time: 1 hour and 45 minutes / *Oven temperature:* 400° then 325°

Preheat the oven to 400°. Rinse and dry the raisins. In a bowl, macerate them with rum and glacéed fruit.

In a large bowl, beat together the sugar and very soft, but not melted, butter until smooth and creamy.

Add the eggs one by one, beating after each addition. Don't worry if the mixture is lumpy. Add the flour, baking powder, and salt, all sifted together over the bowl. Stir rapidly with a wooden spoon. Fold the fruits and macerating liquid in at the end.

Line the inside of the loaf pan with foil or brown kitchen paper. Pour in the batter.

Place in the oven. After 25 to 30 minutes, the cake will begin to puff up. Run a knife lightly down its length and reduce the heat to 325° and bake 1 hour. As soon as the top seems brown enough, cover with foil.

After taking it out of the oven, unmold the cake without removing the foil. Wait 24 hours before tasting.

My advice: This cake keeps well without drying out. You can make two at a time by doubling the ingredients and using two loaf pans.

Caramels au miel et au chocolat   HONEY AND CHOCOLATE CARAMELS

[FOR 40 TO 50 CARAMELS]

3 ounces (3 squares) unsweetened chocolate
½ cup sugar
½ cup honey
3 tablespoons butter
A little oil for the mold

1 rectangular cake pan (with nonstick surface)
Plastic wrap

Preparation and cooking time: 15 minutes / Cooling time: 30 minutes

In a saucepan (preferably with a nonstick surface), place the chocolate, broken in pieces, the sugar, honey, and butter. Simmer 10 minutes, stirring occasionally.

Generously oil the inside of the cake pan with a wad of oiled paper toweling. Pour the hot caramel in it.

When the sheet of caramel is cool but still soft (cooling time: about 30 minutes), unmold it, using a knife or rubber spatula (for a nonstick surface).

Place the caramel on a cutting surface, metal or marble. Use a heavy knife to mark deep squares. Let the caramel harden before cutting it.

Wrap the caramel squares in plastic wrap folded or twisted at the ends.

My advice: If you're afraid the caramels will be hopelessly stuck, use a saucepan and cake pan with nonstick surfaces. The work will be easier.

Charlotte aux fraises et fruits rouges

CHARLOTTE WITH STRAWBERRIES AND RED BERRIES IN SEASON

[FOR 4 TO 6 PEOPLE]

4 to 5 tablespoons *crème fraîche* or whipping cream
1 envelope vanilla sugar or 1 teaspoon vanilla extract
4 tablespoons strawberry or raspberry jam
1½ cups syrup*
3 to 4 tablespoons kirsch
24 ladyfingers
2 pints strawberries
Juice of ¼ lemon

GARNISH
1 cup small strawberries or other berries
Powdered (confectioners') sugar

1 charlotte mold or soufflé mold, about 10 inches in diameter

Preparation time: 15 minutes, plus a few hours in the refrigerator

In a bowl, beat together very cold cream, the vanilla, and the jam until smooth. Refrigerate.

Pour the syrup and the kirsch into a deep dish. Soak the ladyfingers in it on both sides. Arrange them, one by one, side by side, in the mold, with the flat surface against the bottom and sides of the mold. (There should be a few ladyfingers left over for the middle of the charlotte.)

Wash and dry the berries. Stem them and cut them in half, lengthwise. Sprinkle with lemon juice.

Arrange a layer of strawberry-halves, lying flat, on the bottom of the mold. Pour some of the cream-jam mixture over it. Cover with dampened ladyfingers. Spread a second layer of strawberries over it, the cream-jam mixture, ladyfingers, etc., finishing with the ladyfingers.

Place a saucer on top, with a heavy object on it to weigh it down. Refrigerate a few hours or even overnight.

To unmold, run a knife blade around the inside of the mold. Hold a large plate over it and turn it over.

To serve, surround the charlotte with a crown of small strawberries, unstemmed, after dipping the tips in powdered sugar. Or decorate it with other small fresh berries.

*Boil 1 cup of water with ½ cup of sugar exactly 2 minutes. Off the heat, add the kirsch.

Charlotte aux framboises

[FOR 6 TO 8 PEOPLE]

BAVARIAN CREAM

1 cup milk
½ envelope vanilla sugar or ½ teaspoon
  vanilla extract
3 tablespoons sugar
⅛ teaspoon salt
3 egg yolks
1 tablespoon (1 envelope) unflavored
  gelatin

1 pint raspberries or strawberries
1 tablespoon butter
15 ladyfingers

WHIPPED CREAM

1 cup whipping cream or 2 cups *crème
  fraîche*
1 to 2 tablespoons ice water or milk (optional)

BERRY PUREE (COULIS)

2 pints raspberries or strawberries
½ cup sugar / Juice of 1 lemon

1 charlotte mold or soufflé mold, about
  12 inches in diameter

Remarks: You can make the berry puree
with frozen strawberries or raspberries. Simply puree them in a food processor without
adding sugar (if they are presweetened), but
don't use them in the charlotte itself. The
strawberries will shrivel and you'll be disap-
pointed.

RASPBERRY CHARLOTTE

Preparation and cooking time the day before: 1 hour

BAVARIAN CREAM: Over the heat, mix the milk, vanilla, sugar, and salt until
they come to a boil. Off the heat, rapidly whisk in the egg yolks. Place back on the
heat, stirring continuously until the mixture begins to thicken. Remove from the heat
before it boils.

Dissolve the gelatin completely in ⅓ cup of water and mix it into the hot milk-
egg mixture. Let it cool until it begins to thicken. Refrigerate it if necessary. Wash
the berries. Reserve 10 to 20 of the nicest for garnish. Dry them and roll in sugar.
Lightly butter the sides of the mold (not the bottom). Arrange the ladyfingers in it
vertically, the rounded sides against the side of the mold. Press to make them stick.
Sprinkle sugar in the bottom of the mold, which will make unmolding easier.

WHIPPED CREAM: If the *crème fraîche* is too thick, dilute it with ice water or
cold milk. Beat it until it thickens and clings to the beaters.

Beat the Bavarian cream vigorously if it has jelled. Then delicately fold in the
whipped cream with a rubber scraper to achieve a firm, fairly well-blended mousse.
Pour a little of it into the mold garnished with ladyfingers. Then layer the fruit and
cream up to the top. End with pieces of ladyfingers. Cover and refrigerate overnight.

BERRY PUREE: Beat the berries together with sugar and lemon juice.

To serve, dip the bottom of the mold in warm water a couple of seconds only,
then turn it upside down over a round dish. Pour a little berry puree over it. Serve
the rest in a sauceboat.

Clafoutis normand flambé au calvados

APPLE PUDDING FLAMED WITH CALVADOS

[FOR 4 PEOPLE]

2 to 3 apples
Juice of ¼ lemon
2 to 3 tablespoons raisins
3 to 4 tablespoons sugar
⅛ teaspoon salt
1 egg
½ cup *crème fraîche* or whipping cream
1 tablespoon flour
3 tablespoons butter plus ½ tablespoon for the mold
2 tablespoons Calvados

1 found mold (such as a soufflé mold) or 12-inch baking dish.

Preparation and baking time: 45 minutes / *Oven temperature:* 375° then 425°

Peel the apples. Slice them thinly and sprinkle with lemon juice. Rinse the raisins and sponge them dry.

With an electric mixer or food processor, beat together the sugar, salt, and egg. When the mixture is light and creamy, mix in *crème fraîche* and flour. Reserve 3 tablespoons of the mixture.

Fold the apples and raisins into the batter. Pour it into a mold buttered with ½ tablespoon of the butter. Put the *clafoutis* in a hot (375°) oven 15 minutes.

Stir 3 tablespoons of melted butter into the 3 tablespoons of reserved batter. Pour it over the *clafoutis*. Put it back in a hotter (425°) oven an additional 15 minutes. Let it cool slightly before unmolding on to a warm platter. Pour boiling Calvados over it. Flame immediately and serve.

My advice: A *clafoutis* made and baked just before serving will be the right temperature by dessert time.

Coeur tendre en chocolat

[FOR 4 TO 6 PEOPLE]

8 tablespoons (1 stick) butter
3 eggs
4 ounces (4 squares) unsweetened chocolate
¼ cup flour
1⅓ cups sugar

1 heart-shaped mold or soufflé mold or round 8- to 9-inch cake pan

---

Remarks: This chocolate *coeur tendre* ("tender heart") is an attractive dessert for parties and romantic dinners. If you don't have a heart-shaped mold, a round cake pan will do—but the dessert will have to be rebaptized. It has a light meringue crust hiding a soft, lush interior. But if you overheat the oven or bake it too long, the result will be a "dry heart"!

TENDER-HEART CHOCOLATE CAKE

Preparation and baking time the day before: 1 hour and 45 minutes / *Oven temperature:* 325°

Cut the butter into pieces so that it softens rapidly. Separate the eggs. Butter the mold.

Put the chocolate, broken in pieces, into the top of a double boiler, over low heat, without stirring. When it has softened completely, stir it and remove from the heat.

Mix the egg yolks and half the butter into the chocolate, stirring vigorously.

With a fork, mash the remaining butter and the flour together. Then beat them into the warm chocolate mixture.

Preheat the oven to 325°. Beat the egg whites until stiff. Halfway through, add 1 tablespoon of the sugar. When the egg whites are very stiff, add the rest of the sugar, continuing to beat until the mixture is somewhat shiny. Fold delicately into the chocolate mixture, using a spatula (as if making a mousse). Pour into the buttered mold. Place in a pan of boiling water and bake in the oven 1 hour and 15 minutes. Unmold when it cools. Store in the refrigerator overnight.

Crème anglaise à la vanille   VANILLA CUSTARD

[FOR 4 PEOPLE]

2 cups milk
1 envelope vanilla sugar or 1 teaspoon
    vanilla extract
¼ teaspoon salt
5 to 6 egg yolks
4 to 5 tablespoons sugar

Preparation and cooking time: 20 minutes, plus chilling time

In a saucepan, bring the milk, vanilla, and salt slowly to a boil.

In a large bowl, beat the egg yolks and sugar together with an electric mixer for several minutes, or until the mixture lightens somewhat. Blend in the milk, stirring constantly with a wooden spoon (the electric mixer will make it too foamy).

Put the mixture back into the saucepan, over low heat. Stir rapidly with a wooden spoon, scraping the sides and bottom, until it begins to thicken. Remove immediately from the heat without letting it boil, or the custard will separate. Pour it into another container right away to stop the cooking. Let it cool.

My advice: A good trick for beginners is to dissolve 1 teaspoon of cornstarch in the cold milk before following the recipe. Your custard will be a little less delicate in flavor, but there's no risk of it separating. You can even reduce the number of eggs since cornstarch acts as a thickener. In that case, 4 eggs are enough for an economical custard.

Remarks: If the custard overheats and "curdles" by turning grainy, beat it, off the heat, with an electric mixer until it becomes smooth again.

Crème anglaise may be flavored with vanilla, coffee, chocolate, fruit essences (which are very practical, in liquid form), caramel, liqueur, or liquor of your choice.

Crème renversée au caramel

[FOR 4 PEOPLE]

CARAMEL

Store-bought liquid caramel

or

3 tablespoons sugar
2 tablespoons water
A few drops lemon juice

CUSTARD

2 cups milk
¼ teaspoon salt / 3 tablespoons sugar
1 envelope vanilla sugar or 1 teaspoon
    vanilla extract / 4 eggs

1 soufflé mold, about 8 inches in diam-
    eter*

Remarks: For a firm and smooth custard:
• put in enough eggs;
• strain the beaten egg/boiling-milk mixture
through a metal strainer to catch any bits of
egg that might coagulate in cooking;
• bake it in a hot oven in a bain-marie.

To loosen the caramel stuck on the bottom of the mold, pour in 2 to 3 tablespoons
of water. Bring slowly to a boil, scraping the
bottom with a wooden spoon. Let it cool and
pour over the unmolded custard.

CARAMEL CUSTARD

Preparation and cooking time: 45 minutes, plus chilling / *Oven temperature:* 425°

CARAMEL: Coat the inside of the mold with store-bought liquid caramel. If you're making it yourself, boil 3 tablespoons of sugar and 2 tablespoons of water in the mold. When the caramel begins to brown, sprinkle in a few drops of lemon juice. Remove the mold from the heat. Grab it with two potholders and tilt the mold to coat it all around the bottom. Let it cool.

Preheat the oven to 425°.

CUSTARD: Bring the milk, salt, sugar, and vanilla to a boil. Add a little boiling milk to the beaten eggs in a large bowl, then the rest of the milk, whisking con-stantly. Pour this mixture through a fine strainer into the caramelized mold. Put it in a panful of cold water (a bain-marie).

Bake in the oven 30 to 35 minutes. The custard is done when its golden surface resists the pressure of your finger. Unmold when it is completely cold.

My advice: Some people recommend baking caramel custard in a moderate oven. But I prefer a hot oven, which seals the custard surface rapidly, producing a light crust that lowers the risk of boiling the custard, which would be disastrous.

*If you're making caramel in the mold, be very careful. Select a sturdy mold (e.g., a charlotte mold or even a ring mold), and efficient potholders. The boiling sugar is *very* hot, and so is the mold. Add the lemon juice cau-tiously—it sometimes splatters. Inexperienced cooks may prefer to make the caramel in a separate saucepan, then pour it immediately into the mold.

Crêpes soufflées SOUFFLÉED CRÊPES

[For 10 to 12 crêpes]

Preparation and cooking time: 1 hour, plus 30 minutes resting time for the batter
Oven temperature: 350°

CRÊPE BATTER

5 tablespoons flour
2 eggs
½ teaspoon salt
2 cups milk
1 tablespoon sugar
1 tablespoon melted butter

THICK, SWEET BÉCHAMEL SAUCE

1 tablespoon flour
2 tablespoons butter
1 cup milk
¼ teaspoon salt
3 tablespoons sugar
1 envelope vanilla sugar or 1 teaspoon
    vanilla extract or 2 tablespoons li-
    queur
2 eggs, separated

9- to 10-inch skillet
1 rag or paper towel soaked in oil
1 attractive medium-sized baking dish

CRÊPES: See Flamed Crêpes Suzette (p. 220), paragraphs 1 and 2.
Preheat the oven to 350°.

THICK, SWEET BÉCHAMEL SAUCE: In a saucepan, over low heat, blend the flour and just-melted butter together with a wire whisk. Add the cold milk, all at once, whisking constantly, then the salt, sugar, and vanilla. Simmer slowly 2 to 3 minutes, stirring constantly to keep the mixture from sticking to the bottom. Lightly beat the egg yolks in a bowl with a few spoonfuls of the hot sauce. Beat this into the remaining sauce, off the heat, to avoid clumps of cooked egg yolk. Beat vigorously another few seconds.

Beat the egg whites until stiff peaks form. Fold them delicately into the sauce.

Spread the crêpes with the sauce. Roll them up loosely, folding the edges under to keep the filling in. Arrange them in the buttered baking dish. Place in the oven 15 to 20 minutes, until the crêpes have puffed up. Serve immediately in the baking dish.

My advice: Crêpes Soufflées may be filled a little before serving and arranged on the baking dish in which they're to be served. Slip them into the oven halfway through the meal and they'll be ready for dessert.

Crêpes Suzette flambées

[FOR 12 SMALL CRÊPES]

CRÊPE BATTER

5 tablespoons flour
2 eggs / ½ teaspoon salt
2 cups milk or water
1 tablespoon sugar
1 tablespoon melted butter

FILLING

8 tablespoons (1 stick) soft butter
5 tablespoons sugar
3 to 4 tablespoons Grand Marnier or other
    liqueur
2 tablespoons pulverized almonds
1 tablespoon grated orange rind

¼ cup rum or other liqueur for flaming

9 to 10-inch skillet
1 rag or paper towel soaked in oil
1 heatproof serving plate

FLAMED CRÊPES SUZETTE

Preparation and cooking time: 45 minutes, plus 30 minutes resting time for the batter

CRÊPES: Beat the crêpe batter ingredients together with an electric mixer or food processor until the mixture is smooth. If possible, let it rest in the refrigerator 30 minutes.

Make thin crêpes, over high heat, in a very hot skillet. Rub the skillet with a rag or paper towel soaked in oil between each crêpe. Keep the crêpes warm on a plate set above a pan of boiling water.

FILLING: With an electric mixer or in a food processor, beat the ingredients for the filling until the mixture is light and fluffy. Spread the filling on each crêpe before rolling or folding it up on a very hot serving plate. sprinkle each crêpe with boiling rum or liqueur and flame at the table.

My advice: If you make your crêpes in advance—the day before or even 2 days ahead of time—sprinkle them with powdered sugar as you stack each one on top of the other, to keep them from sticking together. Wrap them in foil and refrigerate. This way you'll be able to pull them apart easily before filling them.

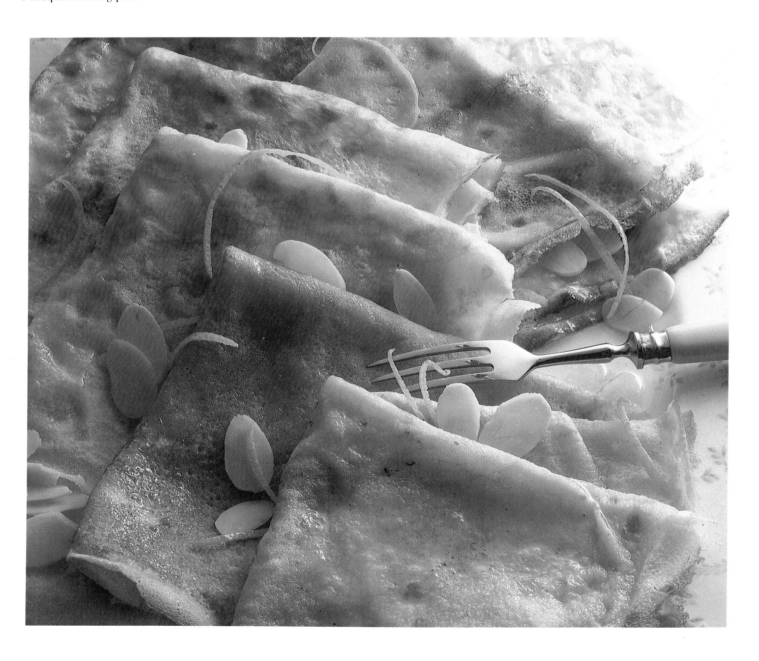

PEARS BAKED WITH CUSTARD AND LADYFINGERS

Délicieux aux poires

[For 6 to 8 people]

1 large (29-ounce) can pears
10 ladyfingers
2 tablespoons pear liqueur (or Benedic-
  tine, Cointreau, Grand Marnier)
2 cups milk
½ teaspoon salt
6 tablespoons sugar
1 envelope vanilla sugar or 1 teaspoon
  vanilla extract
4 eggs
1½ tablespoons butter

1 soufflé mold or other round baking
  dish, about 10 inches in diameter

Remarks: A liqueur should be used to
flavor a dessert that needs cooking, rather than
a hard liquor whose volatile flavor disappears
almost completely during cooking.

Preparation and baking time the day before or a few hours before: 1 hour / *Oven temperature:* 400°

Drain and sponge the pear halves dry. Arrange them in the mold, in a star shape, cut sides down, stem ends in the center.

Sprinkle the ladyfingers with liqueur. Arrange them over the pears. Preheat the oven to 400°.

Heat the milk with the salt, sugar, and vanilla. Beat the eggs. Off the heat, mix in the boiling milk, whisking constantly.

Pour half the mixture into the prepared mold. Press the ladyfingers to help them absorb the liquid. When they are well soaked, pour in the remaining milk-egg mixture. Dot with butter. Bake in the oven in a bain-marie 45 minutes. Cover with foil if the surface browns too fast. Chill completely before unmolding.

My advice: For this recipe, canned pears are preferable to fresh pears, which give off too much juice.

Far breton BRETON FLAN WITH PRUNES

[FOR 4 TO 6 PEOPLE]

1½ cups prunes, preferably pitted
3 to 4 tablespoons rum
5 tablespoons flour
½ teaspoon salt
3 tablespoons sugar
3 eggs
2 cups milk
2 tablespoons butter

Remarks: This is a classic dessert from Brittany, traditionally baked until it is very brown. It is often served accompanied by a pitcher of heavy cream. If you're using prunes that are very dry, soak them 12 hours in water or, even better, in rum.

You can prepare a less expensive flan by leaving out the rum and reducing the number of prunes somewhat or substituting ½ cup of raisins.

Preparation and baking time: 1 hour and 30 minutes / *Oven temperature:* 400° then 375°

A few hours in advance, pit the prunes if necessary and place them in a small bowl. Pour rum over them. Cover and let them macerate until ready to use.

Preheat the oven to 400°.

In a bowl, mix together the flour, salt, sugar, and eggs. Beat in the milk, fairly warm, using an electric mixer to produce a smooth, fluid batter. Stir in the prunes and then rum.

Butter the bottom and sides of a baking dish. Pour in the batter (it should be about 1 to 2 inches deep).

Place in the middle of the oven 1 hour. After 30 minutes, reduce the heat to 375°. Serve the flan, warm or cold, in its baking dish.

My advice: Flan is better warm than completely cold. And since it is very difficult to unmold, consider serving it in its baking dish, so choose an attractive one!

Fraises Melba   STRAWBERRIES MELBA

[FOR 4 PEOPLE]

Preparation time: 15 minutes

2 tablespoons strawberry jam
2 tablespoons kirsch
1 pint strawberries
1 pint vanilla ice cream
1 cup whipped cream (optional)
¼ cup slivered almonds or crushed hazelnuts

4 glass dessert dishes or champagne glasses

Over low heat, stir the jam with the kirsch, just until it melts.

Wash and wipe the strawberries dry. Remove the stems.

Divide the ice cream among the serving dishes. Cover with strawberries, a dollop of whipped cream (if desired), and liquefied jam. Finish by sprinkling with slivered almonds or crushed hazelnuts.

My advice: Raspberries and peaches may be made *à la melba*. Canned peaches may be used, but strawberries and raspberries must be fresh for good results.

Fraisier STRAWBERRY CAKE

[FOR 6 TO 8 PEOPLE]

SPONGE CAKE

4 eggs
½ cup plus 1 tablespoon sugar
1 envelope vanilla sugar or 1 teaspoon
    vanilla extract
⅛ teaspoon salt
3 tablespoons cornstarch
⅓ cup flour

PASTRY CREAM

1 cup milk
2 egg yolks
4 tablespoons sugar
1 tablespoon flour
⅛ teaspoon salt
8 tablespoons (1 stick) butter
2 tablespoons kirsch

SYRUP

½ cup sugar
½ cup water

2 pints strawberries
Powdered (confectioners') sugar or cur-
    rant jelly

10-inch cake pan or square baking dish

Preparation and baking time: 1 hour and 15 minutes, plus chilling time

Prepare the sponge cake according to the recipe on p. 225.

PASTRY CREAM: In a food processor or mixer bowl, place the milk, egg yolks, sugar, flour, and salt. Mix until thoroughly blended. Pour into a saucepan. With a whisk, beat steadily over the heat. Remove the mixture as soon as it comes to a boil. Off the heat, mix in half the butter, bit by bit, beating vigorously. Let it cool a little before beating in the remaining butter and kirsch. Refrigerate to thicken it.

SYRUP: Dissolve the sugar in the water, stirring over heat. Remove from the heat as soon as it comes to a rolling boil.

Cut the cake in half across the width. Place the lower half on a cake plate and moisten it with syrup. Spread half the pastry cream over it.

Cut the strawberries in half, vertically. Arrange them side by side on the layer of pastry cream. Pour the remaining pastry cream over it, spreading it evenly but leaving the berries along the edges very visible. Cover with the second piece of cake, pressing it on lightly.

Sprinkle with powdered sugar or brush on a layer of currant jelly melted over heat with a little kirsch. Chill before serving.

Gâteau de Savoie

[For 6 to 8 people]

4 eggs
½ cup plus 1 tablespoon sugar
1 envelope vanilla sugar or 1 teaspoon
    vanilla extract
⅛ teaspoon salt
3 tablespoons cornstarch
⅓ cup flour

9-inch cake pan or loaf pan

Remarks: Use your food processor or electric mixer for beating egg yolks and sugar together thoroughly and for whipping the egg whites. But use a wooden spoon or rubber spatula for folding the flour into the egg whites as delicately as possible.

Wrapped in foil, store in the refrigerator as long as 3 to 4 days.

SPONGE CAKE

Preparation and baking time: 1 hour and 15 minutes / *Oven temperature:* 350°

Separate the eggs. In a mixing bowl or food processor, place the sugar (reserving 1 tablespoon), the vanilla, and the egg yolks. Beat until the mixture is light and creamy. Lift up a spoonful—it should form a ribbon. The success of the cake depends in large part on this process.

Preheat the oven to 350°.

Wash and carefully wipe the beaters for you'll be using them again right away. In another bowl, beat the egg whites with the salt until they are stiff and somewhat shiny. Halfway through, beat in the reserved tablespoon of sugar.

Sift the cornstarch and flour through a sifter or metal strainer over the creamy sugar-egg mixture. Fold in gingerly with a spatula without being too thorough. Then fold in the egg whites in 2 to 3 delicate strokes.

Butter and lightly flour the pan. Pour in the batter about ¾ full. Bake 35 to 40 minutes in the oven. The top of the cake should be golden brown and dry. Unmold the cake while it is still warm and let it dry on a rack.

My advice: The sponge cake should be served as is or lightly sprinkled with powdered sugar. It goes well with fruit salad or preserves, chocolate mousse, custard (*crème anglaise*), or pastry cream. (See also the recipe for Mocha Cake, p. 232.)

Gelée de coings QUINCE JELLY

[FOR 2 POUNDS QUINCE (OR HALF
QUINCE/HALF APPLE)]

4 cups sugar per quart of juice
Juice of 1 lemon
½ teaspoon vanilla extract (optional)

Plastic wrap

Precooking the fruit: about 30 minutes / *Cooking time:* 20 minutes from the start of boiling

Don't wash the quince unless they are very dirty. Rub them clean instead with a cloth. Cut them up with their skins and seeds and place in a pot. Add enough water to just cover. Boil them until they are soft. Then pour through a strainer placed over a large bowl to catch the juice. Press lightly with your hand.

Measure the juice. Add 4 cups of sugar per quart of juice and, if desired, the vanilla. Boil over high heat, about 20 minutes. Add lemon juice toward the end. (A few drops poured on to a saucer should jell lightly right away. Otherwise, cook a few more minutes.)

Pour into jars immediately and cover.

Gelée de groseilles, mûres ou framboises «à froid» UNCOOKED CURRANT, BLACKBERRY, OR RASPBERRY JELLY

[FOR 4 POUNDS BERRIES (RASPBERRIES,
CURRANTS, OR BLACKBERRIES)]

2 cups water
4 cups sugar per quart of juice

Plastic wrap

Cooking time: 5 minutes over high heat / *Mixing time:* 30 minutes

Place the berries with water over high heat 5 minutes to make them burst open. Squeeze the juice out with a vegetable mill over a large bowl. Measure the resulting juice.

Add 4 cups of sugar per quart of juice. Stir this mixture slowly with a wooden spoon until the sugar has completely dissolved (about 30 minutes). You can use a mixer set on the lowest speed.

Put in jars and cover immediately with plastic wrap.

Île flottante pralinée

[FOR 4 PEOPLE]

CARAMEL

3 tablespoons sugar
3 tablespoons water
Juice of ½ lemon

1 soufflé mold, about 8 inches in diameter

SOUFFLÉ MIX

½ cup pralines*
4 egg whites
½ teaspoon salt
4 tablespoons sugar

CUSTARD (CRÈME ANGLAISE)

1⅓ cups milk
1 teaspoon vanilla extract
⅛ teaspoon salt
4 egg yolks
3 tablespoons sugar

Remarks: The inside of the mold must be carefully caramelized, all the way to the top, because caramel keeps the egg whites from sinking during cooking and subsequent cooling. Since store-bought caramel won't stick as well to the sides of the mold, it isn't suitable for this recipe. Similarly, nonstick molds, so useful for many things, are to be avoided for this soufflé.

COLD ALMOND-CARAMEL SOUFFLÉ

Preparation and baking time: 45 minutes / *Oven temperature:* 350°

CARAMEL: Spread the sugar in the bottom of the mold. Sprinkle with water and lemon juice. Heat it (use a heat diffuser over the burner for a gas flame). When the sugar begins to brown, tilt the mold all around to caramelize it all over.** Remove from the heat before it turns really brown.

SOUFFLÉ MIX: Preheat the oven to 350°. Crush the pralines on a board with a rolling pin. Drape a kitchen towel over them to keep them on the board.

Whip the egg whites with salt until stiff peaks form. As soon as they are firm, add 1 tablespoon of the sugar. Continue beating. As soon as the egg whites are very stiff, add, in two portions, the remaining sugar. Beat the whites another 2 minutes, until they are somewhat shiny. Fold in the crushed pralines, delicately, with a wooden spoon or rubber spatula without crushing the egg whites. Pour into the caramelized mold. Place the mold in a pan of boiling water set in the oven. Bake 20 minutes in the oven. Let cool in the mold. Do not unmold until ready to serve.

CRÈME ANGLAISE: In a saucepan, bring the milk to a boil with vanilla and salt. In a bowl, beat, with an electric mixer, the egg yolks and sugar. Stir in the boiling milk with a spoon. Pour it back into the saucepan. Heat it over low heat, stirring until it begins to thicken, but without letting it boil. Pour the custard immediately into a large container to hasten cooling, then refrigerate it.

Just before serving, unmold the very cold almond-caramel soufflé on to the equally cold *crème anglaise* (dip the bottom of the mold rapidly in hot water to facilitate unmolding it).

*Pralines are caramelized almonds. You can buy them in specialty food stores or make them yourself: Toast ½ cup of slivered almonds 5 to 10 minutes in a 350° oven or a toaster oven. Boil ½ cup of sugar with 2 tablespoons of water until it caramelizes (turns medium brown), then stir the almonds into it and pour the mixture onto an oiled baking sheet or marble slab. In about 10 minutes, it will be cool enough to break into pieces.

**For the faint-at-heart unwilling to face caramelizing a mold over the burner, the caramel may be made in a separate saucepan and poured into the mold. Remember that caramel is *very* hot.

Kougloff KOUGLOFF

[FOR 4 TO 6 PEOPLE]

⅔ cup raisins
2 tablespoons rum
1 cake fresh yeast or 1 tablespoon (1 envelope) powdered yeast
1 cup milk
2 cups flour
12 shelled almonds
½ cup sugar
½ teaspoon salt
5 tablespoons butter
1 egg
Powdered (confectioners') sugar (optional)

1 kougloff mold* or decorative ring mold

Preparation and baking time: 1 hour / *Resting the dough:* 2 hours to 2 hours and 30 minutes
Oven temperature: 350°

Rinse the raisins in very hot water to soften them. Drain them. Then put them in the rum to macerate.

In a large bowl, mix the yeast with ¾ cup of warm milk. Stir in ½ cup of the flour to make a soft dough. Beat well with a wooden spoon. Sprinkle the remaining flour over it without kneading it in. Cover the bowl with a towel. Let rest in a warm spot, about 1 hour, until the yeast pushes the flour up.

Butter the mold. Arrange the almonds on the bottom of it.

When the dough has risen, mix in the sugar, salt, softened butter, egg, remaining milk, and raisins with their macerating rum. Knead vigorously for several minutes. Beat the dough by stretching it up high to give it elasticity. Place the dough in the buttered mold. It should come no more than halfway up. Cover and put it back one final time in a warm spot (the dough should double in volume).

Preheat the oven to 350°. Put the kougloff in the center and bake 35 to 40 minutes. Let it cool before unmolding it on a rack. Sprinkle it with powdered sugar before serving, if desired.

My advice: Using dry baker's yeast, sold in envelopes, makes the preparation of this cake much faster. This yeast gets mixed in, as is, with all the ingredients—flour, egg, sugar, etc.—and kneaded as indicated. It needs only one rising period 1 hour and 30 minutes to 2 hours before baking, so a whole hour is saved.

*A specialty of Alsace, Kougloffs are baked in special round molds that often have a raylike pattern on the bottom and sides.

Langues de chat   CATS' TONGUES COOKIES

[ABOUT 20 COOKIES]

2 egg whites
4 tablespoons soft butter
½ cup sugar
½ envelope vanilla sugar or ½ teaspoon
    vanilla extract
⅛ teaspoon salt
½ cup flour

Baking sheet

Preparation and baking time: 30 minutes / *Oven temperature:* 400°

Preheat the oven to 400°. Heat the unbeaten egg whites a little in a warm, but not hot, double boiler.

Meanwhile beat together with an electric mixer or wire whisk the softened butter, sugar, vanilla, and salt until smooth and creamy.

Fold in, in 3 to 4 batches, the warm egg whites, lightly beaten with a fork.

With a wooden spoon or rubber spatula, fold in the flour without mixing too thoroughly.

Butter the baking sheet and flour it lightly. Spread thin strips of cookie dough over it using a pastry bag. Or, simpler, use a teaspoon to place little knobs of dough about 1 inch apart (you'll get round tongues). Bake in the oven 8 to 10 minutes. Lift the cookies off the baking sheet with a spatula as soon as they come out of the oven. don't delay, because when they cool, *langues de chat* become brittle and break easily. You can store them 1 to 2 days in a tin box.

My advice: Even though *langues de chat* smell delicious right out of the oven, resist the temptation! They'll be even more wonderful the next day and the days following.

Remarks: Don't try to do the job faster by using an electric mixer. You'll get a foamy mixture that way and the cookies, once baked, won't resemble true *langues de chat*.

It is essential to warm the egg whites in a double boiler so that the mixture blends well. But make sure the double boiler doesn't get scalding hot, because anything over 120° to 140° will cook the eggs, which would be catastrophic!

Meringues fourrées au chocolat

[FOR 2 TO 3 DOZEN MERINGUES]

2 egg whites
⅛ teaspoon salt
4 tablespoons sugar

CHOCOLATE FROSTING

2 ounces (2 squares) bittersweet chocolate
¾ cup *crème fraîche*

Small paper fluted cups
Baking sheet covered with foil

Remarks: Do you know why your meringues sometimes fall flat? Since a meringue will brown rapidly, you think it's done and take it out of the oven. But because the inside is still soft, it collapses while cooling off. Meringues need to bake and dry out in the oven. If, in spite of everything, you hope to keep your meringues a day or two, you'll have to keep them closed up—whether or not they're filled—in an airtight container stored in the refrigerator.

MERINGUES FILLED WITH CHOCOLATE

Preparation time: 20 minutes / *Baking time:* 1 hour / *Oven temperature:* 375° then 350°

Preheat the oven to 375°. Cover a baking sheet with a large piece of foil. Lightly butter and flour it.

MERINGUE: In a mixing bowl, place the egg whites and salt. Begin beating them. As soon as they are foamy, add 1 tablespoon of the sugar. Continue beating. When the egg whites are stiff, add the remaining sugar in 2 to 3 portions, beating continuously until they are smooth, shiny, and clinging to the beaters (you should be able to turn the mixing bowl upside down without fear of the beaten egg whites falling out!). Distribute as quickly as possible on the foil-covered baking sheet, using a teaspoon to shape small meringues. Bake 45 minutes at 375°, then lower heat to 350° for 15 minutes.

CHOCOLATE FROSTING: Place the chocolate, broken into small pieces, and the *crème fraîche* in a small heavy saucepan. Bring slowly to a boil, without stirring. Then stir the softened chocolate and remove from the heat. Let it cool a little. Whip with an electric beater until the frosting thickens and doubles in volume. Let cool to room temperature so that it firms up without hardening too much.

Spread half the meringues with a thick layer of frosting, on the flat side. Press the flat side of unfrosted meringues against them. Place them in the refrigerator to harden before eating them, without waiting too long because they'll soften up in a few hours.

My advice: Filled meringues can be attractively presented, like petits fours, in fluted paper cups.

Mini-savarins au rhum

[FOR 6 SAVARINS]

1 tablespoon butter
¼ cup sugar
3 eggs, separated
1 tablespoon milk
1 cup flour
1 teaspoon baking powder
½ teaspoon salt

SYRUP

1 cup prepared sugar syrup (or see *My advice*)
¼ cup rum

GARNISH

2 tablespoons apricot jam
Glacéed cherries and pieces of angelica (optional)
1 cup whipped cream (optional)

6 small ring molds, about 5 inches in diameter*
1 pastry brush

MINI RUM CAKES

Preparation and cooking time: 50 minutes / *Oven temperature:* 350°

Preheat the oven to 350°. Butter the molds. Using an electric mixer, beat the sugar and egg yolks together until they are creamy. Add the milk, then the flour sifted with the baking powder, without blending it in too thoroughly.

Beat the egg whites and salt until stiff peaks form. Fold them carefully into the batter. Pour the batter into the molds, ¾ full. Bake in the oven 15 to 20 minutes.

Unmold the savarins as soon as they emerge from the oven to keep them from sticking, then put them back in the molds. Bring the sugar syrup to a boil. Add the rum. Pour it while it is still very hot over the savarins. Let them soak up the rum syrup for a minute or two. Add more syrup occasionally. Unmold the savarins on a serving platter.

Stir the apricot jam with 1 tablespoon of water over low heat. Simmer 1 to 2 minutes to thicken it. With a pastry brush, paint the savarins with jam to make them shiny. Decorate with halved glacéed cherries and strips of angelica, if desired. If you wish, you might fill the centers with whipped cream.

My advice: You can make the syrup by melting over heat 1 cup of sugar in 1 cup of water. Remove from the heat after a minute of simmering.

*You can bake these in muffin tins or custard cups, in which case they will resemble rum babas more than savarins. Or you can make one large savarin, baking it in a savarin mold or plain ring mold.

Moka MOCHA CAKE

[FOR 6 TO 8 PEOPLE]

Preparation and cooking time: 1 hour and 30 minutes / *Oven temperature:* 375°

GÉNOISE BATTER

4 eggs
½ cup sugar
½ teaspoon salt
½ cup flour
½ cup cornstarch
⅓ teaspoon baking powder
2½ tablespoons butter

MOCHA CREAM

1 tablespoon freeze-dried coffee crystals
1 tablespoon hot water
3 egg yolks
½ cup sugar
12 tablespoons (1½ sticks) very soft butter

DECORATION

Grated chocolate or cocoa
Slivered almonds
Candied violets or other flowers

10-inch cake pan or 12-inch loaf pan

Remarks: Since the cake is easier to slice when it is slightly stale, it's best to make it a day ahead of time.

GÉNOISE: In a double boiler over low heat, beat the eggs, sugar, and salt until the mixture is warm, foamy, and has almost doubled in volume. Transfer it to a mixing bowl and continue to beat until it is cool.

Preheat the oven to 375°. Sift the flour, cornstarch, and baking powder together over the mixing bowl containing the egg mixture. Fold together delicately.

Melt the butter in the mold. Pour in the batter. Bake in the oven 45 to 50 minutes. Unmold and let cool on a rack.

MOCHA CREAM: In an electric mixer bowl, stir the coffee and hot water together. Then add the egg yolks and sugar. Place the mixer bowl in a pan of hot water over medium heat. Beat with an electric mixer until the mixture is smooth and shiny (if you lift it up with a spoon it should fall back in a ribbon). Let cool 10 minutes. Then, still using the electric mixer, beat in the softened butter in small pieces.

Slice the cake in 3 pieces, horizontally. Spread each piece with mocha cream. Put the cake back together again. Cover it entirely, top and sides, with the rest of the cream. Smooth it out with a knife blade dipped in hot water. Then use your imagination to decorate it.

My advice: If you do better with the Sponge Cake (p. 225) than the *Génoise*, you should know that it lends itself as well to mocha cream frosting. For more intense flavor, moisten the pieces of cake with a little kirsch before spreading the mocha cream over them.

Mousse au chocolat pâtissière

[FOR 4 PEOPLE]

4 ounces (4 squares) bittersweet choco-
    late
5 tablespoons very soft butter
3 eggs plus 1 to 2 egg whites
¼ teaspoon salt
1 tablespoon sugar

1 serving bowl or 4 ramekins

Remarks: Chocolate reacts badly to intense heat, which destroys its flavor and makes
it grainy. For that reason, it should be melted
in a double boiler or in front of an open oven
door rather than over direct heat.

No particle of egg yolk should touch the
whites or they will not mount properly in stiff
peaks.

The spoonful of sugar added to the whites
during their beating keeps them from getting
grainy.

CHOCOLATE MOUSSE

Preparation and cooking time: 20 minutes, plus 1 to 12 hours refrigeration

Break the chocolate into a small saucepan. Let it melt over a double boiler for
several minutes without stirring. Remove from the heat. Blend the butter completely
into the very hot chocolate, using a wooden spoon.

Carefully separate the eggs. Mix the yolks, one by one, into the chocolate.

Beat the egg whites with a pinch of salt. When they are thick and foamy, add
the sugar. Continue beating. Stop as soon as stiff peaks have formed and they are
somewhat shiny (egg whites beaten too long become granular, leaving a light deposit
of liquid in the bottom of the bowl).

Place a spoonful of beaten egg white into the cool chocolate mixture. Mix it in
well with a spatula. To keep the rest of the egg whites from deflating, fold them in,
using 2 to 3 large scooping gestures with the spatula.

Pour immediately into a serving bowl or in ramekins. Refrigerate until ready to
serve.

Œufs à la neige FLOATING ISLAND

[FOR 4 PEOPLE]

2 cups milk
6 tablespoons sugar
½ teaspoon salt
1 teaspoon vanilla extract or 1 envelope
    vanilla sugar
5 eggs

Remarks: The egg whites may be prepared several hours ahead of time, but add them to the *crème anglaise* just before serving. Leaving the two mixed together for any length of time is inadvisable.

Overcooked meringue dries up. A few seconds on one side and then the other is enough for them to puff and firm up. And cook them in water rather than milk, which boils over too easily. Finally, milk turns egg whites grayish.

Preparation and cooking time: 45 minutes, plus chilling time

CRÈME ANGLAISE (CUSTARD): In a saucepan, slowly bring the milk to a boil with 4 tablespoons of the sugar, salt, and vanilla. Separate the eggs. Pour a little boiling milk over the yolks, stirring vigorously with a wooden spoon. Pour it all back into the saucepan, off the heat, stirring continuously. Put it back on the stove over low heat. Continue stirring until the custard takes on a somewhat creamy consistency (a film of custard coats the back of the spoon) without ever letting it boil. Chill thoroughly.

To cook the egg whites, put a large potful of water on to boil, or better yet, a large *sauteuse*. Beat the egg whites until stiff peaks form.

Add the remaining sugar halfway through the process. When the water, just ready to boil, begins to shudder, slide 4 to 5 tablespoons of egg white onto it. The whites should cook without touching each other in the still-shuddering water. After no more than 4 to 5 seconds, turn them over, starting with the first spoonful dropped into the water. Drain them after a few moments. Proceed the same way with the rest of the egg whites.

Just before serving, float the well-drained egg white "islands" on top of the chilled custard.

My advice: Decorate with arabesques of caramel or butterscotch drawn on the "islands" at the last minute.

Omelette norvégienne

[FOR 6 TO 8 PEOPLE]

SWISS MERINGUE

4 egg whites
1 cup sugar
½ teaspoon salt

1 *génoise* cake (p. 232)
2 tablespoons kirsch or other liqueur
1 pint vanilla ice cream
Powdered (confectioners') sugar

1 ovenproof flat serving platter

Remarks: If the layer of meringue is thick enough all around the cake and if your oven is hot enough to brown it rapidly, the ice cream inside won't melt.

A layer of glacéed fruit, finely minced and macerated in liqueur, can be spread between the cake and the ice cream.

BAKED ALASKA

Preparation and cooking time: 30 minutes / *Oven temperature:* 500° then 475°

Prepare the Swiss meringue ahead of time. Place the egg whites, sugar, and salt in a heavy saucepan. Beat them with a portable electric mixer over very low heat or in a double boiler until the mixture is shiny and forms stiff peaks. Continue beating, off the heat, until it is cool. Chill the meringue. Cut the *génoise* in half, horizontally. Sprinkle it with liqueur.

Fifteen minutes before serving the dessert, preheat the oven to 500°. Place a piece of *génoise* on the serving platter. Cover it with the ice cream, frozen solid (in 2 to 3 pieces if necessary). Place the second piece of *génoise* on top of it. With your hands, press it down over the sides of the ice cream to completely cover it. Then, with a spatula, coat the surface with a layer of meringue. Don't smooth it down too much; give it a textured surface. Sprinkle with powdered sugar.

Put in the middle of a very hot (475°) oven just long enough to lightly brown the surface of the meringue.

Organization: Whip the Swiss meringue in advance. It can be kept several hours in the refrigerator without deflating. Cover it with a piece of foil so that it doesn't dry out. You can even prepare a Baked Alaska entirely in advance on its serving platter (metal) and put it in the freezer. All that's needed then is to slip it into the oven at the last minute.

My advice: This sumptuous dessert is sure to impress your guests. Yet it is usually successful on the first try!

Pêches pâtissière meringuées

PEACHES WITH CUSTARD AND MERINGUE

[For 4 to 5 people]

Preparation and cooking time: 45 minutes, plus chilling / *Oven temperature:* 350°

1 large (29-ounce) can peach halves

PASTRY CREAM

2 cups milk
½ envelope vanilla sugar or ½ teaspoon
  vanilla extract
½ teaspoon salt
4 tablespoons sugar
4 egg yolks
2 tablespoons flour

MERINGUE

4 egg whites
¼ teaspoon salt
⅓ cup sugar
⅓ cup slivered almonds

1 small soufflé mold, about 9 inches in
  diameter

Drain the peaches thoroughly.

PASTRY CREAM: In a saucepan, bring the milk slowly to a boil with the vanilla and salt. Meanwhile, in a large bowl, beat the sugar and egg yolks with an electric mixer until the mixture is light and syrupy. Fold in the flour, then add the milk, beating continuously. Pour it all into the saucepan. Put it back on the heat. Stir continuously with a wooden spoon, while it simmers slowly 1 to 2 minutes. You should have a smooth cream. Pour it into the soufflé mold.

Preheat the oven to 350°. Blot the peaches dry with paper towels. Arrange them side by side over the pastry cream.

MERINGUE: Beat the egg whites with salt until stiff peaks form. When they begin to thicken, gradually add the sugar. Continue beating until the mixture is stiff and shiny. Carefully fold in the slivered almonds. Pour into the mold without smoothing out the top.

Place in the oven about 10 minutes to lightly brown the meringue. Chill several hours before serving.

Petites marquises au chocolat

[FOR 4 TO 5 PEOPLE]

COFFEE CUSTARD

1½ cups milk
1 tablespoon instant coffee
½ teaspoon salt
1 egg yolk
2 to 3 tablespoons sugar
1 tablespoon cornstarch

4 ounces (4 squares) bittersweet chocolate
8 tablespoons (1 stick) butter
2 egg yolks
Unsweetened cocoa

4 to 5 ramekins

INDIVIDUAL CHOCOLATE CUSTARDS

Preparation and cooking time: 30 minutes, plus chilling

COFFEE CUSTARD: In a saucepan, bring the milk to a boil with the coffee and salt. In a bowl, place the egg yolk, sugar, and cornstarch. Beat until the mixture is slightly foamy. Slowly stir in the hot milk with coffee. Pour the mixture back into the saucepan. Put it back on the stove over low heat, stirring constantly until it begins to thicken. Remove it from the heat just before it reaches a boil and let cool.

Melt the chocolate in a double boiler over low heat, then pour it into a large bowl. Add the butter, egg yolks, and coffee custard. Beat with an electric beater several minutes, or until the mixture is very smooth and pale.

Pour into ramekins. Refrigerate several hours or overnight.

Unmold before serving. Sprinkle with unsweetened cocoa.

My advice: Since unmolding them is not very easy, dip the bottom of the ramekins in hot water a few seconds before turning them over on a plate. Sprinkle the unmolded ramekins with unsweetened cocoa before sliding them onto individual dessert plates or a platter.

Plus-que-parfait glacé au caramel   FROZEN CARAMEL PARFAIT

[FOR 4 PEOPLE]

2 eggs, separated
1 cup whipping cream or *crème fraîche*
1 tablespoon cold milk (optional)
3 tablespoons sugar
1 tablespoon caramel or butterscotch topping

4 ramekins or dessert bowls

Preparation time: 15 minutes, plus 2 or more hours in the freezer (in the freezing compartment of the refrigerator, at least 4 hours)

WHIPPED CREAM: If you're using *crème fraîche*, stir the milk into it (whipping cream does not need thinning). Beat until it is as thick as meringue. Transfer it to another bowl and chill.

In its place, put the egg yolks, 2 tablespoons of the sugar, and the caramel. Beat with an electric mixer until the mixture is pale and falls back in a ribbon. Pour it over the whipped cream without mixing it in. Return it to the refrigerator.

Carefully wash and dry the beaters and bowl before beating the egg whites until stiff peaks form. Add the remaining tablespoon of sugar halfway through. Fold them, delicately, into the first mixture. Pour into the ramekins immediately.

Let the mixture harden in the freezer at least 2 hours (or in the freezer compartment of the refrigerator at least 4 hours). Serve without unmolding.

Remarks: If you prepare this the day before, cover the ramekins with foil to keep their flavor intact and store them in the freezer. Thirty minutes before serving, take them out of the freezer and let them sit in the refrigerator to soften.

Poires Belle-Hélène   PEARS WITH HOT CHOCOLATE SAUCE

[FOR 4 TO 6 PEOPLE]

1 large (29-ounce) can pears

CHOCOLATE SAUCE
5 ounces (5 squares) bittersweet chocolate
1½ tablespoons soft butter

1 pint vanilla ice cream

DECORATION
A few candied violets (optional)

Preparation time: 15 minutes

Drain the pears. Reserve their syrup.

CHOCOLATE SAUCE: In a double boiler, melt the chocolate, broken into small pieces, without stirring. When it has softened, beat in the very soft butter, then 2 to 3 tablespoons of the pear syrup. Beat vigorously with a whisk until the mixture is smooth and creamy.

Put the ice cream in a serving bowl. Arrange the pears around it. Pour the hot chocolate sauce over the pears and serve immediately.

My advice: The simplest way to serve Pears with Hot Chocolate Sauce is in individual glass bowls.

Profiteroles au chocolat

[FOR ABOUT 30 CREAM PUFFS]

PUFF PASTRY

1 cup water
1 tablespoon sugar
¼ teaspoon salt
5 tablespoons butter
4 tablespoons flour
4 eggs

CHOCOLATE SAUCE WITH HONEY

2 ounces (2 squares) unsweetened chocolate
½ teaspoon instant coffee
2 tablespoons butter
1 small (5-ounce) can evaporated milk
3 tablespoons honey

CREAM PUFFS WITH CHOCOLATE SAUCE

Preparation and cooking time: 1 hour / *Oven temperature:* 350°

PUFF PASTRY: In a large saucepan, heat the water with the sugar, salt, and butter cut into pieces. Pour in the flour all at once. Mix it in vigorously with a rubber scraper or spatula. Continue cooking it over medium heat, stirring with a wooden spoon until the dough no longer clings to the spoon or the pan. Off the heat, add the eggs, one by one, continuing to beat vigorously.

Preheat the oven to 350°. Butter a baking sheet. Arrange spoonfuls of the dough on it with enough space between to allow them to puff up.

Bake in the oven 20 to 25 minutes. Take the cream puffs out of the oven as soon as they are hard enough to resist being pressed with your finger.

CHOCOLATE SAUCE WITH HONEY: Simmer all the ingredients in a small saucepan, over low heat, 4 to 6 minutes. Stir occasionally until the sauce is thick and smooth.

Pile the cream puffs into a pyramid in a wide shallow bowl. Pour the chocolate sauce over it and serve.*

*Profiteroles are sometimes filled with whipped cream, pastry cream (p. 236), or vanilla ice cream.

Quatre-quarts de tradition

[FOR 4 PEOPLE]

2 eggs
⅔ cup sugar
1 teaspoon vanilla extract or grated lemon
   or orange peel
8 tablespoons (1 stick) butter
1 cup flour
½ teaspoon baking powder
½ teaspoon salt

10-inch cake or loaf pan

Remarks: Your pound cake will be lighter and smoother if you sift the flour and baking powder together. Use either a flour sifter or a fine metal strainer, shaking it over the batter in the mixing bowl.

Be sure to follow the order in which the ingredients are listed in the recipe.

To unmold your cake without difficulty, sprinkle flour in the buttered pan. Hold it upside down over the sink, tapping lightly to shake out the excess flour. Then pour the batter in.

TRADITIONAL POUND CAKE

Preparation and baking time: 1 hour / *Oven temperature:* 350°

Preheat the oven to 350°.

With an electric mixer, beat the eggs and sugar together until they are pale, creamy, and somewhat frothy. Beat in the vanilla or fruit rind. Put the butter in the cake pan and place it in the oven a minute or two. When it has almost melted, beat it into the batter until it is completely absorbed.

Add the flour mixed with the baking powder and salt, folding it in until just blended. Pour the batter into the cake pan and bake 35 to 40 minutes.

Cover with a piece of foil as soon as the top is lightly browned. Unmold the cake on a rack when it comes out of the oven. Cool completely before serving.

My advice: As soon as the pound cake has cooled, wrap it in foil and refrigerate it until ready to serve. It should keep like this for several days and retain its texture. It can even be put in the freezer for a short time. Defrost it several hours before serving.

The traditional proportions for these home-baked cakes are easy to remember, since the four main ingredients each weigh a quarter of the total, with the weight of the eggs determining the rest.

Riz à l'Impératrice   RICE PUDDING WITH CUSTARD AND GLACÉED FRUIT

[FOR 6 TO 8 PEOPLE]

3½ ounces mixed glacéed fruit, chopped
2 tablespoons kirsch
1 cup rice
3 cups milk
½ teaspoon salt
¾ cup sugar

CRÈME ANGLAISE (CUSTARD)
1 cup milk
½ cup sugar
1 envelope vanilla sugar or 1 teaspoon
  vanilla extract
¼ teaspoon salt
4 egg yolks

1 tablespoon (1 envelope) unflavored
  gelatin
Currant jelly

1 soufflé mold or charlotte mold, 10 to
  12 inches in diameter

Preparation and cooking time the day before: 1 hour and 30 minutes

Macerate the chopped glacéed fruit in the kirsch. Rinse the rice. Boil it 3 minutes in a generous amount of water. Drain it. Place the milk and salt in a saucepan. Bring to a boil. Toss the rice in. Cover partially and simmer until the milk is entirely absorbed, about 30 minutes. Stir in the sugar and put back over very low heat, about 5 minutes.

CRÈME ANGLAISE: In a saucepan, bring the milk, sugar, vanilla, and salt to a boil. In a bowl, pour a little boiling milk over the egg yolks, stirring vigorously. Put back in the saucepan. Stir continuously, over low heat, until the custard thickens slightly. Do not let it boil. Dissolve the gelatin in ⅓ cup of warm water. Whisk it into the very hot custard.

Mix together the rice, glacéed fruit, kirsch, and *crème anglaise.*

Coat the inside of the mold with currant jelly. Pour the hot mixture in it. Chill overnight. Unmold and serve very cold.

My advice: This dessert bears little resemblance to a simple rice pudding. It is a worthy addition to any elegant buffet table. It looks very handsome, unmolded on an attractive platter. And its creamy texture, from the *crème anglaise,* reinforces the mingled flavors of kirsch, glacéed fruit, and vanilla.

Riz aux pommes meringués
[FOR 4 TO 6 PEOPLE]

1 cup rice
3 cups milk
½ teaspoon salt
1 teaspoon vanilla extract
3½ tablespoons butter
3 apples
7 tablespoons sugar
2 tablespoons Cognac (optional)
2 eggs, separated

1 baking dish

APPLE-RICE PUDDING WITH MERINGUE

Preparation and cooking time: 1 hour / *Oven temperature:* 425°

Rinse the rice. Boil it in a saucepan with a generous amount of water 3 minutes. Drain it. Place the milk over the heat with salt and vanilla. As soon as it comes to a boil add the drained rice. Cover partially and simmer over low heat until the milk is almost completely absorbed (30 to 35 minutes).

Meanwhile butter the baking dish with ½ tablespoon of the butter. Peel and slice the apples. Melt the butter in a skillet. Sauté the apples in it 10 minutes over medium heat. Sprinkle with 1 tablespoon of the sugar. Pour the Cognac over it, if desired.

Preheat the oven to 425°. Take the rice off the heat. Stir 4 tablespoons of the sugar and 2 egg yolks into it. Spread the mixture in the baking dish. Cover with apples.

MERINGUE: Beat the 2 egg whites until very stiff peaks form. Halfway through, beat in the remaining 2 tablespoons of sugar. Spread over the apples without smoothing the surface. Place 5 minutes in the top of the oven to brown it lightly. Serve warm or cold.

My advice: If you add 1 to 2 additional egg whites (left over from another recipe), your meringue will be fuller and the dessert even more attractive. Add a little more sugar. Count on 1 tablespoon of sugar per egg white.

Sablés normandes à la cannelle

[FOR 2 DOZEN COOKIES]

2 hard-boiled egg yolks
1 cup flour
7 tablespoons very soft butter
⅓ cup sugar
¼ teaspoon salt
½ teaspoon cinnamon

1 drinking glass or cookie cutter, about
    2 inches in diameter

CINNAMON COOKIES

Preparation and cooking time: 30 minutes, plus 1-hour resting time for the dough
Oven temperature: 375°

Mash the egg yolks. Mix them in a bowl with the remaining ingredients. Knead until the dough is smooth. Shape it into a flattened ball. Wrap it up and refrigerate 1 hour.

Preheat the oven to 375°. Roll the dough out about ¼ inch thick. Dip the rim of a cookie cutter or glass in flour before cutting the dough out in circles. Arrange them on a buttered baking sheet. Bake 10 to 12 minutes in the oven. When the cookies are lightly browned, remove them from the baking sheet. Let them cool on a rack. Eat them immediately or store them in a tightly sealed tin box.

My advice: This cookie dough with its hard-boiled egg yolks is very easy to knead, because the dough will not get tough. On the other hand, since the dough is very flaky (a virtue when eating it!), it is hard to roll out.

I also advise you to divide it into small balls that you roll out one by one, cutting out the cookie circle and arranging them on the baking sheet as you go along. When the baking sheet is full, place it in the hot oven and bake.

Soufflé à la liqueur

[FOR 4 PEOPLE]

3 tablespoons butter
1 tablespoon flour
1 cup milk
3 tablespoons sugar
4 tablespoons Grand Marnier or other
    liqueur of your choice
4 eggs, separated
½ teaspoon salt

1 soufflé mold, 9 inches in diameter

LIQUEUR SOUFFLÉ

Preparation and cooking time: 50 minutes / *Oven temperature:* 375°

In a large saucepan, melt 2 tablespoons of the butter without letting it brown. Then stir in the flour. As soon as it begins to foam, pour in the cold milk all at once. Beat continuously with a whisk until it comes to a boil. Simmer a few seconds. Remove from the heat.

Preheat the oven to 375°. Butter the soufflé mold with the remaining butter.

Add to the saucepan the sugar, liqueur, and egg yolks, stirring constantly. Beat the egg whites with salt until stiff peaks form. Fold them delicately into the egg yolk mixture.

Pour into a soufflé mold, ¾ full (it will puff up). Smooth the top with a spatula or a knife. Bake in the oven about 30 minutes. Serve immediately, for this soufflé collapses very fast.

My advice: Prepare the soufflé mixture before dinner. Pour it into the mold immediately and refrigerate it. Just before sitting down to eat, turn on your oven to 375°. Then, as you're about to serve the main course, place the soufflé in the hot oven. You'll be able to bring a perfectly cooked soufflé to the table for dessert.

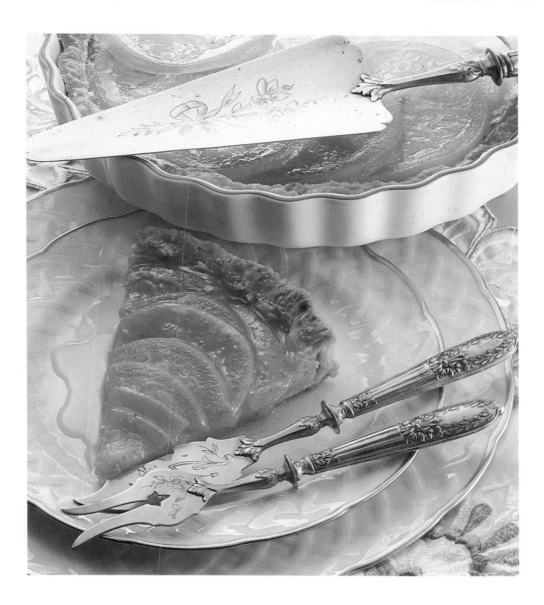

Tarte aux pamplemousses

[FOR 6 PEOPLE]

PASTRY DOUGH

2 cups flour
½ teaspoon salt
6 tablespoons butter or margarine
⅔ cup cold water
2 grapefruit

PASTRY CREAM

2 eggs
1 cup sugar
5 tablespoons butter
Juice of 1 grapefruit, plus grated rind

1 cup water
1 cup sugar

1 pie pan, 12 inches in diameter

GRAPEFRUIT TARTE

Preparation and cooking time: 1 hour, plus resting time for the dough / *Oven temperature:* 375°

PASTRY DOUGH: Mix the flour, salt, and butter (cut in pieces) by pressing and rubbing it between the palms of your hands. Add a little water to this granular mixture. Knead it vigorously. Roll it into a ball, then flatten it with the palm of your hand. Form it again into a loose ball. Do this 3 times, very rapidly. Spread the crust thinly in the pie pan and refrigerate several hours.

Preheat the oven to 375°. Rinse and scrub the grapefruit in cold water.

PASTRY CREAM: With an electric mixer, beat the eggs and sugar together until creamy. Add the melted butter, grapefruit juice, and grated grapefruit rind. Spread it over the bottom of the uncooked pie crust. Bake in the oven about 35 minutes.

Meanwhile cut the other grapefruit, unpeeled, into very thin horizontal slices. Pour water and sugar into a large skillet. Boil, uncovered, 2 minutes to obtain a syrup. Arrange the grapefruit slices in it, side by side, in two layers if necessary. Simmer until the grapefruit rind is shiny and translucent (candied).

Arrange the candied grapefruit slices on the baked tarte. Put back in the oven a few minutes to caramelize it. Serve hot or cold.

Tarte aux poires Bourdaloue

PEAR TARTE WITH ALMONDS

[FOR 4 PEOPLE]

Preparation and cooking time: 1 hour and 30 minutes, plus resting time for the dough
Oven temperature: 400°

PASTRY DOUGH WITH EGG

1 cup flour
5 tablespoons soft butter or margarine
2 tablespoons sugar
¼ teaspoon salt
1 egg

PASTRY CREAM

1 cup milk
½ envelope vanilla sugar or ½ teaspoon
   vanilla extract
¼ teaspoon salt
2 tablespoons sugar
2 egg yolks
1 tablespoon flour or cornstarch

GARNISH

1 large (29-ounce) can pears
1 cup currant jelly
1 tablespoon glacéed fruits
1 tablespoon slivered almonds

1 tarte or pie pan (preferably one with
   removable sides), 10 to 12 inches in
   diameter

PASTRY DOUGH WITH EGG: Mound the flour. Make a well in the center and mix in the softened butter with sugar and salt. Work the egg in until the mixture is creamy. Knead rapidly with the flour. Roll it into a ball and refrigerate it.

PASTRY CREAM: In a saucepan, bring the milk, vanilla, and salt to a boil. Meanwhile beat the sugar and egg yolks together until the mixture turns pale and creamy. Mix in the flour or cornstarch, then, little by little, the boiling milk. Pour back into the saucepan. Stir over low heat until it thickens.

Preheat the oven to 400°. Roll out dough, not too thin. Fit it into the pie pan. Prick the bottom with a fork. Crumple a piece of foil to hold up the sides (remove it halfway through the baking). Bake in the oven 25 to 30 minutes. Remove the sides of the pan, if possible, and let the tarte cool on a rack.

Before serving, spread the tarte with cold pastry cream. Arrange carefully, with the drained pears on it. Melt the currant jelly over low heat with 1 to 2 spoonfuls of the pear syrup. Let boil a few seconds. Pour over the fruit. Decorate with glacéed fruits and almonds.

My advice: This tarte is prepared in three steps: the crust, the pastry cream, and the garnish. It can be almost entirely prepared the day before, but in order to avoid a soggy crust, do not assemble it until just before the meal begins, which will take no more than about 10 minutes.

Tarte Tatin APPLE UPSIDE-DOWN TARTE

[FOR 4 PEOPLE]

Preparation and cooking time in advance: 30 minutes, plus 15 minutes before serving
Oven temperature: 500°

Chilled or frozen pastry dough (regular pie crust or flaky crust)
4 tablespoons sugar
3 tablespoons butter
7 medium-sized firm apples
A pitcher of *crème fraîche* or whipped cream

1 deep mold, about 10 inches in diameter*

In advance, defrost the dough if necessary. (If you're making it yourself, see the recipe for Apple Dumplings, p. 210.) Sprinkle the sugar in the bottom of the mold. Dot with the butter. Peel the apples whole. Cut them in half to remove the cores and seeds. Arrange them in the mold, re-formed whole, upright and tightly packed.

Put the mold over low heat (if necessary, place a heat diffuser between the heat and the mold). When the butter has melted, turn the heat up to medium. Caramel will form and start boiling. Press lightly on the apples to flatten them. Keep a close watch so the caramel doesn't burn. After about 20 minutes, the caramelized juices will have increased, cooking the apples, which become golden brown and shiny. Remove from the heat. Let them cool.

Roll the dough into a circle about ⅛ inch thick and a little larger than the mold. Place it directly over the apples, tucking it all around the inside between the fruit and the mold. Refrigerate until just before baking.

Before sitting down to eat, preheat the oven to 500°. When it is very hot, place the mold in the middle of the oven about 15 minutes. Turn the tarte upside down onto a plate when it comes out of the oven. Keep it warm until it is time to serve it for dessert, accompanied by a pitcher of *crème fraîche* or whipped cream.

My advice: This is the warm upside-down tarte that has brought success to so many lively bistros and restaurants. And if you serve it at your own table, you should know that it can be almost entirely prepared several hours ahead of time and put in to bake at the beginning of the meal.

Remarks: For *tarte tatin*, use apples that stay firm after being cooked. If you find they aren't done after they've been caramelized, put them in a hot oven 5 minutes to tenderize them before covering them with dough.

*The mold must be sturdy, heavy, and able to withstand direct heat. Special *Tarte Tatin* molds are available, usually in copper. A sturdy iron skillet may be used in a pinch.

Tuiles aux amandes

[ABOUT 25 COOKIES]

2 tablespoons butter
2 egg whites
3 tablespoons sugar
½ teaspoon salt
1 tablespoon flour
⅓ cup slivered almonds

1 baking sheet

TILE-SHAPED ALMOND COOKIES

Preparation time and baking time: 30 minutes / *Oven temperature:* 350°

Preheat the oven to 350°. Butter the baking sheet with 1 teaspoon of the butter.

In a bowl, with a wooden spoon, mix the unbeaten egg whites, sugar, salt, flour, almonds, and remaining butter melted.

On the baking sheet, arrange half-teaspoonfuls of the cookie dough. Space them 2 finger-widths apart, for they spread into very thin cookies.

Place them in the oven 8 to 10 minutes. When the cookies start browning on the edges but are still pale in the center, take them out of the oven. Pry them off the baking sheet with a table knife or spatula and immediately drape them over a rolling pin to cool in the shape of curved roof tiles. Let them cool completely and stiffen on a rack.

My advice: The thickness of the dough depends to some extent on the size of the egg whites and the type of flour. If the dough is fairly solid, the cookies won't be excessively brittle. If it's runny, the very thin cookies that result will taste even better but will be much more fragile. It's your choice.

Turinois à la chantilly

CHOCOLATE CHESTNUT CAKE WITH WHIPPED CREAM

[FOR 6 TO 8 PEOPLE]

1 pound unsweetened chestnut puree (canned)

3 ounces (3 squares) unsweetened chocolate

4 tablespoons powdered (confectioners') sugar

½ envelope vanilla sugar or ½ teaspoon vanilla extract

6 tablespoons very soft butter

CRÈME CHANTILLY (WHIPPED CREAM)

1 cup *crème fraîche* or whipping cream

1 to 2 tablespoons cold milk or water (to thin *crème fraîche*)

1 envelope vanilla sugar or 1 tablespoon vanilla extract

DECORATION

Walnuts, hazelnuts, candied flowers, or cocoa

1 cake pan, 9 inches in diameter

Preparation time: 40 minutes, plus 12 hours refrigeration

In a saucepan, over low heat, work the chestnut puree with a wooden spoon, mashing and stirring it to keep it from sticking.

Grate the chocolate with a dull knife or the grating attachment of a food processor. Transfer the hot chestnut puree to a mixing bowl or food processor bowl and beat it with the grated chocolate, the sugar, and the vanilla until smooth. Cool. Then beat in the softened butter. Continue beating until thoroughly mixed and light.

Cut a circle the size of the cake pan out of brown paper or wax paper. Butter it and place in the bottom of the pan, buttered side up. Pour the chestnut mixture over it. Smooth out the surface. Cover and refrigerate overnight.

CRÈME CHANTILLY: Dilute very cold *crème fraîche* with milk, or use plain whipping cream. Add the vanilla. Beat with electric beaters or use a whisk, whipping in as much air as possible with wide sweeping gestures. Increase the speed at the end. As soon as the cream is thick and clings to the beaters, stop whipping it, for it could rapidly turn to butter. Refrigerate until ready to use.

Unmold the cake on a serving plate. Peel off the circle of paper. Decorate with nuts or candied flowers or sprinkle with bitter cocoa. Pass whipped cream separately.

My advice: You won't get good results with melted chocolate. Grate it.

The quality of the cake depends on the vigorous and prolonged mixing of the various ingredients. A food processor or electric mixer will save you time and effort.

MISCELLANEOUS NOTES

Andouillettes: Small fresh sausages made with chitterlings and flavored with mustard, shallots, salt, and pepper. They are difficult to find in the U.S., but any mild, fresh sausage can be used in their stead. Just simmer first in shallots and wine. Served with Mashed Potatoes with Cheese and Garlic (see p. 176), they make a delicious entrée for a brunch or light supper.

Bain-marie: A kind of multiple double-boiler. You can make one by partially filling a pot larger than the one containing your stew with hot water. Keep the stew warm over the simmering water. It will not dry out the way it would over direct heat.

Calamary: Either cuttlefish or squid. Although enjoyed in Mediterranean countries, cuttlefish is rarely found in the U.S. If you're adventurous, and can get any, make sure you pound it well with a mallet before cooking to tenderize it. After pounding, cuttlefish will take the same amount of time as squid to cook. Squid can be cooked quickly *or* simmered for 45 minutes or longer. Between the quick sauté time and the 45-minute time period, the squid goes through a tough phase. If you wish to sauté quickly, add the cooked squid to the sauce for the last five minutes of cooking; otherwise, simmer for 45 minutes.

Chevrotins: These small goat cheeses are perfect for single servings of salad. Slices from a goat cheese log, such as Montrachet or Lezay, may be substituted.

Fish for Bouillabaisse and Fish Soup: The traditional Mediterranean fish called for in this recipe—red mullet, weever, monkfish (also called lotte or tilefish), conger eel, whiting, sea robin, and rascasse—are difficult to find in the U.S. Equally excellent substitutes easily found here include: cod, bass, flounder, haddock, hake, rockfish, scrod, snapper, sole, and any kind of shellfish. Try to use as many varieties as possible, but avoid fatty fish such as mackerel, herring, or sardines.

Fresh pork fatback: Slices of pork fat used in barding or covering duck, goose, and chicken to keep them from drying out. Also used in pâtés. It is available in butcher stores, but you may substitute thin slices of salt pork or slices of bacon, if necessary. Just be sure to blanch the bacon or salt pork to remove their strong smoky, salty flavor.

Langoustines *(Nephrops norvegicus):* A variety of small lobster found in cold European waters, occasionally imported to the U.S. Large shrimp or prawns are a good substitute.

Tomme de Cantal: A fresh, soft cheese, difficult to find in the U.S., except in gourmet cheese shops. Substitute another soft cheese, such as Boursin.

INDEX

Thanks to **M. Boutron** for the design of pages 14, 23(R), 28(L), 39, 44, 47, 72(R), 84, 96, 108, 110, 127, 132(L), 134, 176(L), 192, 199, 224, 234, 236, and to **Melles Scotto** for the design of pages 13, 24, 43, 80(L), 213.

For collaboration with the table settings, thanks to the following: **Antiquités-Curiosités**, **M. Berger** (Courbevoie), **Bernardaud** (Limoges), **Cadeaux Ménage** (Courbevoie), **Dior** (Paris), **Habitat** (Paris-La Défense), **Pier Import** (Paris-La Défense), **Salins** (Paris), **Utilux** (Courbevoie), **Villeroy et Boch** (Paris), **Porcelaine Blanche** (Courbevoie), **Cotte** (63250 Chabreloche), **Dior** (Paris), **3 Suisses** (Roubaix), **Scoff** (Centre international des Arts de la table, Paris), **Laura Mars** (Centre international des Arts de la table, Paris), **3 Suisses** (Roubaix), **Descamps Style Primerose Bordier** (Paris), **Le Jacquart Français Style Primerose Bordier** (Paris), **Textil Décor** (Courbevoie).